D1238365

The Economics of Immigration

The Economics of Immigration

Market-Based Approaches, Social Science, and Public Policy

Edited by Benjamin Powell

OXFORD

UNIVERSITY PRESS

OXFORD
UNIVERSITY PRESS

Oxford University Press is a department of the University of Oxford.
It furthers the University's objective of excellence in research, scholarship,
and education by publishing worldwide. Oxford is a registered trade mark
of Oxford University Press in the UK and in certain other countries

Published in the United States of America by Oxford University Press
198 Madison Avenue, New York, NY 10016, United States of America

© Oxford University Press 2015

All rights reserved. No part of this publication may be reproduced, stored in
a retrieval system, or transmitted, in any form or by any means, without the prior
permission in writing of Oxford University Press, or as expressly permitted by law,
by license, or under terms agreed with the appropriate reproduction rights organization.
Inquiries concerning reproduction outside the scope of the above should be sent
to the Rights Department, Oxford University Press, at the address above.

You must not circulate this work in any other form
and you must impose this same condition on any acquirer

Cataloging-in-Publication data is on file at the Library of Congress

9780190258788 (hbk.)
9780190258795 (pbk.)

CONTENTS

ACKNOWLEDGMENTS

I have debated immigration policy in public lectures and summer semi-
nars, on the radio and television, and in the pages of newspapers and
other popular outlets for more than a decade. Over that time I came to
realize that there was a wide gap between the debates that reasonable
social scientists had over the costs and benefits of immigration and the
popular fallacies that plagued public discourse. The motivation for this
book was inspired by, and will hopefully narrow, that gap. So, my first debt
is to almost all of the people who have hosted me in public lectures or have
invited me to participate in public discourse on this important topic.[1]

I am most grateful to the contributors to this volume. Their collective
expertise was invaluable, and I believe the joint product is of even greater
value than a summation of the parts. I could not have hoped to author
nearly as comprehensive or compelling a book on my own.

I am grateful for the environment and support that Texas Tech Univer-
sity has given me. This book resulted from a research project of Texas
Tech's Free Market Institute (FMI), which I direct. President M. Duane
Nellis, Provost Lawrence Shovanec, and Vice President of Research Robert
Duncan have all provided crucial support and guidance for the institute,
which is an ideal entity in which to conduct research projects such as this.
The chapters in this volume were presented as working papers at a one-day
research conference hosted by FMI in May 2014. As editor, I benefited
greatly from the feedback that the contributors and my colleagues at
Texas Tech provided on each of these chapters at the conference. Special
thanks goes to my colleague and the Director of the Center for the Study
of Western Civilization, Stephen Balch, for making a public debate at
Texas Tech possible on the evening prior to the conference. Also, a special
thanks to FMI's senior administrator Charles Long, who was involved in

1. I exclude Lou Dobbs from this category because his version of public discourse
does not amount to much more than name calling. https://www.youtube.com/
watch?v=zoDb3D7B2Zo.

every stage of the entire project. Thanks are also due to my research assistant Audrey Redford, who provided assistance in preparing the final manuscript and valuable research for my own chapters.

I also thank the Charles G. Koch Charitable Foundation for the financial support that allowed FMI to commission these chapters and host the conference. Allison Kasic and Adam Kissel, in particular, deserve credit for spearheading the collaboration between FMI and the Koch Foundation that made this project possible.

Oxford University Press was an ideal publisher to work with to bring the final product together. My thanks to three anonymous reviewers and Oxford's senior delegate, who all provided valuable revision suggestions that greatly improved this volume. My thanks to Oxford's senior editor, Scott Parris, for his support of this project and the invaluable guidance he provided in final revision stages of publication. I also thank David Theroux and Roy Carlisle for involving the Independent Institute in the final stages of publication.

Finally, I thank my family, Lisa and Raymond, for their love and support. Equally important, for projects like this, I appreciate their willingness to not just tolerate the endless stream of guests we host at FMI but to genuinely enjoy interacting with them.

The Economics of Immigration

CHAPTER 1

Introduction

BENJAMIN POWELL

Immigration policy is one of the most contentious and emotionally charged public policy issues in America today. Unfortunately, the debate surrounding immigration policy—in Congress, the media, public policy think tanks, and among the general public—is often conducted in ignorance of the enormous amount of academic research in scientific journals investigating almost every aspect of immigration. An appreciation of this academic literature changes the substance of the immigration policy debate, but it does not necessarily dictate a particular policy conclusion.

Economist Henry Simons said, "Economics is primarily useful, both to the student and to the political leader, as a prophylactic against popular fallacies" (Simons 1983). That is the purpose of the first half of this book: to make research from academic economics, and other social sciences, accessible and intelligible to people concerned with immigration policy and, in doing so, to serve as a prophylactic against popular fallacies. Serious debate about what the appropriate immigration policy is for the United States, or other countries, can occur once we move beyond the popular fallacies. That is the purpose of the second half of the book.

The importance of what is at stake, in economic and human terms, is impossible to understate. Hundreds of millions of people are trapped, by accident of birth, in countries with bad governance and dismal living conditions. As Chapter 8 reports, many of them want to move:

> Gallup has conducted worldwide polls since 2010 asking adults whether they would move to another country immediately if allowed. Over 600 million

adults—14 percent of the world adult population—wish to permanently move to another country. Over a billion want to seek temporary work abroad. For comparison, 232 million people currently live outside their country of birth. The United States is the first-choice destination for over 100 million adults. Gallup has used these polls to estimate population gain and loss for each country if everyone migrated to their first-choice destination. The effects are huge: Haiti would lose half its population. Australia, Singapore, and New Zealand would more than double. Even the United States, the world's third most populous country, would see population increase by 60 percent. (Caplan and Naik, Chapter 8 of this volume)

Yet, right now only about 3 percent of the world's population live in countries where they were not born. In the United States, about 40 million residents are foreign born, and nearly a third of them are in the United States illegally. Significant changes to US immigration policy, as well as the policies of other developed countries, would have a dramatic effect on the welfare of many of the world's poorest citizens. These changes could also have an enormous impact on the world's economy.

Economists estimate that the complete removal of immigration restrictions to wealthy countries could add roughly $50 trillion to $150 trillion to the world's economy (see Chapter 2). Even a much smaller policy change that results in only 5 percent of the population of the world's poorest countries moving to richer countries would raise world GDP more than the complete elimination of all remaining barriers to trade in goods and services and capital flows. Much of that gain would go to the world's poor who choose to migrate. This raises many questions about how such a change would impact others, particularly those in immigrant-receiving countries.

1   SOCIAL SCIENCE

The next three chapters of the book explore how immigrants impact the countries that receive them. In each chapter, the authors summarize and assess the body of academic research on their topic. The chapters are not merely summaries, cataloging everything that has been published. Instead, the authors, each an expert in a specific aspect of immigration, highlight what they think the best scholarship is on their topic, weigh the pros and cons of various studies, and try to assess what the overall scientific consensus should be on each of their questions.

How does immigration impact the economies of receiving countries? One popular belief, that immigrants "steal our jobs," is so prevalent that it has even been turned into the subject of an entire episode of Comedy Central's *South Park*.[1] Will they depress the wages of the native born? Will they, as Lou Dobbs frequently claims, turn our economies into something no better than that of a third world country? What about brain drain? Do emigrants contribute to the impoverishment of the countries they leave behind, or do they do more for the welfare of their origin countries when they are able to work abroad? These are the questions addressed by Peter Leeson and Zachary Gochenour in Chapter 2 of this volume, "The Economic Effects of International Labor Mobility."

What about the fiscal impact of immigration on the government's budget? Free market economist and Nobel Laureate Milton Friedman famously said, "It's just obvious that you can't have free immigration and a welfare state" (1998). Is he right? Are immigrants a fiscal drain because of tax-funded benefits like welfare, schooling, and Medicaid? Would more liberal immigration policies balloon the budget deficit? In Chapter 3, Alex Nowrasteh explores the vast and complex literature examining the impact that immigrants have on tax revenue and government expenditures.

What about assimilation? Do immigrants learn English, intermarry with native-born citizens, and "Americanize?" What about their children? Are today's immigrant groups different on these margins from nineteenth-century immigrants? Jacob Vigdor explores these questions in Chapter 4 and finds that immigrants today are much like immigrants of prior generations.

Chapter 5 examines the hot-button topic of temporary and permanent work visas for both high-skilled and low-skilled workers. In the United States, temporary visas for high-skilled workers become available on April 1 for the following fiscal year. Each of the last 10 years, even during the recession, the visa quota was reached before the end of the fiscal year. For fiscal year 2014, the quota was reached in the first five days. Low-skilled agricultural visas (H-2A) are so cumbersome to obtain that few employers bother, and many low-skilled workers come to the United States illegally instead. Chapter 5 begins the book's transition from pure social science to public policy advocacy. In it, Alexandre Padilla and Nicolás Cachanosky survey work visa policies across Organisation for Economic Co-operation and Development (OECD) countries in order to evaluate best practices. The chapter surveys the policies that exist, but also puts some emphasis on which policies work better than others.

1. https://www.youtube.com/watch?v=768h3Tz4Qik.

2   PUBLIC POLICY

Immigration reform has been on the US political agenda for more than a decade without a single comprehensive piece of legislation becoming a law. More than 11 million people reside in the United States illegally. Many millions more desire to migrate, either temporarily or permanently, to the United States, and there are thousands of businesses that desire to hire them. Meanwhile, there is a severe mismatch of the supply and demand for work visas (Powell and Gochenour 2013). There is a clear need for policy reform, yet politics seems incapable of coming up with any viable solutions.

Shortly before this book went to press, President Obama issued an executive order that prioritizes illegal immigrants who have committed crimes or are suspected of having terrorist ties for deportation. More importantly, the order establishes that illegal immigrants who were brought to the United States as children or parents of people who are US citizens will not be deported and will also have permission to work legally. The executive order caused an uproar; Republicans in Congress and 24 states have challenged it in federal court. However, no one expected that Obama, or anyone else, had the will or ability to deport more than 11 million illegal immigrants over the next few years. So, some form of selectivity regarding who is processed for deportation, even if random, was inevitable. The executive order did not change that. All it did was make explicit who will be targeted for deportation and who will not, and it let those who are not targeted work while they are here. The executive order was only issued because Congress has yet to pass a comprehensive immigration reform bill. But the blowback from this relatively minor policy change via executive order illustrates why passing a more comprehensive reform is difficult.

During the 113th Congress, more than a dozen immigration bills were introduced in the House of Representatives alone. It is beyond the scope of this introduction to review all of them and the many other immigration reform proposals made over the last decade. But before reviewing what social scientists believe are appropriate policy changes, it is at least worth reviewing the features of a couple of the most significant recent policy proposals made in the political arena.

"Comprehensive" immigration reform is usually used to connote a reform that deals with three major areas of immigration policy: what to do with the current illegal immigrants residing in the United States; how to handle future legal migration; and how to secure the border against future illegal migration. The Senate's Border Security, Economic Opportunity, and Immigration Modernization Act of 2013 (S. 744) was the most recent attempt at a comprehensive reform. The bill would have introduced the following measures: a "registered provisional immigrant" status (RPI) for current illegal immigrants who resided in the United States before 2012 and an eventual path toward legal permanent residency for them; a new agricultural worker visa program; expanded family- and employment-based visas and a new points-based merit visa; and it would have provided funding for hiring more border patrol agents and building more fencing, while also authorizing the use of the National Guard in border enforcement. The issuing of RPI status and the transition from RPI status to legal permanent residency were both contingent on meeting certain border security goals. The bill passed the Senate but failed to be adopted by the House of Representatives or reconciled with their various proposals.

In 2007 the Senate passed a similar bipartisan bill sponsored by Senators McCain and Kennedy. That bill also would have increased border security, provided a path to legal residency for current illegal residents after paying a fine, and it would have created 400,000 new guest worker visas. The bill also failed to become law. Scores of other bills have been introduced in Congress that deal with single aspects of immigration reform. Some of these have simply funded greater border security. Others, such as the DREAM Act, which would help those who were brought to the United States illegally as minors obtain legal status, have dealt with a subset of current illegal immigrants. How do the various political proposals compare to what social scientists think are the appropriate public policy reforms?

Once one appreciates the scholarly research that is assessed in the first half of the book, the terms of the immigration policy debate may be changed, but this does not necessarily lead those who appreciate the literature to agree on what policy should be. The authors of three of the last four chapters of the book each propose a different policy change. The final chapter of the book reviews the policy views of other prominent immigration scholars and then offers my own take on the direction that public policy should head in light of the social science.

Richard Vedder argues for a "market-based" approach to immigration in Chapter 6. He recognizes the economic benefits that immigration creates for both the immigrants and the native-born population, but also recognizes the political backlash that often accompanies high levels of immigration. He recommends expanding our legal immigration quota up to roughly the peak, in absolute numbers, that it reached in the twentieth century. However, unlike our current system, he argues for a system that would auction off immigration permits to the highest bidder. He argues that an auction system would be more efficient, fair, and better for our economy than the current system in which bureaucratic rules determine who gains admission. Vedder also suggests ways to integrate currently illegal immigrants into the auction system and how to include temporary workers.

Herbert London is more pessimistic about our ability to "Americanize" immigrants than the other contributors. In Chapter 7, he argues that legal immigration should be cut in half in order to better assimilate immigrants, and he hints toward possibly biasing that immigration toward higher skilled workers. However, he also proposes a "grand bargain" in which the US government would legalize a large portion of the current illegal immigrant population in exchange for cutting legal immigration in half.

Bryan Caplan and Vipul Naik make a case for complete open borders in Chapter 8. They find that the estimated economic gains of open borders are so large, and most of the feared negative consequences are so small, that even with very wide confidence intervals, open borders is always the best policy. Positive science, as summarized in the first part of the book, establishes chains of consequences and empirical relationships, but it does not tell us whether any particular outcome is "good" or "bad." For that, we need normative philosophy. Caplan and Naik take positive science and couple it with moral philosophy, arguing that, in light of the empirical evidence, *every* major moral philosophy argues for open borders. More than 90 percent of people in most countries disagree with Caplan and Naik. They recognize this and try to consider which empirical claims produce the disagreements.

My own concluding chapter surveys the policy views of other prominent immigration economists. The chapter reviews some of the main reasons that scholars disagree about the desirability of various immigration policies. It then examines the policy views of three scholars, George Borjas, Paul Collier, and Victor Davis Hanson, who are generally critical of increased immigration, and then examines the views of three scholars, Gordon Hanson, Lant Pritchett, and Michael Clemens, who are generally supportive of increased legal immigration. The chapter concludes with my assessment of the relative merit of their policy positions and briefly indicates my own position.

Most readers probably will not completely agree with any of the reform proposals in the final four chapters. But agreement with the particulars of any of these proposals is not the point (at least not my point in inviting them; the chapter authors may disagree). The point is to show how reasonable scholars can appreciate the positive science and then come to different policy conclusions. The debate between any of these three chapters is significantly different from the misinformed rants about immigration that appear on talk radio, in Lou Dobb's newsroom, or in congressional campaigns.

If readers believe the scholarly literature that is evaluated in the first half of this book, then they should update what they view as desirable immigration policy, regardless of whether they agree with any of the particular policy proposals outlined in the second part of this book. Popular and widely held fallacies about the impact of immigration on jobs, wages, the budget, and assimilation are simply out of step with the majority of scholarship on these topics. To the extent that a reader's preference for any particular immigration policy was influenced by these fallacies, their desired immigration policy should change in light of the empirical findings presented in this volume.

That does not imply embracing any policy proposal put forth by the authors of this volume. But it does imply moving one's position on the margin in light of newly obtained information, and it changes the terms of the debate about optimal immigration policy. It is my sincere hope that this volume can help bring some reasonable dispassionate discourse to a policy debate that is so often emotionally charged and devoid of decent scientific evidence. Potential immigrants, our countrymen, and our descendants deserve as much.

REFERENCES

Friedman, Milton. 1998. "Milton Friedman Soothsayer," interview by Peter Brimelow. *Hoover Digest*, no. 2.

Powell, Benjamin, and Zachary Gochenour. 2013. *Broken Borders Government, Foreign-Born Workers, and the U.S. Economy.* Oakland, CA: Independent Institute.

Simons, Henry. 1983. *Simons' Syllabus*, ed. Gordon Tullock. Fairfax, VA: Center for the Study of Public Choice.

Social Science

CHAPTER 2

꙳

The Economic Effects of International Labor Mobility

PETER T. LEESON AND ZACHARY GOCHENOUR

1 INTRODUCTION

In *The Wealth of Nations* (1776: Book IV, Chap. II) Adam Smith famously observed: "If a foreign country can supply us with a commodity cheaper than we ourselves can make it, better buy it of them with some part of the produce of our own industry, employed in a way in which we have some advantage." The principle underlying Smith's observation is simple. To create more wealth, carry out production activity where it is most productive: where it yields the most output for the least expense. This principle is called *comparative advantage*.

Today, the importance of comparative advantage for wealth creation is recognized by nearly all economists. It stands at the foundation of the case for free trade—a case that in the second half of the twentieth century largely won over policymakers in the developed world, who increasingly liberalized the movement of goods and services across borders (see, for instance, Shleifer 2009). There remains, however, a critical exception to the relatively free movement of goods and services internationally: the movement of labor.

Virtually every developed country in the world severely restricts the movement of people born outside its borders who desire to move inside them. Roughly 3 percent of the world's current population—about 200 million people—live in countries in which they were not born. However, a dramatically larger percentage would like to but cannot. According to the World

Gallup Poll, for instance, 40 percent of adults who currently inhabit the poorest quintile of the world's nations would move permanently to another country if they could (Pelham and Torres 2008; Torres and Pelham 2008).

The desire to relocate that these persons express is not cheap talk. In fiscal year 2013, 14.6 million persons applied for 50,000 visas granting permanent residency in the United States via the US Diversity Lottery (US Department of State 2014). High-skilled migrants often pay thousands of dollars in legal expenses to expedite the process of immigration to destination countries. And many workers migrate illegally, risking imprisonment, deportation, or worse.

Some of these workers pay professional smugglers hefty fees to move them across national borders—$3,000 to be smuggled across the United States–Mexico border, for example, $16,000 to be smuggled to the United States from Brazil, and $50,000 to be smuggled to the United States from China (Mexican Migration Project 2010; Havocscope Global Black Market Information 2014). These figures reflect only a small part of the cost that would-be migrants from the developing world are willing to bear to relocate to the developed one. They are also willing to leave their homes, families, and jobs to move to countries with unfamiliar languages, customs, and cultures.

The reason that migrants are happy to bear such costs is economic. Compared to the wage-earning opportunities available to them in the countries in which they were born, those available to them in popular destination countries, such as the United States, the United Kingdom, Canada, France, Germany, and Australia, are tremendous. Clemens, Montenegro, and Pritchett (2008) conservatively estimate the welfare gain available to a moderately skilled worker in a typical developing country who moves to the United States at $10,000 (PPP) per year. This is roughly double the per capita income in the average developing country.

The enormous wage gains available to such migrants reflect the enormous productivity gains their labor enjoys in developed countries where capital is more abundant and institutional quality, such as private property protection, is much higher. By reallocating labor to regions where it is more productive, international labor migration exploits the wealth increases possible via the principle of comparative advantage.

To get a sense of the magnitude of the increases that are available globally by permitting labor reallocation through unfettered international migration, consider the results of research that empirically investigates the efficiency improvements of eliminating policy barriers to international labor mobility (Hamilton and Whalley 1984; Iregui 2005; Klein and Ventura 2007; Moses and Letnes 2004). This research suggests that eliminating such barriers would increase global wealth by between *50 and 150 percent of world GDP.*

This improvement is an order of magnitude larger than the efficiency improvement that researchers estimate would be achieved by eliminating policy barriers to the movement of commercial merchandise and capital internationally (see, for instance, Anderson and Martin 2005; Dessus, Fukasaku, and Safadi 1999; Hertel and Keeney 2006; World Bank 2001). Indeed, even far more modest reductions of policy barriers to international labor mobility would add more to global wealth than completely eliminating policy barriers to the movement of "ordinary" goods and capital across countries. Current estimates suggest that the migration of less than 5 percent of poor countries' populations to the developed world would accomplish as much (Clemens 2011).

Although it is uncontroversial among economists that the free movement of labor across countries would dramatically enhance welfare globally, the economic effects of international labor mobility for various subpopulations of the world—in particular, native workers in the countries migrants move to and citizens who stay behind in the countries migrants depart—are subjects of considerable controversy. This is unsurprising. That freer labor movement would improve global efficiency follows obviously from the principle of comparative advantage. The distributional consequences of such movements, however, do not.

This chapter, which surveys the state of knowledge about the economic effects of international labor mobility, is therefore especially concerned with considering labor mobility's economic effects for potentially vulnerable subpopulations. In focusing on labor mobility's influence on these subpopulations, we aim to come to some conclusions for thinking about policy relating to international migration that take account of both the distributional impacts of migration and its more straightforward global impact discussed above.

2 THE ECONOMIC EFFECTS OF IMMIGRATION

2.1 Theory

Most research that investigates the economic effects of international labor mobility studies the economic effects of immigration: how migration from poor countries to wealthy ones influences wages and job opportunities in migrant-receiving nations.

To get a sense of how immigration might impact these economic variables theoretically, a natural starting place is a simple economic model of a labor market, such as that depicted in Figure 2.1. This model has several assumptions: wages are set competitively; labor is homogeneous, meaning that all workers are economically identical from the perspective of employers, and thus are perfectly substitutable for one another; and changes affecting this market do not affect others.

Analyzing immigration's economic effects in this context is straightforward. Immigration increases the supply of labor, shifting supply rightward from S_0 to S_1. This leads competing native workers' wages to fall by the amount W_0-W_1 and their employment to fall by the amount Q_0-Q_2. Immigration's influence on native workers would appear to be unambiguously negative.

Using a model like that in Figure 2.1 to predict immigration's effect on native workers is problematic, however, for two reasons. First, while the assumption of homogeneous labor and thus perfect immigrant-native substitutability may make sense for certain subpopulations of native workers and certain subpopulations of immigrants, it is clearly violated for other subpopulations of these groups of labor. For example, unskilled immigrants who have little or no education are not perfectly substitutable for highly skilled native workers whose labor tasks are human-capital intensive, such as professionals. Indeed, in many cases unskilled immigrants may not be perfectly substitutable even for unskilled native workers. The latter typically have far better command over the language used in their country, for example, and such command is important for many unskilled tasks.

Some subpopulations of immigrant labor are in fact likely to be *complementary* to some subpopulations of native labor. Consider, for instance,

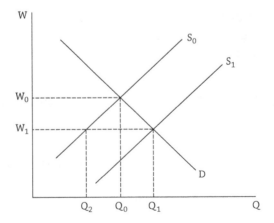

Figure 2.1
A Simple Model of the Labor Market

immigrant manual laborers who perform physical tasks, such as hanging drywall on construction projects, and native "cognitive" workers who perform more complex, human-capital intensive tasks, such as engineering for construction projects. If one were to depict the economic effects of an influx of the former subpopulation of immigrants on the latter subpopulation of natives using a model similar to that in Figure 2.1, demand would shift rightward, *raising* native wages and employment rather than reducing them.

The second difficulty of using such a model to predict immigration's economic effects is that, because it is a partial-equilibrium model, this model ignores potentially important general-equilibrium effects of immigration. For example, in response to an immigration-induced fall in the relative price of unskilled labor in an economy, additional capital is likely to flow to that economy, restoring the capital-to-labor ratio, and with it, native wage rates and employment. Moreover, an influx of immigrants to an economy increases not only that economy's supply of labor. It also increases its demand for labor—both through immigrants' consumption and when some immigrants become employers themselves—putting upward pressure on native wages and employment.

Because of such factors, contrary to what some have suggested (see Borjas 2003), the fact that the "the labor demand curve is downward sloping" is not sufficient to permit one to know a priori that immigration harms natives. As we discuss below, alternative appraisals of these factors' importance in practice play an important role in the ongoing debate about immigration's economic effects empirically.

2.2   Evidence

2.2.1   Native Wages

An extensive literature considers immigration's effect on native wages empirically.[1] As Card (2005) describes, this literature reflects two main approaches, which parallel a long-standing debate about immigration's influence on natives in the United States in particular. We consider several of the most important and influential studies under each approach, which represent the basic results found using each method.

---

1. For relatively recent reviews of this literature, see Kerr and Kerr (2011) and Card (2005). For somewhat older reviews, see Friedberg and Hunt (1995) and Borjas (1994).

Grossman (1982) introduced the first major approach to estimating immigration's effect on native wages, which examines the relationship between differences in the relative structure of wages and differences in the relative supply of immigrants across local labor markets. Studies using this regional-comparison method may rely on important immigration events, such as political changes that permitted an influx of new foreign labor, to identify exogenous changes in immigration. In an influential study that applies this approach, Card (1990), for instance, compares labor market conditions in Miami and other cities before and after an influx of Cuban immigrants, the *Marielitos*, increased Miami's workforce by 7 percent following the Cuban government's decision to permit 125,000 citizens to emigrate in 1980. Despite the large influx of new foreign labor, Card finds no discernible effect on wages in Miami's labor market.

The regional-comparison approach takes advantage of the many local labor markets that exist in countries such as the United States, which exhibit substantial variation in their proportions of immigrants. An important drawback of this method, however, is that goods and factors of production are mobile between cities. If their flows are highly sensitive to differences in local prices, the regional-comparison method may have difficulty finding effects from immigration. Borjas, for example, who has most vocally criticized results obtained via the regional-comparison method, and most vocally advocated the alternative method of estimating immigration's effect on native wages discussed below, argues that the endogeneity of immigrants' settlement choices and the response of native capital owners and workers to immigration-induced changes in relative prices across localities are likely to prevent the regional-comparison method from detecting immigration-caused reductions in native wages (see, for instance, Borjas 1994; Borjas, Freeman, and Katz 1992, 1996).

The second major approach to estimating immigration's effect on native workers uses time-series data to examine the relationship between changes in immigrant densities over time and economy-wide measures of relative labor market outcomes. In an influential study that applies this method, Borjas (2003), for instance, uses time-series data on aggregate relative wages in the United States between 1960 and 2001 to estimate how immigration-driven increases in the labor supply of particular skill groups influence economic outcomes for native workers in those skill groups. In contrast to the implications of Card's (1990) study, Borjas finds that an influx of immigrants that increases the supply of workers in a particular skill group by 10 percent reduces the wages of natives in that skill group by 3–4 percent.

By shifting the unit of analysis to the national level, the aggregate time-series method circumvents the difficulties confronted by the regional-comparison approach in light of the movement of people and capital between localities in response to immigration-generated changes in relative prices. A potentially important problem for studies that rely on this method, however, is the absence of a counterfactual, which can render interpretations of estimates achieved via the aggregate time-series approach sensitive to assumptions about how important economic variables move over time. Card (2005), for example, argues that without knowledge about the rate of growth of relative demand for high-school dropouts versus high-school graduates, Borjas's (2003) aggregate time-series data on relative wages are uninformative about immigration's effect on natives.

Perhaps surprisingly, given the intense methodological disagreement one finds in the foregoing literature, it may not matter greatly which approach to estimating immigration's effect on native wages one finds most appealing. Consider Table 2.1, the third column of which summarizes the main findings of 10 representative studies that investigate immigration's effect on native wages in the United States over the last 50 years.

Despite differences in the methods these studies use, the time periods they consider, and the subpopulations they consider, they display a clear pattern: immigration has a small, but negative, effect on native wages.[2] This pattern is not limited to studies that consider the United States. It is also found in the literature that considers immigration's effect on native wages in Europe (see, for instance, Brücker and Jahn 2011; De New and Zimmermann 1994a, 1994b; Gang and Rivera-Batiz 1994; Pischke and Velling 1994; Zorlu and Hartog 2005).

Borjas (2003) and Borjas and Katz (2007), whose estimates are the largest in the literature, deserve special attention, since their findings are the two exceptions to the pattern of small effects found by others and reported in Table 2.1. For example, although Borjas and Katz (2007) find that Mexican immigration to the United States between 1980 and 2000 had *zero* effect on the *typical* native's wage in the long run, they also find

---

2. Because of the differences across these studies pointed to above, and because they measure changes in immigration differently (e.g., as a share of total population vs. as a share of the workforce), it is not possible to use their results to neatly summarize a lower and upper bound of immigration's influence on native wages. In lieu of such a summary, to get a better sense of the range of these results, we discuss in greater detail the largest estimates in the literature below.

Table 2.1 IMMIGRATION'S EFFECT ON NATIVE WAGES AND EMPLOYMENT
IN THE UNITED STATES, 1960–2006

Study	Year	Finding for Native Wages	Finding for Native Employment
Grossman (1982)	1970	10 percent increase in the number of immigrants reduces wages of natives by 1 percent.	No discernible effect
Card (1990)	1980	No discernible effect	No discernible effect
LaLonde and Topel (1991)	1970, 1980	No discernible effect	No discernible effect
Altonji and Card (1991)	1970, 1980	1 percentage point increase in immigrant population share reduces wage of less-skilled natives by 1.2 percent.	1 percentage point increase in immigrant population share reduces unemployment rate of less-skilled natives by 0.23 percent.
Borjas, Freeman, and Katz (1992)	1967–1987	1 percentage point increase in immigrant share of labor force reduces wage of native high-school dropouts by 1.2 percent.	
Borjas and Ramey (1995)	1977–1991	1 percentage point increase in immigration share of labor force reduces wage of native high-school dropouts relative to college graduates by 0.7 percent.	
Card (2001)	1990	Immigrant inflows between 1985 and 1990 reduce wage of low-skilled natives by 1–3 percentage points.	Immigrant inflows between 1985 and 1990 reduce employment of low-skilled natives by 1–3 percentage points.
Borjas (2003)	1960–2001	Immigrant inflows that increase the supply of workers in a particular skill group by 10 percent reduce wages for natives in that group by 3–4 percent.	Immigrant inflows that increase the supply of workers in a particular skill group by 10 percent reduce weeks worked by natives in that group by 2–3 percent.
Borjas and Katz (2007)	1980–2000	Immigrant inflows between 1980 and 2000 reduce wages of native high-school dropouts by 8.2 percent in the short run and 4.2 percent in the long run; and reduce wage of typical native 3.4 percent in the short run and 0.0 percent in the long run.	

		Table 2.1 (CONTINUED)	
Study	Year	Finding for Native Wages	Finding for Native Employment
Ottaviano and Peri (2008, 2012)	1990–2006	Immigrant inflows between 1990 and 2006 reduce wages of natives without high-school degrees by 0.7 percent in the short run and increase their wages by 0.6–1.7 percent in the long run.	

that it reduced the wage of American high-school dropouts by 8.2 percent in the short run and 4.2 percent in the long run.[3]

Given that the literature's two largest sets of estimates are found in studies that use the aggregate time-series approach, it is tempting to attribute the results in Borjas (2003) and Borjas and Katz (2007) to their reliance on this method. But this would be a mistake. Recent work suggests that their larger estimates are instead the result of two important assumptions these studies make: first, that the labor market is defined by four education groups (high-school dropouts, high-school graduates, people with some college, college graduates), and second, that immigrants and natives in the same skill group are perfect substitutes.

Ottaviano and Peri (2008, 2012) use the same method as Borjas (2003) and Borjas and Katz (2007) to estimate immigration's effect on native wages in the United States, but modify these two assumptions. Instead of defining the labor market using four education groups, they define it using two education groups (high-school equivalents and college equivalents). And instead of treating immigrant labor of a given skill level as perfectly substitutable for native labor of the same skill level, they treat them as imperfectly substitutable. Doing so, these authors find that immigration's large negative effects on native wages, per Borjas (2003) and Borjas and Katz (2007), disappear. Indeed, Ottaviano and Peri's (2008, 2012) results suggest that immigration to the United States between 1990 and 2006 reduced the wages of natives without high-school degrees by only 0.7 percent in the short run and *increased* their wages by 0.6–1.7 percent in the long run.

The case for modifying the two assumptions in Borjas (2003) and Borjas and Katz (2007) that appear to drive their larger estimates, per Ottaviano

3. "Typical" refers to the group "all native workers"—that is, without regard to workers' education group.

and Peri (2008, 2012), is persuasive.[4] The conventional division of labor-market education groups in labor economics uses two groups: "high education" (college or more) and "low education" (high school or less), not four. Further, as Card (2012) points out, if high-school dropouts and high-school graduates are separate skill groups with the same degree of substitutability as between high-school graduates and college graduates, as Borjas (2003) and Borjas and Katz (2007) assume, we should observe a systematic negative relationship between the relative wage of dropouts versus high-school graduates and their relative supply. However, in the post-1960 US period that Borjas (2003) and Borjas and Katz (2007) consider, no such relationship exists.

There is equally strong reason to think that immigrant and native labor within the same skill group are imperfect substitutes for one another, rather than perfect substitutes as Borjas (2003) and Borjas and Katz (2007) assume. The simple fact that, as alluded to above, immigrants' language skills are often significantly inferior to those of natives points to imperfect substitutability, and the empirical evidence seems to support this claim (see, for instance, Card 2009; Dustmann, Frattini, and Preston 2013; Ferrar, Green, and Riddell 2006; Peri 2007; Peri and Sparber 2009).

Ottaviano and Peri's (2008, 2012) work offers to reconcile the most divergent results in the literature that examines immigration's effect on native wages. In doing so it affirms the typical finding in this literature: immigration has little effect on those wages.

2.2.2   Native Employment

The literature that considers immigration's effect on native employment empirically is smaller than that which considers native wages, but finds similar results. Consider the fourth column of Table 2.1, which presents the findings of a half-dozen influential studies that examine this relationship in the United States over the past 50 years.

Immigration's effect on native employment in America is minimal. In four of the six studies in Table 2.1, immigration's estimated effect on native employment is zero or positive. In the other two, it is negative but modest. According to Borjas (2003), who finds the largest effect of immigration on native employment in this literature, an influx of immigrants that increases the supply of workers in a particular skill group by 10 percent reduces the weeks worked by native laborers by 2–3 percent. The same pattern is found again in the literature that considers immigration's

4. For a more detailed analysis of why this is so, see Card (2009).

effect on native employment in Europe, whose estimates cluster around zero (see, for instance, Angrist and Kugler 2003; Gross 2002; Mühleisen and Zimmermann 1994; Winkelmann and Zimmermann 1993; Winter-Ebmer and Zimmermann 1999; Winter-Ebmer and Zweimüller 1996).

The tone of contestation one finds in much of the empirical literature that studies immigration's economic effects obscures the quite consistent, broader picture this literature seems to reflect. All but the most pessimistic estimates of immigration's influence on native wages suggest a small effect, and aberrations to this pattern cease to be so under the appropriate assumptions. Recent meta-analyses of the substantial literature that generates these estimates support this conclusion (Longhi, Nijkamp, and Poot 2005, 2008a). Further, research agrees that most, if not all, of immigration's negative effect on native wages is temporary. Over a longer period in which capital is able to adjust to immigration-induced relative price changes, small native wage reductions become smaller still and may become wage increases, even for the most vulnerable subpopulations. Nearly all of the work that estimates immigration's influence on native employment also finds small effects. This impression, too, is confirmed by recent meta-analyses of the literature that examines this question, which suggest that native employment is largely unaffected by immigration (Longhi, Nijkamp, and Poot 2008a, 2008b).

Finally, it bears emphasis that there appears to be no disagreement among researchers that the net economic benefit of immigration for natives as a whole is positive, albeit perhaps modest. Even Borjas (1995, 2001), whose work on the distributional consequences of US immigration discussed above is the most pessimistic in the literature, estimates that immigration to the United States generates an annual efficiency gain for Americans of between $5 billion and $10 billion. The free movement of factors of production benefits the economies of the countries to which those factors move, and thus their native inhabitants, by enabling them to better exploit the principle of comparative advantage. Labor is no exception.

3   THE ECONOMIC EFFECTS OF EMIGRATION

3.1   Theory

The economic effects of emigration refer to the consequences of migration for citizens who remain behind in countries from which migrants depart. In the most basic economic labor-market model, considered in Figure 2.1, emigration's economic effects on such citizens move oppositely to their effects on natives in emigrants' destination countries. Thus when the migration of workers from one country to another reduces the wages of competing native workers in the latter country, it raises the wages of competing workers who remain behind in the former country—albeit at the expense of capital owners in that country, who must pay more for labor. Mishra (2007), for example, finds that Mexican emigration to the United States between 1970 and 2000 increased the wages of high-school-educated workers who remained in Mexico by 15 percent, but harmed the welfare of Mexican owners of fixed factors of production more than it benefited Mexican workers.

Of particular interest is what happens to citizens who remain behind when their compatriots who emigrate are highly skilled, such as doctors and engineers (the so-called brain drain).[5] These emigrants have human capital that may make their labor complementary to the labor of many of their compatriots. Thus a highly simplified partial-equilibrium model like that in Figure 2.1 suggests that such citizens who remain behind will be harmed by emigration.

However, for essentially the same reasons that this model can have difficulty predicting how an influx of immigrants affects economic outcomes for natives, it can also have difficulty predicting how an outflow of emigrants affects economic outcomes for non-emigrating citizens. For example, while the simplest labor-market model treats human-capital investments by citizens in migrant-origin countries as exogenous, in practice it seems likely that citizens' investments in such capital are endogenous to the prospect of emigration.

Because the returns on human capital in migrant-origin countries are typically low, and in migrant-destination countries are typically high, citizens anticipating emigration have an incentive to invest in human capital that makes their labor more highly skilled. If some portion of would-be emigrants who invest in human capital for this purpose do not ultimately emigrate, emigration may raise the average level of human capital among citizens that remain, creating the opposite effect of that predicted above for citizens with complementary labor skills who do not emigrate. This explains how the Philippines, for instance, which sends more nurses abroad than any other developing country, still manages to enjoy more nurses per capita at home than the United Kingdom (Clemens 2009). While the prospect of emigration in part drives human capital acquisition, many do not emigrate.

---

5. For a more comprehensive review of this literature than we provide below, see Docquier and Rapoport (2012).

The simple labor-market model in Figure 2.1 also ignores the possibility that high-skilled emigrants may remit part of the income they earn abroad to their origin countries; that they may develop or strengthen international networks that contribute to trade with origin countries; and that they may ultimately return to their origin countries not only wealthier, but also with additional human capital they acquired in residency abroad—each of which also stands to improve the economic situation of their compatriots who remain at home.

Of course introducing complications to the most basic labor-market model can also generate welfare-reducing effects of brain drain for citizens who remain behind. For example, Bhagwati and Hamada (1974) develop a model in which internationally integrated labor markets can increase unemployment in countries from which skilled workers emigrate. The particular assumptions one makes about a wide range of factors that may influence how brain drain operates thus strongly influence its theoretical effect on remaining citizens. Much like the case of establishing immigration's economic effects, then, establishing emigration's economic effects in practice— including those of the brain drain—requires empirical investigation.

3.2 Evidence

3.2.1 *Human Capital*

In a series of recent cross-country studies, Beine, Docquier, and Oden-Defoort (2011), Beine, Docquier, and Rapoport (2001, 2008, 2010), Easterly and Nyarko (2009), and Docquier, Faye, and Pestieau (2008) study how the emigration of highly skilled individuals affects human capital formation in their home countries. Their results suggest that the prospect of brain drain may in fact generate "brain gain": the emigration of highly skilled persons is associated with higher levels of gross human capital formation in origin countries rather than less.

Recent micro studies of the brain drain's effect on human capital formation in origin countries corroborate this finding. For example, Batista, Lacuesta and Vicente (2012) find that brain drain drives most of Cape Verde's human capital formation. Gibson and McKenzie (2011), who study New Guinea and Tonga, find that the overwhelming majority of top highschool students in these countries consider emigration, which leads them to invest more in their schooling. Similarly, Chand and Clemens (2008) find evidence that brain drain enhances human capital investment among those with Indian ancestries in Fiji.

These studies furnish evidence for the potential importance of emigration's incentive effects on human capital investment and lend credence to the idea that such investment in migrant-origin countries is indeed endogenous to the prospect of emigration. They suggest that, rather than depleting migrant-origin countries of human capital, emigration is likely to enhance it.

3.2.2   Remittances

In 2014 estimated global flows of remittances to developing countries were $404 billion (World Bank 2014). To put the size of these flows in perspective, consider the fact that in 2011 official development assistance to the developing world was approximately a third of this amount—$133 billion. In 2012 remittances to Tajikistan equaled more than 50 percent of this country's GDP, and in eight other developing nations they equaled 20–30 percent of their respective nations' GDP.

As Clemens and McKenzie (2014) point out, remittances are generally unimportant contributors to economic growth in migrant-origin countries. Nevertheless, their importance to the welfare of citizens who remain behind in such countries is substantial. Much of the money that emigrants return is sent to alleviate the poverty of family members and friends who rely on emigrants' assistance for their support.

How brain drain in particular may affect remittances remains unclear. Faini (2007), Niimi, Ozden, and Schiff (2010), and Dustmann and Mestres (2010) provide evidence that suggests high-skilled emigrants may remit less than their low-skilled counterparts. On the other hand, Bollard et al. (2011) find that, conditional on remitting, more educated emigrants in fact remit more. Although a dearth of empirical work that focuses on high-skilled emigrants' remittance practices in particular makes it difficult to draw strong conclusions about brain drain in this regard, anecdotal evidence seems to comport better with the finding of Bollard et al. (2011). According to Kangasniemi, Winters, and Commander (2007), for instance, nearly half of Indian medical doctors in the United Kingdom send remittances to India, and among the half that remit, the average remitter sends 16 percent of his income.

While the emigrant-specific source of the tremendous flow of remittances going to citizens who remain behind in migrant-origin countries is an important question for the literature that considers brain drain, in terms of evaluating emigration's effect on poverty reduction for citizens who remain behind in migrant-origin countries, what seems more important is the volume of remittances, which is assuredly positively related to the number of emigrants, regardless of skill level.

3.2.3   Trade

Indeed, because many emigrants are low-skilled workers, it is important not to ignore how emigration affects citizens who remain at home more generally. Perhaps the best-documented such effect is that of improving trade between migrant-destination and migrant-origin countries. A large empirical literature finds that emigration facilitates such trade (see, for instance, Combes, Lafourcade, and Mayer 2005; Gould 1994; Head and Ries 1998; Rauch and Trindade 2002; Rauch and Casella 2003). Emigrant-created diasporas in migrant-destination countries create and strengthen trade networks with migrant-origin nations, contributing to larger commercial flows between such countries that benefit origin-country traders and consumers.

Additional evidence suggests that such diasporas may also facilitate the international transfer of knowledge, and thus technology and innovation, from emigrant-destination countries to emigrant-origin countries. Using data on patent citations, Kerr (2008), for instance, finds that emigrant-created ethnic diasporas in the United States enhance the international transfer of knowledge between the United States and emigrants' origin countries. In contrast, in a related study focusing on "innovator emigrants" from India, Agrawal et al. (2011) find that emigration may reduce origin-country access to knowledge on net by removing valuable innovators from the local knowledge network. However, these authors express some skepticism about what their finding may ultimately mean for the welfare of citizens who do not migrate.

Much empirical work remains to be done to evaluate emigration's economic effects for citizens in migrant-origin countries who do not migrate. Considered together, however, the literature on emigration's economic effects is optimistic. The evidence that this literature adduces points to a highly probable welfare-enhancing effect of emigration on citizens who remain behind.

4   ADDITIONAL ECONOMIC EFFECTS OF INTERNATIONAL LABOR MOBILITY

4.1   Institutional Reform

Political economists have long recognized the potential importance of "voting with one's feet" as a means through which citizens may be able to improve public officials' accountability to their wishes (Tiebout 1956). So-called "Tiebout competition" acts as a feedback mechanism in political markets akin to the profit-and-loss feedback mechanism in actual markets, which both informs producers (political officials) about how well they are satisfying consumers' (citizens') demands and incentivizes producers (political officials) to respond to what they learn. If citizens are mobile and political authorities are concerned with enlarging, or at least preserving, their tax bases, the prospect of inter-jurisdictional migration may improve their incentive to follow those policies their citizens demand.

Traditionally, inter-jurisdictional competition is considered in domestic contexts with reference to the movement of a country's citizens between federal jurisdictions, such as states, or within states, between municipalities. However, the mobility of citizens internationally may also be useful to citizens for improving the quality of their countries' governments.

International labor mobility is nowhere near as great as labor mobility domestically—because of the much more substantial policy barriers to international movement as well as the considerably larger cost of moving to another country for many citizens. Thus Tiebout competition's potential to improve governmental quality at the national level is surely much weaker than its potential to do so at the local level. Still, since some citizens in developing countries do in fact migrate internationally, and many more desire to do so, there is reason to think that inter-jurisdictional competition at the international level may be able to affect national governmental quality to some degree and that reducing policy impediments to international migration could strengthen this effect.

We are unaware of any empirical research that examines the effect of international Tiebout competition on governmental quality. However, a handful of studies consider how international labor mobility may affect governmental quality in migrant-origin countries through alternative mechanisms. Mahmoud et al. (2013), for example, argue that emigration creates political spillovers from migrants' destination countries to their countries of origin. Emigrants' exposure to alternative political institutions in destination countries provides them with new information about these institutions, which they may share with contacts in their countries of origin. This information diffusion has the power to alter the political tastes of citizens in migrant-origin countries who do not emigrate, strengthening their support for institutional reform. To examine this hypothesis, Mahmoud et al. (2013) examine emigration from Moldova to Western Europe, which began in the late 1990s. They find that this emigration was pivotal in bringing about the end of Communist government in Moldova in 2009 through the political spillover channel described above.

Emigration's potential influence on democracy in migrant-origin countries has been the subject of interest in the small literature that considers migration's effect on institutional quality and reform. Spilimbergo (2009), for instance, examines the influence of foreign education on democracy and finds that migrants who are educated in democratic countries and return home promote democracy in their origin countries. Using experimental evidence, Batista and Vicente (2011) similarly find support for the possibility that emigrants promote democratic institutions in their origin countries. Their results suggest that migrants who temporarily live abroad in nations with high-quality governance institutions increase the demand for political accountability in their origin countries when they return. In a still more recent study, Docquier et al. (2014) find that greater emigration leads to stronger democracy and more economic freedom in migrant-origin countries.

In principle, at least, it is also possible for emigration to affect institutions in migrant-origin countries negatively. Hansen (1988) and Ferguson (2003), for example, speculate that emigration from Mexico and Haiti may contribute to the delay of institutional reform in these countries by, for instance, facilitating large remittance flows that prop up dysfunctional economies, or by creating "safety valves" through which such economies can unburden themselves of unemployed workers. Thus far, however, the literature that considers migration's influence on institutions empirically unanimously finds evidence for the opposite effect: in practice, greater emigration appears to contribute to institutional reform in poor countries rather than contributing to reform's delay.

4.2 Environment

Although not a concern in the scholarly literature, some environmental advocates have expressed concern that the movement of people from poor countries to wealthy ones may have significant negative environmental effects.[6] According to those who harbor such fears, because wealthy people produce and consume many more goods than poor people, the ecological footprint of wealthy people is much larger. The movement of people from poorer countries to wealthier ones, which enriches those who move, may therefore contribute to accelerated environmental degradation.

The relationship between income and environmental impact may be more subtle than that described by those who express this concern, however. According to one hypothesis, for example, the relationship between

6. See, for instance, Kraly (1998).

economic development and environmental impact is hump-shaped—a relationship known as the "environmental Kuznets curve" (Shafik 1994).

The logic underlying this curve is straightforward. At subsistence levels of development, because production is nearly nonexistent, so too is the environmental impact of a country's economic activity. As an economy grows, production increases, contributing to a rise in environmental degradation. With still further economic growth, however, environmental degradation declines: production again increases, but now tends to be undertaken in more environmentally friendly ways. For example, clean-burning fuels are substituted for dirty ones, renewable resources are relied on more heavily than non-renewable ones, and investments in pollution-reducing technologies are undertaken. Unlike economies just beginning to experience economic growth, which are not yet rich enough to afford more environmentally friendly production processes, those that have grown more substantially, and thus are wealthier, are able to adopt them, leading to improved environmental quality.

A large literature debates the evidence for an environmental Kuznets curve.[7] Much of the controversy surrounds the level of development a country needs to reach before it exhibits production activity that reduces its environmental footprint, as well as how this relationship may vary depending upon the particular pollutant one considers. Nevertheless, even the possibility of a Kuznets-curve type of relationship between development and environmental impact suggests that the fears that migration from poor countries to wealthy ones will wreak havoc on the environment are, at the very least, premature.

It is possible, and indeed likely, that migration from poor counties to rich ones improves global environmental quality on at least some dimensions because of environmental Kuznets curve relationships. Migration from middling developing countries to developed countries may move people from the top of the environmental Kuznets curve, where environmental degradation is greatest, to its "wealthy tail," where degradation is less severe. Similarly, migration from countries that are so undeveloped that they are located at the "impoverished tail" of the environmental Kuznets curve may move people who, with the eventual growth of their economies, would have otherwise contributed more to global environmental damage, at least temporarily, directly to the "wealthy tail" of the curve where environmental degradation is lower, bypassing the curve's middle portion where degradation is greatest. More empirical work is required to

7. See, for instance, Tisdell (2001), Dasgupta et al. (2002), and Harbaugh et al. (2002).

understand how migration from poor countries to rich ones may affect environmental quality. However, at this stage we see little theoretical reason to expect a negative impact, let alone a large one, and even less evidence for such an effect.

4.3   Urban Renewal

An underappreciated, and understudied, economic effect of international labor mobility is the influence of migrants on urban centers. The ethnic-enclave communities, such as "Chinatown," "Little Italy," and others, that populate major metropolitan areas in the United States in particular are among the most popular city destinations for tourists and residents. Such communities contribute to the diversity and cosmopolitan dynamics that give major urban areas their particular "feel" and are partly responsible for making such areas vibrant centers of commercial and social activity.

Recent research suggests that immigrants may benefit the economies of urban areas in another way as well: by facilitating declining cities' revival. According to Vigdor (2014), the population and financial decline of New York City in the 1970s was ultimately reversed by immigrants who moved there in the 1980s and 1990s. While native-born citizens continued to exit the city during these decades, immigrants entered in still greater numbers. Vigdor (2014) contends that this immigrant-fueled reversal in city population growth played an important role in supporting the tax base required for the city's operation, stabilizing housing prices in the metropolitan area, and generating the density required for the city to thrive economically.

Vigdor's (2014) study is the only work we are aware of that considers immigrants' effect on urban renewal, so it is unclear to what extent immigrants may have played a role in revitalizing other major metropolitan areas in the United States or elsewhere. Nevertheless, his study points to the potential importance of immigration for such revitalization and will hopefully spur additional research in this area that sheds light on the generalizability of his findings.

5   CONCLUSION

Our analysis of the economic effects of international labor mobility leads to several conclusions. First, if creating additional wealth is the goal, it is hard to argue with the principle of comparative advantage. The implication of this principle for immigration policy interested in maximizing global wealth is straightforward: eliminate policy barriers to the international movement of labor.

Getting the most of out the world's labor force requires permitting labor to move to those areas where it is most productive. At the moment, the developing world is very much overpopulated relative to this benchmark, and the developed world is very much underpopulated. The unsurprising result is substantial economic inefficiency relative to what is achievable with even moderately more liberal immigration policy. There is no great mystery here. Adam Smith pointed to the logic underlying the necessity of international labor mobility for realizing the world's wealth-creating potential in 1776, and the point has been reiterated by various economists over the course of the subsequent 230 years.

Since it seems unreasonable at this point to believe that the message has not been heard, the most sensible inference to draw from the continuation of severe restrictions on the international movement of people by developed countries is that policymakers in such countries are not in fact interested in maximizing global wealth. This should not come as any great surprise since, as James Buchanan and Gordon Tullock pointed out some decades ago, policymakers, like everyone else, aim to serve their own interests rather than society's (see, for instance, Buchanan 1979). How much more true this must be when society refers to the world's population instead of a nation's.

The tremendous increases in wealth that freer international migration policy would generate would not accrue equally to every subpopulation. Indeed, in the short run some individuals are likely to lose from freer migration policy, albeit in most cases minimally. In our view these distributional considerations—or rather popular perceptions of them—are the major reason that countries such as the United States have not done more to liberalize their immigration policies. This observation brings us to the second conclusion of our analysis of the literature that considers the economic effects of international labor mobility.

To the extent that policymakers are reluctant to liberalize international migration policy despite its clear global welfare-enhancing effect because they believe that potentially vulnerable native subpopulations in their countries would suffer significantly, they are mistaken. Our examination of the research that investigates immigration's effects on native wages and employment suggests that, while perhaps negative, these effects are (a) small and (b) temporary. This is little solace to an American worker whose wage falls for some time, or whose work hours diminish, in light of increased immigration. However, the considered policymaker will take note that other American workers will experience a rise in their wages and increased employment opportunities because of increased immigration, and in the long run it seems that the American-worker beneficiaries of increased immigration gain more, or at least not less, than American-worker losers suffer.

Of course self-interested policymakers are unlikely to be moved by these facts, since the losses experienced by American workers of the former group in the face of increased immigration are readily seen and thus complained of, while those experienced by American workers of the latter group in the absence of increased immigration go unseen and thus undiscussed. Ultimately, then, it seems that immigration liberalization in a country such as the United States would require policymakers to put more weight on the welfare gains of the immigrants, which dwarfs any net welfare gain or loss to natives. As would-be immigrants do not have the ability to vote or contribute to political officials' campaigns, however, we are not optimistic about this prospect.

Third, although we doubt seriously that the economic effects of emigration play any role in policymakers' thinking about international migration policy, it bears noting that, here too, evidence that more liberal policy would negatively affect citizens who do not migrate in migrant-origin countries is scant, and evidence that more emigration, which a more liberal migration policy would of course achieve, would improve the welfare of citizens who do not move is substantial.

It does not seem insane to think that in a well-functioning democracy governed by sensible and informed policymakers, we should expect the implementation of a policy reform that would almost certainly improve the long-run welfare of its average citizen and, in the worst case, leave him no worse off, and perhaps double the income of some of the poorest people in the world, while almost certainly leaving none of them worse off—particularly when the losses experienced by any losing subpopulations as a result of the reform are likely to be small and transitory. This is precisely the situation the United States confronts with respect to the liberalization of policy relating to international labor mobility. Yet no reasonable person expects dramatic change to this policy in the direction of liberalization anytime soon. As noted above, this situation should not puzzle students of political economy. That does not mean, however, that it should not frustrate them.

REFERENCES

Agrawal, Ajay K., Devesh Kapur, John McHale, and Alexander Oettl. 2011. "Brain Drain or Brain Bank? The Impact of Skilled Emigration on Poor-Country Innovation." *Journal of Urban Economics* 69: 43–55.

Altonji, Joseph G., and David Card. 1991. "The Effects of Immigration on the Labor Outcomes of Less-Skilled Natives." In *Immigration, Trade and Labor*, eds. John Abowd and Richard B. Freeman, pp. 201–234. Chicago: University of Chicago Press.

Anderson, Kym, and Will Martin. 2005. "Agricultural Trade Reform and the Doha Development Agenda." *World Economy* 28: 1301–1327.

Angrist, Joshua D., and Adriana Kugler. 2003. "Protective or Counter-Protective? Labor Market Institutions and the Effect of Immigration on EU Natives." *Economic Journal* 113: 302–331.

Batista, Catia, Aitor Lacuesta, and Pedro C. Vicente. 2012. "Testing the 'Brain Gain' Hypothesis: Micro Evidence from Cape Verde." *Journal of Development Economics* 97: 32–45.

Batista, Catia, and Pedro C. Vicente. 2011. "Do Migrants Improve Governance at Home? Evidence from a Voting Experiment." *World Bank Economic Review* 25: 77–104.

Beine, Michel, Frédéric Docquier, and Cecily Oden-Defoort. 2011. "A Panel Data Analysis of the Brain Gain." *World Development* 39: 523–532.

Beine, Michel, Frédéric Docquier, and Hillel Rapoport. 2001. "Brain Drain and Economic Growth: Theory and Evidence." *Journal of Development Economics* 64: 275–289.

Beine, Michel, Frédéric Docquier, and Hillel Rapoport. 2008. "Brain Drain and Human Capital Formation in Developing Countries: Winners and Losers." *Economic Journal* 118: 631–652.

Beine, Michel, Frédéric Docquier, and Hillel Rapoport. 2010. "On the Robustness of Brain Gain Estimates." *Annals of Economics and Statistics* 97/98 January/June: 143–165.

Bhagwati, Jagdish, and Koichi Hamada. 1974. "The Brain Drain, International Integration of Markets for Professionals and Unemployment: A Theoretical Analysis." *Journal of Development Economics* 1: 19–42.

Bollard, Albert, David McKenzie, Melanie Morten, and Hillel Rapoport. 2011. "Remittances and the Brain Drain Revisited: The Microdata Show That More Educated Migrants Remit More." *World Bank Economic Review* 25: 132–156.

Borjas, George J. 1994. "The Economics of Immigration." *Journal of Economic Literature* 32: 1667–1717.

Borjas, George J. 1995. "The Economic Benefits from Immigration." *Journal of Economic Perspectives* 9: 3–22.

Borjas, George J. 2001. "Does Immigration Grease the Wheels of the Labor Market?" *Brookings Papers on Economic Activity* 2001: 69–119.

Borjas, George J. 2003. "The Labor Demand Curve *Is* Downward Sloping: Reexamining the Impact of Immigration on the Labor Market." *Quarterly Journal of Economics* 118: 1335–1374.

Borjas, George J., Richard B. Freeman, and Lawrence F. Katz. 1992. "On the Labor Market Impacts of Immigration and Trade." In *Immigration and the Workforce: Economic Consequences for the United States and Source Areas*, eds. George J. Borjas and Richard B. Freeman, pp. 213–244. Chicago: University of Chicago Press.

Borjas, George J., Richard B. Freeman, and Lawrence F. Katz. 1996. "Searching for the Effect of Immigration on the Labor Market." *American Economic Review* 86: 246–251.

Borjas, George J., and Lawrence F. Katz. 2007. "The Evolution of the Mexican-Born Workforce in the United States." In *Mexican Immigration to the United States*, ed. George J. Borjas, pp. 13–56. Chicago: University of Chicago Press.

Borjas, George J., and Valeria A. Ramey. 1995. "Foreign Competition, Market Power, and Wage Inequality: Theory and Evidence." *Quarterly Journal of Economics* 110: 1075–1110.

Brücker, Herber, and Elke J. Jahn. 2011. "Migration and Wage-Setting: Reassessing the Labor Market Effects of Migration." *Scandinavian Journal of Economics* 113: 286–317.

Buchanan, James M. 1979. "Politics Without Romance: A Sketch of Positive Public Choice Theory and Its Normative Implications." *IHS-Journal* 3: B1–B11.

Card, David. 1990. "The Impact of the Mariel Boatlift on the Miami Labor Market." *Industrial and Labor Relations Review* 43: 245–257.

Card, David. 2001. "Immigrant Inflows, Native Outflows and the Local Labor Market Impacts of Higher Immigration." *Journal of Labor Economics* 19: 22–64.

Card, David. 2005. "Is the New Immigration Really so Bad?" *Economic Journal* 115: F300–F323.

Card, David. 2009. "Immigration and Inequality." *American Economic Review* 99: 1–21.

Card, David. 2012. "Comment: The Elusive Search for Negative Wage Impacts of Immigration." *Journal of the European Economic Association* 10: 211–215.

Chand, Satish, and Michael A. Clemens. 2008. "Skilled Emigration and Skill Creation: A Quasi- Experiment." Center for Global Development Working Paper No. 152.

Clemens, Michael A. 2009. "Skill-Flow: A Fundamental Reconsideration of Skilled-Worker Mobility and Development." Center for Global Development Working Paper No. 180.

Clemens, Michael A. 2011. "Economics and Emigration: Trillion-Dollar Bills on the Sidewalk?" *Journal of Economic Perspectives* 25: 83–106.

Clemens, Michael A., and David McKenzie. 2014. "Why Don't Remittances Appear to Affect Growth?" World Bank Policy Research Working Paper No. 6856.

Clemens, Michael A., Claudio E. Montenegro, and Lant Pritchett. 2008. "The Place Premium: Wage Differences for Identical Workers across the U.S. Border." Center for Global Development Working Paper No. 148.

Combes, Pierre-Phillippe, Miren Lafourcade, and Thierry Mayer. 2005. "The Trade-Creating Effects of Business and Social Networks: Evidence from France." *Journal of International Economics* 66: 1–29.

Dasgupta, Susmita, Benoit Laplante, Hua Wang, and David Wheeler. 2002. "Confronting the Environmental Kuznets Curve." *Journal of Economic Perspectives* 16: 147–168.

De New, John P., and Klaus F. Zimmermann. 1994a. "Blue Collar Labor Vulnerability: Wage Impacts of Migration." In *The Economic Consequences of Immigration to Germany*, eds. Gunter Steinmann and Ralf E. Urich, pp. 81–99. Heidelberg: Physica-Verlag.

De New, John P., and Klaus F. Zimmermann. 1994b. "Native Wage Impacts of Foreign Labor: A Random Effects Panel Analysis." *Journal of Population Economics* 7: 177–192.

Dessus, Sébastien, Kiichiro Fukasaku, and Raed Safadi. 1999. "Multilateral Tariff Liberalisation and the Developing Countries." OECD Development Centre Policy Brief 18.

Docquier, Frédéric, Ousmane Faye, and Pierre Pestieau. 2008. "Is Migration a Good Substitute for Subsidies?" *Journal of Development Economics* 86: 263–276.

Docquier, Frédéric, Elisabetta Lodigiani, Hillel Rapoport, and Maurice Schiff. 2014. "Emigration and Democracy." CEPREMAP Working Paper No. 1406.

Docquier, Frédéric, and Hillel Rapoport. 2012. "Globalization, Brain Drain, and Development." *Journal of Economic Literature* 50: 681–730.

Dustmann, Christian, Tommaso Frattini, and Ian P. Preston. 2013. "The Effect of Immigration along the Distribution of Wages." *Review of Economic Studies* 80: 146–173.

Dustmann, Christian, and Josep Mestres. 2010. "Remittances and Temporary Migration." *Journal of Development Economics* 92: 62–70.

Easterly, William, and Yaw Nyarko. 2009. "Is the Brain Drain Good for Africa?" In *Skilled Immigration Today: Problems, Prospects and Policies*, eds. Jagdish Bhagwati and Gordon Hanson, pp. 316–360. Oxford: Oxford University Press.

Faini, Riccardo. 2007. "Remittances and the Brain Drain." *World Bank Economic Review* 21: 177–191.

Ferguson, James. 2003. *Migration in the Caribbean: Haiti, the Dominican Republic and Beyond*. London: Minority Rights Group International.

Ferrar, Ana, David A. Green, and W. Craig Riddell. 2006. "The Effect of Literacy on Immigrant Earnings." *Journal of Human Resources* 41: 380–410.

Friedberg, Rachel M., and Jennifer Hunt. 1995. "The Impact of Immigrants on Host Country Wages, Employment and Growth." *Journal of Economic Literature* 9: 23–44.

Gang, Ira N., and Francisco L. Rivera-Batiz. 1994. "Labor Market Effects of Immigration in the United States and Europe: Substitution vs. Complementarity." *Journal of Population Economics* 7: 157–175.

Gibson, John, and David McKenzie. 2011. "Eight Questions about Brain Drain." *Journal of Economic Perspectives* 25: 107–128.

Gould, David M. 1994. "Immigrants' Links to the Home Country: Empirical Implication for U.S. Bilateral Trade Flows." *Review of Economics and Statistics* 76: 302–316.

Gross, Dominique M. 2002. "Three Million Foreigners, Three Million Unemployed? Immigration Flows and the Labor Market in France." *Applied Economics* 34: 1969–1983.

Grossman, Jean B. 1982. "The Substitutability of Natives and Immigrants in Production." *Review of Economic and Statistics* 64: 596–603.

Hamilton, Bob, and John Whalley. 1984. "Efficiency and Distributional Implications of Global Restrictions on Labour Mobility." *Journal of Development Economics* 14: 61–75.

Hansen, L. O. 1988. "The Political and Socio-Economic Context of Legal and Illegal Mexican Migration to the U.S. (1942–1984)." *International Migration* 26: 95–107.

Harbaugh, William T., Arik Levinson, and David Molloy Wilson. 2002. "Reexamining Evidence for the Environmental Kuznets Curve." *Review of Economics and Statistics* 84: 541–551.

Havocscope Global Black Market Information. 2014. "Prices Charged by Human Smugglers." http://www.havocscope.com/black-market-prices/human-smuggling-fees/.

Head, Keith, and John Reis. 1998. "Immigration and Trade Creation: Econometric Evidence from Canada." *Canadian Journal of Economics* 31: 47–62.

Hertel, Thomas, and Roman Keeney. 2006. "What Is at Stake: The Relative Importance of Import Barriers, Export Subsidies, and Domestic Support." In *Agricultural Trade Reform and the Doha Development Agenda*, eds. Kym Anderson
and William Martin, pp. 37–62. Washington, DC: World Bank.

Iregui, Ana María. 2005. "Efficiency Gains from the Elimination of Global Restrictions on Labour Mobility." In *Poverty, International Migration and Asylum*,
eds. George J. Borjas and Jeff Crisp, pp. 211–238. New York: Palgrave
Macmillan.

Kangasniemi, Mari, L. Alan Winters, and Simon Commander. 2007. "Is the Medical
Brain Drain Beneficial? Evidence from Overseas Doctors in the UK." *Social
Science and Medicine* 65: 915–923.

Kerr, Sari Pekkala, and William R. Kerr. 2011. "Economic Impacts of Immigration:
A Survey." *Finnish Economic Papers* 24: 1–32.

Kerr, William R. 2008. "Ethnic Scientific Communities and International Technology Diffusion." *Review of Economics and Statistics* 90: 518–537.

Klein, Paul, and Gustavo Ventura. 2007. "TFP Differences and the Aggregate Effects
of Labor Mobility in the Long Run." *B.E. Journal of Macroeconomics* 7: Article
10.

Kraly, Ellen Percy. 1998. "Immigration and the Environment: A Framework for Establishing a Possible Relationship." *Population Research and Policy Review* 17:
421–437.

LaLonde, Robert J., and Robert H. Topel. 1991. "Immigrants in the American Labor
Market: Quality, Assimilation, and Distributional Effects." *American Economic
Review* 81: 297–302.

Longhi, Simonetta, Peter Nijkamp, and Jacques Poot. 2005. "A Meta-Analytic Assessment of the Effects of Immigration on Wages." *Journal of Economic Surveys*
19: 451–477.

Longhi, Simonetta, Peter Nijkamp, and Jacques Poot. 2008a. "Meta-Analysis of Empirical Evidence on the Labor Market Impacts of Immigration." IZA Discussion Paper No. 3418.

Longhi, Simonetta, Peter Nijkamp, and Jacques Poot. 2008b. "The Impact of Im-
migration on the Employment of Natives in Regional Labour Markets: A
Meta-Analysis." In *Migration and Human Capital*, eds. Jacques Poot, Brigitte
Waldorf, and Leo van Wissen, pp. 173–194. Cheltenham, UK: Edward
Elgar.

Mahmoud, Toman Omar, Hillel Rapoport, Andreas Steinmayr, and Christoph Treb-
esch. 2013. "The Effect of Labor Migration on the Diffusion of Democracy:
Evidence from a Former Soviet Republic." CReAM Discussion Paper Series
No. 1320.

Mexican Migration Project. 2010. Database MMP128. mmp.opr.princeton.edu.

Mishra, Prachi. 2007. "Emigration and Wages in Source Countries: Evidence from
Mexico." *Journal of Development Economics* 82: 180–199.

Moses, Jonathon W., and Bjørn Letnes. 2004. "The Economic Costs to International
Labor Restrictions: Revisiting the Empirical Discussion." *World Development*
32: 1609–1626.

Mühleisen, Martin, and Klaus F. Zimmermann. 1994. "A Panel Analysis of Job
Changes and Unemployment." *European Economic Review* 38: 793–801.

Niimi, Yoko, Caglar Ozden, and Maurice Schiff. 2010. "Remittances and the Brain
Drain: Skilled Migrants Do Remit Less." *Annals of Economics and Statistics*
97/98 January/June: 123–141.

Ottaviano, Gianmarco I. P., and Giovanni Peri. 2008. "Immigration and National Wages: Clarifying the Theory and the Empirics." NBER Working Paper No. 14188.

Ottaviano, Gianmarco I. P., and Giovanni Peri. 2012. "Rethinking the Effect of Immigration on Wages." *Journal of the European Economic Association* 10: 152–197.

Pelham, Brett, and Gerver Torres. 2008. "A Country's Richest Citizens Report Greatest Desire to Migrate." *Gallup*. July 30. http://www.gallup.com/poll/109144/countrys-wealthiest-citizens-report-greatest-desire-migrate.aspx.

Peri, Giovanni. 2007. "Immigrants' Complementarities and Native Wages: Evidence from California." NBER Working Paper No. 12956.

Peri, Giovanni, and Chad Sparber. 2009. "Task Specialization, Immigration and Wages." *American Economic Journal: Applied Economics* 1: 135–169.

Pischke, Jorn-Steffen, and Johannes Velling. 1994. "Wage and Employment Effects of Immigration to Germany: An Analysis Based on Local Labour Markets." CEPR Discussion Paper No. 935.

Rauch, James E., and Alessandra Casella. 2003. "Overcoming Informational Barriers to International Resource Allocation: Prices and Ties." *Economic Journal* 113: 21–42.

Rauch, James E., and Vitor Trindade. 2002. "Ethnic Chinese Networks in International Trade." *Review of Economics and Statistics* 84: 116–130.

Shafik, Nemat. 1994. "Economic Development and Environmental Quality: An Econometric Analysis." *Oxford Economic Papers* 46: 757–773.

Shleifer, Andrei. 2009. "The Age of Milton Friedman." *Journal of Economic Literature* 47: 123–145.

Smith, Adam. 1776. *An Inquiry into the Nature and Causes of the Wealth of Nations.* London: W. Strahan and T. Cadell.

Spilimbergo, Antonio. 2009. "Democracy and Foreign Education." *American Economic Review* 99: 528–543.

Tiebout, Charles M. 1956. "A Pure Theory of Local Expenditures." *Journal of Political Economy* 64: 416–424.

Tisdell, Clement. 2001. "Globalisation and Sustainability: Environmental Kuznets Curve and the WTO." *Ecological Economics* 39: 185–196.

Torres, Gerver, and Brett Pelham. 2008. "One-Quarter of World's Population May Wish to Migrate." *Gallup*. June 24. http://www.gallup.com/poll/108325/onequarter-worlds-population-may-wish-migrate.aspx.

US Department of State. 2014. "D 2014 – Selected Entrants." http://travel.state.gov/content/visas/english/immigrate/diversity-visa/dv2014-selected-entrants.html.

Vigdor, Jacob L. 2014. *Immigration and New York City: The Contributions of Foreign Born Americans to New York's Renaissance, 1975–2013.* New York: AS/COA.

Winkelmann, Rainer, and Klaus F. Zimmermann. 1993. "Ageing, Migration and Labour Mobility." In *Labour Markets in an Ageing Europe*, eds. Paul Johnson and Klaus F. Zimmerman, pp. 255–282. Cambridge: Cambridge University Press.

Winter-Ebmer, Rudolph, and Klaus F. Zimmermann. 1999. "East-West Trade and Migration: The Austro-German Case." In *Migration: The Controversies and the Evidence*, eds. Ricardo Faini, Jaime de Melo, and Klaus F. Zimmermann, pp. 296–327. Cambridge: Cambridge University Press.

Winter-Ebmer, Rudolph, and Josef Zweimüller. 1996. "Immigration, Trade, and Austrian Unemployment." CEPR Discussion Paper No. 1346.

World Bank. 2001. *Global Economic Prospects and the Developing Countries 2002.* Washington, DC: World Bank.

World Bank. 2014. "Migration and Development Brief 22." April 11.

Zorlu, Aslan, and Joop Hartog. 2005. "The Effect of Immigration on Wages in Three European Countries." *Journal of Population Economics* 18: 113–115.

CHAPTER 3

୶

The Fiscal Impact of Immigration

ALEX NOWRASTEH

1 INTRODUCTION

The fiscal impact of immigration—how immigrants and their descendants affect government budgets—is a widely debated and contentious issue. Economists overwhelmingly accept the economic gains of immigration, but are less certain about immigrants' impact on government budgets. Gauging the fiscal effects of immigration is a very complex and difficult endeavor. Despite the difficulty and the raft of studies that attempt to measure the fiscal impact, the results tend to find relatively small effects that are mostly positive—immigrants slightly increase net government revenue. Even in situations where immigrants increase budget deficits, those negative effects are likely swamped by the large economic benefits elsewhere in the economy. Contention over this issue is fueled by the numerous methods and complexity of analysis that obscure the fiscal costs of immigration.

The complexities are many. Each layer of the United States' federal structure of government—federal, state, and local—is funded by different types of taxes, and each spends its budget on different programs and in different ways. Many government spending programs are directed at specific age groups. Public education is one example of a front-loaded cost, expended on children and young adults at the beginning of their life span, while Medicare and Social Security are back-loaded costs, expended closer to the end of the recipient's life span (MaCurdy et al. 1998: 61-62). The intertemporal structure of many government programs makes age a relevant factor in analyzing the fiscal costs of immigration, but so do other factors such as the skill level, fertility, and language ability of the immigrants themselves. This is similar to estimating the fiscal impact of newborn children, who consume vast amounts of public schooling before paying taxes. However, the working life of an immigrant can be shorter than that of a native because immigrants often immigrate later in life, meaning that they also consume less government-funded education as a result (Rowthorn 2008: 563–564).

The types of public goods consumed by immigrants also affect their fiscal impact. If the public goods are "pure," meaning that they are non-rivalrous and non-excludable, then more taxpayers in the form of immigrants spread out the tax cost without diminishing the quality of the goods. Immigrants lower the tax burden of providing pure public goods such as national defense and servicing the national debt. But if the public goods are "congestible," more immigrants could decrease the quality of the goods, prompting the government to spend more tax dollars to maintain the quality. Some congestion occurs for most government-supplied goods such as roads or education whenever pop-ulation increases, by immigration or through procreation, but the fiscal impact varies widely.

Immigrants also impact the US economy. They can displace US-born workers, complement them, or have little impact on their employment opportunities, all of which alter tax revenue and government welfare expenditures in different ways. Immigrants are also consumers of real estate and other goods and services in the United States, boosting ag-gregate demand and spurring investment that further grows the taxable economy. In short, the fiscal impact of immigration is a deceptively simple question that obscures a complex reality: Is the extra tax reve-nue *created* by immigrants more or less than the cost of the extra government-supplied goods and services they consume? If it is more, then the fiscal impact of immigration is positive, and immigrants de-crease the budget deficit or produce a budget surplus. If less, then the fiscal impact of immigration is negative, and immigrants increase the budget deficit.

The methods employed to study the fiscal impact of immigration are also numerous and complicated (see Rothman and Espenshade 1992 for a literature review of the earliest attempts to measure the net fiscal impact of immigration). This chapter will examine these methods' relative merits and demerits, and present the common findings of the major studies using the various methods.

2 DYNAMIC ECONOMIC AND FISCAL EFFECTS

Studies that estimate the economic impact of immigration, how that economic impact affects tax payments, and how immigrants increase expenditures over time are worth serious consideration. Such studies are called "dynamic," as they rightly assume that immigrants impact all of those budget areas over time (Preston 2013: 20). Studies that assume immigrants do not affect the taxable economy are "static" and can reveal the net fiscal impact of a stock of immigrants in a given year. While there are some insightful static analyses, those that do not state their methods, only count fiscal costs, or only calculate tax revenue will be ignored in this chapter.

Dynamic fiscal impact estimates must also be longitudinal, or forward-looking, because large government expenditures are either front-loaded or back-loaded on individual life cycles. Young immigrants of working age may pay more in taxes than they consume in government benefits today, but, when they retire, they will become net consumers of benefits. Longitudinal studies analyze immigrants' long-term impact on the economy and government expenditures—including their descendants, if possible. They then discount their net fiscal contribution to the present, expressed as a net present value, and compare the effects to a projected fiscal baseline (Lee and Miller 1998: 183–184; National Research Council 1997: 339–340; Rowthorn 2008: 566). A problem with longitudinal studies is that they are based on forecasts of future government expenditures, the economic impact of immigrants and their descendants, and future tax rates—three variables that are constantly in flux and *ex ante* unknowable. Changes in policy, such as the creation of new entitlement programs and unanticipated surges in economic growth, can quickly eviscerate even the most thoughtful fiscal projection. Furthermore, many longitudinal studies assume that the government will balance its budget at some point in the future. Adjusting the date at which the government will balance its budget, whether it will balance its budget through tax increases or budget cuts or a combination, or even assuming that it will not balance its budget all impact the result (Auerbach and Oreopoulos 2000: 151).

Another type of study uses a relatively easier static accounting methodology that seeks to explain how current immigrants affect the economy and government budgets today or at a specific point of time in the past. Static accounting studies do not involve assumptions and projections for the future, a characteristic that makes them more accurate than longitudinal studies, but they cannot indicate how future immigrants will affect budget deficits (Lee and Miller 1998: 200–201). The static accounting methodology largely misses accumulated fiscal costs and benefits over time, but it is useful in answering questions such as, "What would happen this year if all illegal immigrants disappeared?" (Lee and Miller 1998: 184). This chapter will discuss a handful of static accounting studies before delving into the more complex dynamic models.

All manner of fiscal impact studies need to grapple with identifying their variables. The first is to decide who the immigrants are. Much of the fiscal impact that immigrants have is through their children. An immigrant may not consume public education, but his or her children likely will. For long-term estimates, the public education costs of those children are important, but so is the long-term tax revenue paid by those children after they finish school—especially for the entitlement programs. If the children are counted when they are young and costly, then they need to be counted when they are middle-aged and paying taxes, too (Kandel 2011: 6–7; Lee and Miller 1998: 184). Deciding when to stop counting the fiscal impact of descendants is difficult and, the more generations that are counted, the more speculative the economic growth and demographic assumptions become (National Research Council 1997: 342–343).

Immigrants can also be counted as individuals or as members of a household. Counting the net fiscal contribution of households headed by immigrants biases the cost estimates upward, because it counts the costs of children enrolled in public schools until they leave home and start working, ignoring their future tax revenue (Lee and Miller 1998: 184). Another reason dynamic longitudinal studies are best completed by estimating the fiscal impacts of individuals is that the size of households changes over time, producing a variable that changes and thus is difficult to analyze (National Research Council 1997: 256, 305). Net fiscal cost calculations of households are highly misleading (Lee and Miller 2000: 350–351).

Accumulated net fiscal cost estimates over long periods of time also have to be represented in an understandable way because of the time value of money. One hundred dollars today is not the same as one hundred dollars in 50 years due to inflation, interest rates, return on investment, and numerous other factors. Therefore, longitudinal dynamic studies over *long* time periods need to show the net fiscal impact in present value. Two other ways to portray the long-run net fiscal costs are through estimating what percentage of future government budget deficits or surpluses can be attributed to immigrants and through estimating the size of the immigrant surplus or deficit in relation to the entire economy (see Rector and Richwine 2013 for a study that ignores the time value of money).

2.1 Estimating Future Tax Revenue Effects

Estimating the economic gains from immigration is essential to estimating future additional tax revenue that will be collected due to immigrant economic activities. The most obvious one is the skill level of immigrants. The more high-skilled the immigrants, the higher the wages, and the more they pay in taxes, *ceteris paribus*. The incidence of taxation is important here, as counting only the taxes directly paid by immigrants likely understates the taxes that immigrants "pay." Immigrants are generally, but not always, complementary to American workers and other factors of production, thus increasing incomes for many American workers and the American owners of capital and land. For instance, a low-skilled immigrant might not pay income tax, but his or her employer will likely make a higher profit and pay additional taxes as a result of hiring the worker. If those effects are not included, then the benefits will be underestimated.

Immigrants affect the supply side of the economy by directly increasing the supply of labor. Judging the net fiscal impact requires looking at wages, the labor force participation rate (LFPR), employment rates, and the other variables examined by labor economists. But other factors unique to immigration, like English language fluency, greatly impact earnings and tax payments. English fluency boosts wages by 21 percent on average, all else remaining equal (Lewis 2011: 7), and is a good predictor of future wages, especially since immigrant wages will rise over time as they and their descendants learn English (Access Economic Pty Limited 2008: 11). Low-skilled immigrants generally have an initially lower rate of English proficiency and have a slower rate of linguistic assimilation over their lifetimes, but their children are nearly uniformly fluent in English, which explains part of the rapid rise in incomes from the first to the second generation. Higher skilled immigrants are usually English fluent upon arrival. Immigrant labor substitutability or complementarity, depending on skill level and other factors, must also be factored into any estimates (see Borjas 2003; Borjas and Katz 2007; Borjas et al. 2011; Kerr and Kerr 2011; Lewis 2011; Ottaviano and Peri 2012; Peri and Sparber 2009).

Immigrants also boost the demand side of the economy through buying goods and services in the United States. One such area of demand is the housing and real estate market, which is likely more affected by immigration than the labor market because the supply of real estate is relatively inelastic (Saiz 2003: 20). For instance, a 1 percent increase in a city's population causes a citywide increase in rents by about 1 percent (Saiz 2007: 345). When the increase is unexpected, a 1 percent rise in population increases rents by 3.75 percent with the effect of also pushing up housing prices and increasing local and state tax revenue from property tax (Saiz 2007: 345), as well as stimulating additional construction to meet the demand. Jacob Vigdor estimates that each individual immigrant out of America's roughly 40 million immigrants adds, on average, 11.6 cents to the value of each home in their local county, boosting the national US taxable housing value by an estimated $3.7 trillion (Vigdor 2013: 2). Interestingly, much of the added housing value is located on the outskirts of the most expensive cities (Vigdor 2013: 14). The increase in real estate prices has a bigger tax effect on states and local governments who collect property tax than on federal government tax revenues. The prices for other goods and services are likely affected by a demand effect that varies by elasticity in different sectors of the economy.

Further indirect economic effects are likely important, but are very difficult to estimate. Immigrants tend to increase productivity through a further division of labor and increase the quantity of skilled native-born workers (see Cortés and Tessada 2011). Higher-skilled immigrants are very innovative, inventive, and entrepreneurial (Fairlie 2014: 11–14; Hanson 2012: 26–27). Lower-skilled immigrants increase returns to owning capital that, in turn, increases investment that boosts production and labor demand (see Lewis 2010).

2.2 Estimating Future Government Expenditure Effects

Estimating the future economic effects and extra tax revenue collected because of immigration is difficult, but it is only half of the calculation. Future additional government expenditures must also be factored in. As mentioned earlier, the per-capita fiscal burden of supporting some pure public goods, such as national defense and the public debt, will decrease as the population increases due to immigration (Cully 2012: 6; Lee and Miller 1998: 187). Congestible publicly provided goods, like public education, must also be considered.

Education is a congestible government-supplied good that is primarily funded by state and local governments and is often their largest budget expenditure (Congressional Budget Office 2007: 7). Many immigrant children are non-English speakers, which increases the cost of educating them, while many move to other states after graduation to begin their working lives—denying the state and local governments that educate them tax revenue to cover the costs of their education. A large increase in the number of immigrants could increase education costs substantially for state and local governments, explaining why some studies find that immigration increases budget deficits for those levels of government.

Immigrant income is a powerful predictive tool in estimating how much means-tested welfare benefits are likely to be consumed. Higher-skilled immigrants consume few means-tested welfare benefits (see Desai et al. 2009). Lower-skilled immigrants are more likely to consume means-tested welfare and greater quantities of it, compared to higher-skilled immigrants, similar to the US-born population. However, the legal status and laws governing access to means-tested welfare shape the use rates and the dollar value of those benefits. Legal migrant workers and illegal immigrants generally have no recourse to public benefits except for Emergency Medicaid, which is a relatively small expenditure (see DuBard and Hessing 2007). Also, many unauthorized immigrants and legal migrant workers return to their home countries when they face unemployment in the United States, decreasing the chance that they will consume welfare benefits as their income drops (Rowthorn 2008: 563). Due to the circular flow of some unauthorized immigrants and legal migrant workers, even the lowest-skilled immigrants can be net fiscally positive. However, expanded immigration enforcement in recent years has largely halted this return movement because it has increased the cost of those migrants, once they leave the United States, of returning to the United States in the future (Massey 2011: 29).

Depending on the state, means-tested welfare benefits are generally unavailable to legal immigrants during their first five years of residency, are unavailable to unauthorized immigrants, and are denied to lawful migrant workers (Schwartz and Artiga 2007: 1). As mentioned above, the major exception is Emergency Medicaid. Specific rules on immigrant access to some means-tested welfare vary by state. It is therefore not surprising that immigrants below 200 percent of the poverty line are much less likely to use welfare than similarly poor natives (Ku and Bruen 2013: 6–7). Even when poor immigrants do use means-tested welfare, they consume a lower dollar amount than similarly poor natives (Ku and Bruen 2013: 6–7). Laws that diminish immigrant welfare accessibility going forward will have two effects. First, such a legal change will alter immigrant self-selection, so that those who want to work and believe they will be able to work will be more likely to come, decreasing the demand for welfare. Second, welfare restrictions will decrease government expenditures and the fiscal costs of immigration (Nowrasteh and Cole 2013: 6).

It is also important not to understate the welfare costs of immigrants. Borjas and Trejo (1991) noted that an average immigrant family, unadjusted for poverty, consumed about twice as much in government services as the average US-born family before the 1996 Welfare Reform Act. Borjas's use of household estimates is problematic for numerous reasons, and the timing of his paper makes his findings inapplicable today. Regardless, the poor US-born children of immigrants consume more welfare than non-citizen children, although still less than the poor children of natives for Supplemental Security Income (SSI), food stamps, and other cash assistance programs (Ku and Bruen 2013: 6–7; Skinner 2012: 661). Despite varying levels of welfare benefits across states, there is little evidence that migrants choose their state destination based on the generosity of the welfare system (see Levine and Zimmerman 1999; McKinnish 2005). New immigrants are mainly choosing to reside in states with low levels of social welfare spending and growing economies and are moving away from states with high levels of social welfare spending and low economic growth (Griswold 2012: 161).

Healthcare spending is another vital component of government expenditures that immigrants can affect, especially since it is such a large and growing proportion of the US budget (Access Economic Pty Limited 2008: 14–15). With the exception of Medicare, which will be discussed below, immigrants generally under-consume healthcare compared to natives. A study from 2000 of immigrants in Los Angeles County, which are 45 percent of the county's 18–64-year-old population, consumed only 33 percent of healthcare benefits for that age bracket (Goldman et al. 2006: 1700). Unauthorized immigrants in Los Angeles were 12 percent of the city's population in the same age bracket, but were only responsible for 6 percent of healthcare spending for that bracket (Goldman et al. 2006: 1708). In the same study, immigrants were twice as likely as natives to never have had a medical checkup. Twenty percent of immigrant women who have never been pregnant have not had a checkup compared to just 4 percent of US-born females who have not been pregnant. For all women, 5 percent of US-born females have not had a checkup compared to 19 percent of immigrant females. The percentages for males are similar: 30 percent of all immigrant males and 40 percent of all unauthorized immigrant males have never had a checkup compared to just 21 percent of US-born males (Goldman et al. 2006: 1706). Although unauthorized immigrants have generally been in the United States for a shorter period of time than US-born individuals, they do not disproportionately consume public healthcare benefits. Unauthorized Mexican immigrants had far fewer physician visits than US-born persons of Mexican descent (see Ortega et al. 2007: 2354). One reason that immigrants are less likely to see doctors is that they are less likely to have a chronic health condition. For Los Angeles residents between 18 and 64 years of age, 27 percent of all immigrants and 19 percent of unauthorized immigrants report having a chronic health problem compared to 38 percent of natives (Goldman et al. 2006: 1705).

Fewer doctor visits for immigrants is correlated with lower government health expenditures. Twenty-one percent of all healthcare spending on the US-born was paid for by government programs, compared to 16 percent for immigrants, regardless of income level (Goldman et al. 2006: 1708). Looking again at the Los Angeles study, 23 percent of healthcare expenditures for immigrant women were covered by government programs compared to 27 percent for US-born women. Twenty percent of healthcare expenditures for immigrant men were paid for by the government compared to 29 percent of healthcare expenditures for US-born men (Goldman et al. 2006: 1707). The different healthcare and doctor usage rates generally hold across California (see Ortega et al. 2007) and the United States (see Schwartz and Artiga 2007). Immigrants are less likely to have private insurance than US-born persons, but they also use emergency rooms less often than US citizens and are more likely to pay out of pocket for medical services (Schwartz and Artiga 2007: 2, 6).

Welfare reform had an enormous effect on immigrant welfare usage in the United States. In 1996, Congress tightened welfare eligibility requirements for legal permanent residents (LPR), a subcategory of immigrants here on green cards. Between 1994 and 1999, LPR use of means-tested welfare per family declined dramatically. Temporary Aid to Needy Families (TANF) declined by 60 percent, food stamps by 48 percent, Medicaid by 15 percent, and SSI by 32 percent. For TANF, SSI, and General Assistance[1] combined (the three major cash benefit programs generally thought of as "welfare"), participation rates fell by 44 percent (Fix and Passel 2002: 15). Such large and unanticipated declines in LPR welfare use would make a large difference in fiscal projections.

Immigrants have a positive long-run fiscal impact on the entitlement programs: Medicare and Social Security. From 2002 to 2009, immigrants made 14.7 percent of contributions to Medicare Part A, but consumed only 7.9 percent of all expenditures, contributing $13.8 billion more annually to Medicare Part A than they consume in benefits. Natives produced $30.9 billion in deficit annually (Zallman 2013: 1). Among Medicare enrollees, average expenditures were $1,465 lower for immigrants than for US-born enrollees: $3,923 compared to $5,388 (Zallman 2013: 3). The differentials are largely the result of return migration and differences in the age structures between the US-born, who are typically older, and younger immigrants.

---

1. Cash aid.

Estimated impacts on the Social Security system vary widely. According to one paper, immigrant men by retirement paid 76 percent of the taxes that a comparable US-born male paid, but received 83 percent of the amount in benefits that a native received (Gustman and Steinmeier 2000: 330). The shares for women are 78 percent and 80 percent, respectively (Gustman and Steinmeier 2000: 330). Based on actuarial information provided by the Social Security Administration, Stuart Anderson ran numerous different immigration scenarios to test their impact on Social Security's actuarial debt (see Social Security Administration 2004 and Anderson 2005). Anderson found that a moratorium on legal immigration beginning in 2005 would balloon the size of the actuarial debt by 31 percent over a 50-year period (Anderson 2005: 1). However, an increase in legal immigration by 33 percent would reduce the actuarial debt by 10 percent over 50 years, boosting revenues to Social Security by a present value of $169 billion over 50 years and $216 billion over 75 years (Anderson 2005: 9). Unauthorized immigrants provide a potentially greater boost, assuming they are not legalized, because they will continue to pay into Social Security but will not be able to legally draw down benefits in the future (see Feinleib and Warner 2005).

Of course, immigrants in the United States age just as everyone else does, meaning that many of them will be net consumers of entitlements in the future, even though they might be net contributors today. Critical in estimating how much immigrants will use in the future is the percentage of immigrants who move back to their home countries before retirement and forgo Social Security[2] and Medicare benefits. The standard estimate of immigrants who return before they can collect entitlements is 30 percent (Duleep 1994: 38; National Research Council 1997: 330). Such a high return rate contributes mightily to making long-run immigrant Social Security contributions a net positive under most estimates. Changed rates of return could, however, substantially shift immigration's impact on the fiscal shape of entitlement programs.

3   BEGINNING WITH THE BASICS: STATIC ACCOUNTING MODELS

The static accounting models differ from the later dynamic models because they attempt to study the net fiscal contribution of immigrants for

---

2. The United States has agreements with some countries that allow return migrants to receive Social Security benefits after leaving. For other migrants, many are able to receive a refund of their FICA taxes after leaving.

a specific slice of time, place, or immigrant group. This method simply compares the taxes paid directly and indirectly by immigrants to the public services consumed by immigrants in a year. Crucially, static accounting methods only measure the fiscal impact of all immigrants currently living in the United States and do not indicate how future immigrants might affect the fiscal condition of the government. Static accounting analyses can also base government expenditures on households because they are the primary unit through which public services are delivered and do not change in size under a static analysis (National Research Council 1997: 254). Before explaining the benefits of static models, there are four major downsides that need to be considered (National Research Council 1997: 297–298).

First, static accounting models only measure existing immigrants, irrespective of any changes that could occur in the future due to age, skills, or changes in income. Future immigrants will undoubtedly be different from today's immigrants, and demographics have an enormous effect on future government budgets. Second, government policies change over time. A static accounting analysis completed for 1995, one year before welfare reform became law, would produce a much more negative fiscal impact result than a static analysis completed in 1997, even though the population would be largely unchanged. Third, static accounting ignores the life-cycle tax contributions and consumption of government benefits. Fourth, government budget deficits or surpluses during the year of analysis considerably skew the final result (National Research Council 1997: 257–720; OECD 2013: 137–139). Government budgets do not need to be balanced over the short term, but there is no obvious way to assign the incidence of a budget deficit or surplus in a static accounting model. Static accounting methods have their limitations for all of the reasons mentioned above, but they are easier to construct and can be a decent starting point for studying how immigrants impact budgets (OECD 2013: 133–137).

In their static accounting analysis, Lee and Miller found that the net fiscal contribution of immigrants and their concurrent descendants in 1994 was a positive $23.5 billion for state and federal governments combined (Lee and Miller 1998: 198). That figure included a $27.4 billion net deficit produced by immigrants at state and local government levels and a $50.9 billion net surplus produced in the federal government (Lee and Miller 1998: 198) (see Table 3.1). The total fiscal surplus was equal to about 0.35 percent of GDP that year (Lee and Miller 1998: 198). Interestingly, Lee and Miller admit that longitudinal studies are superior (Lee and Miller 1998: 199).

Table 3.1 HOW THE AGGREGATE FISCAL IMPACT DEPENDS ON THE
DEFINITION OF THE STUDY POPULATION (1994 IN 1994 $ BILLIONS)

A. Aggregate Fiscal Impact

Study Population	Overall	Federal	State and Local
Immigrants Only	32.4	28.2	4.2
Immigrant Households	–13.3	16	–29.3
Immigrants and Concurrent Children	29.5	48.9	–19.3
Immigrants and Concurrent Descendants (Children and Grandchildren)	23.5	50.9	–27.4

B. Population Subtotals

Study Population	Number	Cumulative Total
First Generation	22,766,711	22,766,711
Second Generation under age 20	8,201,368	30,968,079
Concurrent Second Generation age 20 and over	5,597,759	36,565,838
Concurrent Third Generation	3,862,610	40,428,448

Source: Lee, Ronald, and Timothy Miller (1998), "The Current Fiscal Impact of Immigrants and Their Descendants: Beyond the Immigrant Household," in *The Immigration Debate*, edited by James P. Smith and Barry Edmonston, Washington, DC: National Academy Press: 198.

The Organisation for Economic Co-operation and Development (OECD) produced a static accounting analysis of households in the United States and other OECD countries using data pooled from the years 2007–2009 (OECD 2013: 146–147). The net fiscal contribution of a household with two US-born Americans at the head was a positive $8,533.96. The same amount for a household headed by two immigrants was a positive $8,274.01. For mixed households, with one immigrant and one US-born American as the heads, the net fiscal contribution was $17,157.63. This analysis excluded immigrants who returned to their home countries and immigrants who had been residing in the United States for less than a year (OECD 2013: 147) (see Table 3.2).

The OECD analysis found that immigrants contributed less in taxes and under-consumed Social Security, Medicare, and housing subsidies compared to natives, but they over-consumed social assistance, unemployment benefits, and family allowances compared to natives (OECD

Table 3.2 AVERAGE NET DIRECT FISCAL CONTRIBUTION OF HOUSEHOLDS
BY MIGRATION STATUS OF THE HOUSEHOLD HEAD, 2007–2009 AVERAGE

Country	Average Net Contributions—Using EU-SILC		
	Only native-born household head(s)	"Mixed"	Only immigrant household head(s)
Switzerland	$14,967	$21,434	$14,545
Iceland	$12,272	$17,558	$9,292
Netherlands	$9,940	$21,303	$2,544
Belgium	$9,159	$16,830	$5,560
United States	$8,534	$17,158	$8,274
Canada	$7,552	$15,494	$5,167
Denmark	$7,362	$17,713	$2,368
Sweden	$6,815	$13,473	$896
Germany	$5,875	–$4,453	–$5,633
Finland	$5,706	$12,265	$1,314
Norway	$5,055	$20,366	$4,505
Greece	$5,008	$10,511	$7,728
OECD average	$4,840	$9,942	$3,283
Estonia	$4,514	$5,877	–$2
Slovenia	$4,450	$2,368	$3,006
Italy	$3,980	$12,126	$9,148
Australia	$3,778	$8,355	$2,305
Czech Republic	$3,474	$1,116	–$184
Austria	$3,375	$6,443	$2,353
Spain	$3,106	$9,830	$7,497
United Kingdom	$2,604	$11,954	$3,029
France	$2,407	$9,131	–$1,451
Slovak Republic	$2,148	$752	–$2,171
Hungary	$1,081	$1,915	$1,864
Portugal	$950	$9,800	$4,479
Poland	$291	–$4,630	–$5,691
Luxembourg	–$1,228	$7,232	$9,178
Ireland	–$2,487	$6,511	–$1,274

Source: OECD, http://dx.doi.org/10.1787/888932822940

2013: 155). Immigrants in the United States are so fiscally positive in this
static accounting model, despite the official deficits at the time, because
they made large contributions to the off-budget Social Security system as
well as Medicare in the 2007–2009 period, increasing net tax revenue to
the federal government by an amount equal to 0.03 percent of GDP (OECD
2013: 159). In their analysis of the fiscal impact, the OECD authors found
that improving the employment rates of immigrants would produce the

largest fiscal gain (OECD 2013: 161). The OECD study concludes by stating that the fiscal impact of immigration is neither a fiscal burden nor so much of a fiscal benefit that immigration should be decided on these grounds (see Table 3.3).

Table 3.3 ESTIMATED NET FISCAL IMPACT OF IMMIGRANTS AS PERCENTAGE OF GDP

	Baseline	Baseline excluding pensions	Baseline plus per capita allocation of collectively accrued items (excluding defense and debt services)	Baseline plus per capita allocation of collectively accrued items (excluding defense)
Australia	0.00	0.82	..	..
Austria	0.12	0.89	−0.37	−0.80
Belgium	0.76	0.96	0.06	−0.43
Canada	−0.06	−0.06	..	..
Czech Republic	−0.01	0.07	−0.28	−0.31
Denmark	0.11	0.23	−0.31	−0.39
Estonia	0.49	1.15	..	..
Finland	0.16	0.02	−0.08	−0.13
France	−0.52	0.30	−0.52	−0.84
Germany	−1.13	0.21	−1.93	−2.32
Greece	0.98	0.86	..	..
Hungary	0.08	0.12	−0.11	−0.18
Iceland	0.90	0.96	..	..
Ireland	−0.23	−0.39	−1.23	−1.41
Italy	0.98	0.91	0.97	0.61
Luxembourg	2.02	2.20	0.37	0.24
Netherlands	0.40	0.74	−0.01	−0.14
Norway	0.42	0.50	0.60	0.49
Poland	−0.32	0.01	−0.42	−0.45
Portugal	0.52	0.56	0.27	0.13
Slovak Republic	−0.06	0.04	−0.16	−0.18
Slovenia	0.76	1.00	..	..
Spain	0.54	0.21	0.07	−0.05
Sweden	0.20	0.62	−0.37	−0.57
Switzerland	1.95	2.00	1.42	1.16
United Kingdom	0.46	1.02	−0.01	−0.26
United States	0.03	−0.51	−0.64	−1.00
Average	**0.35**	**0.57**	..	..
Average (2)	**0.30**	**0.49**	**−0.12**	**−0.31**

Source: OECD (2013): 159.

Many static accounting studies focus on individual US states during specific years. A fiscal analysis of New Jersey based on 1980 census data found that a typical immigrant-headed household imposed an average net fiscal burden of $350 on local governments compared to a net fiscal burden of $225 for each native-headed household during a year when the state ran a budget deficit. On the state level, immigrant-headed households imposed a net fiscal burden of $841 compared to a net fiscal cost of $846 imposed by native-headed households (Espenshade and King 1994: 225). The study also divides up immigrant households by ethnicity, finding that Hispanic American households impose the largest net fiscal cost (Espenshade and King 1994: 225).

Another study of New Jersey focused on the impact of immigrant households on the state and local levels for the 1989–1990 fiscal year (Garvey and Espenshade 1998: 77). Average net state fiscal costs in 1990 per immigrant household, where the head of the household was under the age of 65, was $1,821 compared to a net state cost of $1,249 for an average native-born household whose head was in the same age range (Garvey and Espenshade 1998: 78–79). Immigrant-headed households from Europe, Canada, and Asia imposed net fiscal costs that were 39 percent to 52 percent of the size of the net fiscal cost imposed by Hispanic immigrant households, who were, again, the biggest net consumers of state provided benefits in those years (Garvey and Espenshade 1998: 79).

On the local level, the study found that the average net fiscal cost for local governments for immigrant households, where the head of household was under the age of 65, was $2,526 compared to an average net fiscal cost of $1,581 for households headed by the native born (Garvey and Espenshade 1998: 84–85). European and Canadian immigrants had net fiscal costs that were 62 percent of the size of Hispanic immigrant households, while Asian households cost 5 percent more than Hispanic immigrant households (Garvey and Espenshade 1998: 85). Large local and state budget deficits in that year made all households seem particularly burdensome on the state and local levels.

Garvey et al. (2002) looked at the same New Jersey data that Garvey and Espenshade (1998) did, but came to a different conclusion. Garvey et al. (2002: 546, 550) discovered that immigrant households consume $366 less in government benefits and contribute about $516 more in local taxes than similarly well-off natives did in that year. Garvey et al. (2002: 537) attributed the differences between natives and immigrants to different socioeconomic characteristics, rather than country-of-origin effects that the Garvey and Espenshade (1998) study identified.

Shifting to the West Coast, Clune (1998: 122) looked at federal, state, and local contributions for households in California for the fiscal year of 1994–1995. The study excluded the budget deficit in California that year, which would have made all households appear to be net fiscal drains. Clune found that native households contributed a net $2,229 to the federal government, $1,126 to the state government, and $267 to local government (1998: 156). In contrast, immigrant households imposed a net fiscal cost of $1,835 to the federal government, $2,217 to the state government, and $787 to the local government (Clune 1998: 156).

The rest of the literature about state governments is fairly poor, and most studies are either fiscal cost analyses or fiscal benefit analyses. The studies that attempted to estimate the net fiscal benefits on the state level were largely produced by think tanks, state governments, and universities.

An analysis of the fiscal impact of immigration in Arkansas used the Impacts for Planning (IMPLAN) model that tracked consumer spending across 500 sectors of Arkansas's economy and how it affected state GDP (Appold et al. 2013: 15–16). This model produced an estimate of the economic impact of immigration on the size of the economy and state employment, as well as productivity spillovers on other workers in the state. It then compared the extra tax revenue from these additional sources of income to the additional public costs incurred by the immigrants and their children, producing a net fiscal cost of $127 per immigrant resident or $31 million for the state budget in 2010 (Appold et al. 2013: 27). In contrast, Gans used the same IMPLAN model to estimate that immigrants contribute $940 million more in tax revenue than they consumed to the state government of Arizona in 2004 (Gans 2007: 57–58).

Heet et al. (2009) estimated the impact of immigration on US-born wages in the state of Indiana for the year 2007. He included the wages of immigrants but excluded indirect economic effects that would affect tax revenue. Its conservative estimates of public benefits consumption and tax payments still revealed an unambiguously positive impact on state and local budgets of $750 million in 2007, finding that only unauthorized immigrants produced a net negative fiscal impact on the state (Heet et al. 2009: vii–1). The estimated lower wages earned by unauthorized immigrants substantially lowered the estimated tax revenue paid by that cohort in Indiana.

Eisenhauer et al. (2007: 5) pooled data in Florida for the years 2002–2005. They relied on an Institute on Taxation and Economic Policy model to estimate taxes paid by immigrants, based on income-level data and their consumption of public goods and services according to the Current Population Survey's Annual Social and Economic supplement (Eisenhauer et al. 2007: 31). Their model did not include the indirect economic effects.

Regardless of that omission and their model's limitations, they found that immigrant individuals paid $506.22 less in taxes per year than natives, but also consumed $614 less in benefits (Eisenhauer et al. 2007: 34–35). Overall, the positive net fiscal contribution of average individual immigrants was $1,500, compared to an average US-born individual's net fiscal contribution of $1,390 to the state of Florida (Eisenhauer et al. 2007: 35).

Static analyses generally find that immigration increases net tax revenue to the federal government, but can have a slightly negative or positive impact on state and local governments. The OECD (2013) and Lee and Miller (1998) both found that immigration slightly decreases the federal budget deficits. Lee and Miller (1998) went on to find a negative fiscal impact on state and local governments in the United States that is far smaller than the positive fiscal impact on the federal government. Studies of Indiana and Florida found that immigrants decreased budget deficits there, while studies of Arkansas, California, and New Jersey found varying degrees of negative net fiscal impacts imposed by immigrants and their households.

4   THREE DYNAMIC METHODS FOR MEASURING THE FISCAL EFFECTS OF IMMIGRATION

There are three main ways to dynamically estimate the fiscal impact of immigration. The first method is by using macroeconomic models—variants of general equilibrium models—to predict the economic effects of immigration relative to a pre-immigration trend line, additional tax revenue, and additional government expenditure. The second is through generational accounting that pays particular attention to the government's intertemporal budget constraints. The third is though a net transfer profile that starts with a static accounting model in a base year and then builds a life-cycle net transfer profile for individual immigrants. These are only quasi-rigid categories, with the possibility of mixing and matching certain characteristics of each methodology, but each one has its own benefits and drawbacks; there are several studies that employ each method, sometimes mixing them.

4.1   Macroeconomic Models

Most macroeconomic modeling approaches use a computable general equilibrium model (CGE). They first estimate economic growth caused by immigration or a shift in immigration policy. CGE models take into account all of the economic factors mentioned earlier, as well as the economic shock caused by a sudden and sustained increase in population (see Dixon and Rimmer 2009; Hinojosa-Ojeda 2012). The assumption is that tax revenue collected by the government will be a proportion of the size of the total economy going forward, so in order to estimate tax revenue, the size of the economy is critical. For instance, the federal tax to GDP ratio in the United States has been steady over recent decades regardless of the actual tax rates. The specific economic growth rates and tax revenue caused by immigration are heavily subjected to assumptions about the future and highly sensitive to policy shifts in areas of economic policy not related to immigration.

Storesletten (2000: 300) used a calibrated general equilibrium model of overlapping generations to investigate whether changes in immigration policies alone could resolve the projected entitlement deficit caused by the imminent retirement of the baby-boomer generation, then discounted the net fiscal contributions of marginal immigrants based on their skill levels. According to his estimates, admitting 1.6 million additional high-skilled immigrants annually who are between the ages of 40 and 44 would pay for the entitlement system (Storesletten 2000: 302). He finds that the net present value (NPV) for the average low-, medium-, and high-skilled legal immigrants are –$36,000, –$2,000, and +$96,000, respectively (Storesletten 2000: 302). He assumes that the age group of skilled immigrants who would be admitted without spouses are unlikely to have children and are likely to pay a high level of taxes due to high incomes and to consume relatively little in welfare. Storesletten found relatively negative results for low- and mid-skilled workers compared to the following studies, because he assumed that there will be no future changes in tax rates or benefit rates, and that the budget will never be balanced (2000: 302).

Lee and Miller (2000: 352) found that the initial budgetary impact is usually negative, but becomes positive over time as the children of immigrants grow to working ages and contribute to Social Security. The main fiscal benefit of young and low-educated immigrants is that they produce more children than natives. Those children will eventually pay more taxes into Social Security, shoring up the entitlement system by creating a younger age distribution that lasts for generations. Specifically, they tested raising net immigration to the United States by 100,000 a year. Based on numerous different policy and economic impact estimates over a 75-year time period, the federal government always experiences a net increase in federal revenues after expenditure and the states experience a small net decline. The greatest positive tax-revenue gain for the federal government is equal to 0.7 percent of federal revenue, and the greatest loss for the states is equal to a negative 0.5 percent of the state's net tax revenue (Lee and Miller 2000: 352). Lee and Miller conclude that "the overall fiscal consequences of altering the volume of immigration would be quite small and should not be a consideration of policy" (Lee and Miller 2000: 352–353).

The Congressional Budget Office (2013a and 2013b) ran two models of the impact of the proposed US Senate 2013 immigration reform bill (S. 744). The first was a less dynamic model that assumed minimal economic impact of immigration besides the addition of more workers. That model assumed that if S. 744 became law, it would lower the projected federal government deficit by $875 billion by the year 2033 (Congressional Budget Office 2013a: 2–3). In the model, the CBO found a large increase in federal tax revenue, but a very slight increase in expenditure, largely because immigrants would have little access to welfare benefits.

The second model run by the CBO was an enhanced Solow model—a more dynamic model—and the first instance of one being used by the CBO in estimating the budgetary impact of legislation. This second model assumed that S. 744 will increase GDP by adding workers, affecting the earnings of American workers, boosting total factor productivity (TFP), and stimulating an increase in investment (Congressional Budget Office 2013b: 2–3). Taking all of those dynamic economic factors into account, the CBO found that S. 744 would boost GDP by 5.1 percent to 5.7 percent over the baseline by 2033 (Congressional Budget Office 2013b: 14). This extra GDP growth was estimated to lower the total federal deficit by $1.197 trillion by 2033, a $300 billion greater reduction than under the less dynamic version of the CBO's model.

Following on the heels of the CBO, the Bipartisan Policy Center (BPC) used a similarly enhanced Solow model. As opposed to the CBO's projections, the BPC estimates assumed that a higher percentage of the legalized unauthorized immigrants would eventually become citizens and thus eligible for government benefits. BPC also did not assume that S. 744 would lead to an increase in TFP. Regardless of those changes, the BPC's findings were similar to those of the CBO. BPC found that S. 744 would decrease net government deficit by $180 billion in the first 10 years after passage and would further decrease federal deficit by $990 billion in the second decade, while causing similar increases in GDP (Bipartisan Policy Center 2013: 7). More interestingly, BPC ran an alternative "attrition through enforcement" projection that was successful at removing more unauthorized immigrants, a strategy desired by many immigration restrictionists. That scenario resulted in an increased federal deficit of $800 billion and a drop in GDP of 5.7 percent compared to the baseline by 2033 (Bipartisan Policy Center 2013: 23). BPC ran numerous varying scenarios and the only one that produced more deficits relative to the baseline was "attrition through enforcement."

CGE models can also form the basis for evaluating the fiscal impact of previous immigration waves. Chojnicki et al. (2011) examined the net fiscal contribution of immigrants during the 1950–2000 period of US history. According to their findings, immigration grew the US economy and produced more net tax revenue. Their model showed that the biggest gains for the US economy and net tax revenue came from the generations of the descendants of immigrants born in the United States (Chojnicki et al. 2011: 323). The low-skilled first generation consumed more welfare than they paid in taxes, but their descendants more than compensated for that initial deficit by producing a more positive dependency ratio for entitlement programs, leading to a slightly positive contribution to the federal budget in the long run (Chojnicki et al. 2011: 323).

Most CGE models find that immigrants increase net tax revenue to the federal government. Many CGE models also find that immigrants slightly diminish net tax revenue for state and local governments, but that the federal net tax revenue increase is larger than the state and local decrease. The CGE models used by the CBO and BPC forecast the net budgetary impact of the proposed Senate immigration reform bill in 2013. They found that immigrants would have decreased deficits by about $1.2 trillion over 20 years if that bill had become law. Storesletten (2000) found that highly skilled immigrants pay far more in tax revenue than they consume in benefits, while low and moderately skilled immigrants consume more in benefits than they pay in taxes. Lee and Miller (2000) found that the federal government always sees a fiscal benefit from immigration, while state and local governments always see a slight loss, but the gain to the federal government is *always* bigger than the loss to state and local governments. Historically, removing the fiscal impact of immigrants from the last half of the twentieth century would have increased the budget deficit over that time period (Chojnicki et al. 2011).

4.2 Generational Accounting

The generational accounting approach estimates the present value of the government's future spending liabilities plus its future projected purchases of goods and services. It then subtracts from those cost estimates the estimated present value of projected future net tax payments of current generations to arrive at the present value of the net tax burden facing future generations under current or projected policy (Auerbach et al. 1999: 1–2). If this method discovers that the tax burden faced by future generations is higher than that currently faced by newborns, then it is impossible to sustain current fiscal policy without raising taxes (Auerbach et al. 1999: 2).

Generational accounting attempts to estimate the degree to which different generations will finance government expenditures or increase government debt, assuming that the debt will always be paid off. Estimating population growth in subsequent generations and future government fiscal policy over the same period are essential to this approach. Demographic shocks, like the addition or subtraction of millions of immigrants, can change the age-structure of society and affect the outcomes of generational accounting. Immigrants, like everybody else, are either net taxpayers or net consumers of government benefits at different points in their lives, but immigrants add peculiar wrinkles to generational accounting that do not occur with population growth through procreation.

Much of the US government's spending commitments are for old-age entitlements. The extent to which immigration affects the age structure of society by lowering the average age, which subsequently improves the dependency ratio for the entitlement, can have a large impact on long-term government finances (Rowthorn 2008: 561). As Rowthorn reported in his literature survey (2008: 562), the dependency ratio is only modestly affected by a large increase in temporary migrants. According to his estimates, a rolling stock of 3.5 million temporary guest workers at working age in the United Kingdom reduces the old-age dependency ratio from 0.431 to 0.395—an improvement but one incapable of sustaining the entitlements. That modest improvement in the dependency ratio should also be kept in perspective, as 3.5 million guest workers is far larger than the number of Poles who stirred up so much controversy by moving to the United Kingdom in 2004 (Rowthorn 2008: 562).

Rowthorn found that the large fiscal effects, which he defines as producing a net fiscal present value contribution or loss of greater than 1 percent of GDP, only occur under two different scenarios. The first is an unrealistically large demographic decline in the destination country, such as a large and sudden drop in the native birth rate. In such a scenario, an increase in guest workers or immigrants can make a substantial difference in the dependency ratio. The second is an unrealistically large surge of immigration (Rowthorn 2008: 577).

Auerbach and Oreopoulos (1999) set up different fiscal accounts for natives and immigrants and ran various future projections varying the size of immigrant flows and fiscal policy. They found that the fiscal impact of both groups is almost entirely driven by fiscal policy. Critical to their findings is their selection of which generation will pay for the fiscal imbalances—current or future residents. If the entire fiscal imbalance is placed on future generations, then the presence of new immigrants reduces the fiscal burden borne by natives by spreading the debt. The more irresponsible the government's fiscal policy, the more positive impact immigrants have on reducing long-run debt. But if the government's budget is balanced to begin with, there is no fiscal gain from immigration. In both scenarios, the impact of immigration on the fiscal balance is extremely small relative to the size of the imbalance itself. Immigration is neither a source of fiscal deficits nor a cause of them (Auerbach and Oreopoulos 1999: 180). In more realistic scenarios with smaller immigrant flows, immigration has a very small impact on the budget, partly depending on whether defense is a pure public good or not in the accounting (Auerbach and Oreopoulos 2000: 151).

Methodology varies slightly between studies, and though most have focused on European countries, their findings are worth mentioning. Bonin et al. (2000), Collado et al. (2004), Moscarola (2001), Fehr et al. (2004), and Mayr (2005) all used different generational accounting methods, adjusting tax revenue and immigrant inflow scenarios over time. They all found that immigration helped balance long-term government finances for Germany, Spain, Italy, the European Union, and Austria, respectively. For France, the average life-cycle contribution of an immigrant is negative according to Chojnicki et al. (2010).

Generational accounting models generally find that immigration more positively impacts public finances than other methods (see Razin and Sodka 2004), partly because they implicitly assume that the entire burden of financing today's fiscal deficit can be pushed to future generations (Rowthorn 2008: 560). It is also important to mention some of the criticisms of generational accounting. The first is that it ignores potential policy-induced changes in factor returns that can alter the long-term fiscal impact. The second is that generational accounting estimates assume that the incidence of taxation falls on those who pay taxes. This assumption makes the calculation easier, but is more likely to lead to incorrect findings (Fehr and Kotlikoff 1999: 44). The third is that this method assumes that all deficits need to ultimately be paid off by resident taxpayers, ignoring other government options like default or inflation to pay debts.

4.3   Net Transfer Models

Net transfer profiles start with the static accounting model mentioned above and then build that out into a life-cycle net transfer profile of immigrant groups by country of origin and their descendants that presents the fiscal impact as a net present value (Cully 2012: 7). The first step is to calculate the net fiscal contribution for each immigrant group under consideration for a single year, depending upon all of the economic and demographic considerations discussed in the previous sections. The second step is to project future income growth and demographic change for the immigrant group. The third step is to take those projections and to extend them over the life cycles of the immigrants themselves and their descendants. The fourth step is to set a time horizon—out to the year 2100, for instance—to estimate the net fiscal contribution over the period.[3] The fiscal cost and tax payment of each generation must be counted in order to avoid biasing the result, at least counting the second generation into old age. The fifth step is to take into account basic financial economics by discounting the future cash flows back to the base year to produce a net present value that describes the fiscal impact (OECD 2013: 137–139).

The age expenditure profile of immigrants during the three life phases of fiscal contribution is crucial to arriving at the most accurate outcome (Access Economic Pty Limited 2008: ii, 12; Kandel 2011: 6). The first phase of life is childhood, where there is a high consumption of government services, such as education and welfare, but a low or zero tax payment. During the childhood phase, substantial fiscal cost is incurred by the person or immigrant being studied. The next phase is the working life. During this phase, the worker pays quite a bit more to the government in taxes than he consumes in social services and welfare. Educational attainment in the childhood phase and the LFPR are very important for determining how positive the worker phase is and how much it makes up for the net fiscal cost incurred during the childhood and the last phases. The last phase is retirement. During this last phase, tax contributions are limited, but consumption of public pensions and healthcare is very high. Estimated life span, demographics, and the quantity of taxes paid during the working phase determine whether the person in question is a net fiscal cost or burden by the end of his life.

So far, a net-transfer model can apply equally well to either a native or an immigrant. The immigrant age of arrival adds a confounding factor

---

3. The Social Security Administration makes 75-year projections.

that is important in gauging the net fiscal impact (Access Economic Pty Limited 2008: 7–10). The age of arrival, which minimizes the amount of public schooling that the immigrant consumes in the source country, but maximizes the length of his working life, is more likely to make a positive fiscal contribution. A younger immigrant worker with only a high school degree who immigrates at the age of 18 makes a positive contribution, in present value, to public finances according to Cully (2012: 4). Cully (2012) goes into greater detail, comparing the present value of fiscal contribution at various ages of arrival and immigrant skill level, but many ambiguities exist. For instance, a 15-year-old refugee and a 40-year-old skilled worker are difficult to compare (Cully 2012: 7). The refugee has his whole working life ahead of him, but the skilled worker will likely have a higher income over the remaining years of his work life. Many other details, like the availability of welfare and the LFPR, make a large impact.

Another consideration for immigrants that rarely applies to the US-born is return migration. A migrant who comes during the working years of his life and then leaves to retire in his home country and who cannot transfer government-subsidized healthcare or old age pension payments will make a more positive fiscal contribution, all else remaining equal. Return migration can help to make the net present value of contributions more positive by reducing the public cost of retirement. However, return migration can also diminish the long-run fiscal impact of additional American-born children. In such a scenario, the legality of the worker also matters. An unauthorized immigrant might or might not pay taxes, although 75 percent in the United States filed a tax return, had taxes withheld from their paycheck, or both (see Cornelius and Lewis 2007), but he almost certainly consumes less welfare than similarly poor natives or legal immigrants. A departing unauthorized immigrant will typically not contribute children who will pay taxes and consume future government benefits.

The descendants of immigrants, when they are included, make a large and positive net fiscal contribution under net transfer models. The National Research Council's net transfer analysis (1997: 297–362) analyzed the net present value fiscal impact of the immigrants themselves, as well as the immigrants and their descendants, for all levels of government in the United States. They found that a typical immigrant imposes a net fiscal cost of $3,000 himself, but the descendants of the immigrant have a positive net fiscal contribution of $83,000 in present value, producing an $80,000 fiscal surplus (National Research Council 1997: 334). Subsequent generations more than make up for the net fiscal cost of the first generation. According to their model, the total fiscal impact for the typical immigrant does not turn positive until 22 years after the arrival of the

Table 3.4 AVERAGE FISCAL IMPACT OF AN IMMIGRANT OVERALL
AND BY EDUCATION LEVEL (1996 DOLLARS)

| Group | Education Level of Immigrant | | | |
	< High School	High School	> High School	Overall
Immigrants (baseline)[a]	–$13,000	$51,000	$198,000	$80,000
Immigrants themselves	–$89,000	–$31,000	$105,000	–$3,000
Descendants	$76,000	$82,000	$93,000	$83,000

[a]Based on estimated educational transition probabilities.
Source: National Research Council (1997): 334.

immigrant, while it takes 40 years for the state and local impact to turn positive (National Research Council 1997: 342). Comparing the results to natives, immigrants generally receive about the same quantity of welfare in these models but pay less in taxes (National Research Council 1997: 349). The National Research Council then makes numerous assumptions about future education, income, duration of welfare benefits, and other relevant factors to estimate the fiscal net present value under different scenarios that reach positive results over time (National Research Council 1997: 358–361) (see Table 3.4).

The further out the projections are, the less certain are the results. A controversial portion of the National Research Council study estimates the fiscal net present value out to the year 2300 (1997: 341–347). The authors admit that such a long-run forecast is not very reliable, and they adjust the discount rate by more heavily discounting the longer run effects (National Research Council 1997: 342). To give an idea of how absurd it is to fiscally forecast out that far, it is the equivalent of trying to forecast today's fiscal conditions in 1729, when there hadn't yet been an industrial revolution and the United States was still a colony of Great Britain. How accurate could our long-run economic and fiscal forecasts possibly be over such a long time scale? George Borjas (1999) echoes this criticism, especially harping on the poor track record of even short-term economic forecasts. He also admits the quandary of not including the descendants, which is necessary to get an accurate fiscal net present value (Borjas 1999: 123–125).

5 A NOTE ABOUT UNAUTHORIZED IMMIGRATION

Most of the fiscal impact studies mentioned in this chapter include unauthorized immigrants as a subset of immigrants. Due to a large and likely-to-increase population of unauthorized immigrants in most developed countries, especially if lawful immigration is not liberalized, there is increasing interest in studying the fiscal impact of this specific subgroup. The main problem, however, is measuring the fiscal impact and economic circumstances of a population that does not want to be found (Kandel 2011: 3). The US General Accounting Office (GAO)[4] reviewed 13 studies on the fiscal impact of unauthorized immigrants that were published between 1984 and 1993. The main result of the studies is that they could not come to a firm conclusion about the fiscal cost and benefit of unauthorized immigration (see General Accounting Office 1995). Generally, the unknowns are so large that it is difficult to judge the reasonableness of studies prior to 1995.

6 CONCLUSION

It is difficult to predict the impact of immigration on government budgets currently or in the future. Based on the few studies that have tried to systematically examine the impact on government budgets, taking into account immigration's impact on the size of the economy and the pace of economic growth, as well as the impact of immigration on government budgets, the longitudinal and static studies reveal a very small net fiscal impact clustered around zero (OECD 2013: 125). Each dynamic model is sensitive to the demographic, economic, and budgetary assumptions built into it, but dynamic models are all we have to judge the long-term fiscal impact. Many of the different models discussed are similar and clearly borrow methods from each other, the main emphasis being on which government-supplied goods are counted, how and if government budgets will be paid off, and the level of rivalry in consumption of certain public goods. The outcome of static models also largely depend on the economic effects of immigration, immigrants' degree of substitutability or complementarity with their US-born counterparts, their indirect economic effects, age characteristics, government budget deficits or surpluses, and estimates of public benefit consumption.

The economic benefits of immigration are unambiguous and large, but the fiscal effects are dependent upon the specifics of government policy over a long time period, which means that the net fiscal impact of immigration could be negative while the economic benefit is simultaneously positive. Looking at the results of all of these studies, the fiscal impacts of immigration are mostly positive, but they are all relatively small. They are

4. It has since been renamed the US Government Accountability Office.

rarely more than 1 percent of GDP in dynamic models (Rowthorn 2008: 568). Even dramatic changes in the level of immigration have small effects on government budgets and deficits (Auerbach and Oreopoulos 2000: 151). Besides the net present value of the individual immigrant or group fiscal contribution, immigrant-caused deficits or surpluses could also be represented as a percentage of future economic growth or projected budget deficits. Regardless of those details and nuances, there is no strong fiscal case for or against sustained large-scale immigration.

The enormous economic gains from immigration described in Chapter 2 indicate that an open borders policy of the type proposed in Chapter 8 is not likely to lead to large government deficits or surpluses. Tax revenue would certainly increase dramatically under an open borders policy, but so would government expenditures on education, roads, and other congestible government-supplied goods. There is no reason to suspect that such an increase in tax revenue and government spending would not continue under a radically liberalized immigration policy. However, the federal, state, and local governments could reform their spending and tax policies to increase the fiscal gains from such a large economic gain. The federal government could institute a head tax or tariff on all immigrants or shift toward flatter taxes that place more of a burden on lower-skilled immigrants. States and local governments could also decrease the amount they spend on public education and thus lower the cost of their most expensive budget item. Congestible public goods could also be privatized, decreasing government spending without decreasing revenues. Generally, governments at all levels in the United States could balance their budgets and pursue a more responsible spending policy, a wise choice regardless of immigration policy. The fiscal impact of radically liberalized immigration or open borders would be determined by the government's fiscal policy.

Even if the fiscal costs of immigration were consistently larger than the fiscal benefits, there are far easier and cheaper methods to lower the cost than scaling back or outlawing immigration. Reforming welfare, charging immigration tariffs, or allowing more immigrant workers could all redress a possible net fiscal cost. The United States has reformed welfare before, but has never succeeded in halting unauthorized immigration except when aided by a Great Depression and World Wars. Reforming the fiscal system to fit the specifics of America's population is actually achievable and more beneficial than attempting to alter the country's population through fiddling with immigration policy to fit the government's fiscal goals.

This chapter leaves aside the wisdom of judging the benefits of immigration based on the immigrant's fiscal impact largely because the fiscal impact is so small. A worldview that seeks to judge whether immigrants are beneficial based on their fiscal impact, where the chief value of an additional American is determined by the size of his net tax contribution, is fundamentally flawed and a testament to how dehumanizing a large welfare state can be. The fiscal impact of immigration is neither a proper evaluating metric, nor a particularly meaningful one upon which to base support for or opposition to immigration.

REFERENCES

Access Economics Pty Limited. 2008. "Migrants Fiscal Impact Model: 2008 Update." Prepared for the Australian Department of Immigration and Citizenship.

Anderson, Stuart. 2005. "The Contribution of Legal Immigration to the Social Security System." National Foundation for American Policy.

Appold, Stephen J., James H. Johnson, Jr., and John D. Kasarda. 2013. *A Profile of Immigrants in Arkansas: Economic and Fiscal Benefits and Costs*, Volume 2. Winthrop Rockefeller Foundation: Little Rock, AR.

Auerbach, Alan J., Laurence J. Kotlikoff, and Willi Leibfritz, eds. 1999. *Generational Accounting around the World*. NBER Volume. Chicago: University of Chicago Press.

Auerbach, A., and P. Oreopoulos. 1999. "Analyzing the Fiscal Impact of U.S. Immigration." *American Economic Review* 89: 176–180.

Auerbach, Alan J., and Philip Oreopoulos. 2000. "The Fiscal Effect of U.S. Immigration: A Generational Accounting Perspective." *Tax Policy and the Economy* 14: 123–156.

Bipartisan Policy Center. 2013. "Immigration Reform: Implications for Growth, Budgets, and Housing." Washington DC: Bipartisan Policy Center.

Bonin, H., B. Raffelhueschen, and J. Walliser. 2000. "Can Immigration Alleviate the Demographic Burden?" *Finanz Archiv* 57: 1–21.

Borjas, George J. 1999. *Heaven's Door: Immigration Policy and the American Economy*. Princeton, NJ: Princeton University Press.

Borjas, George. 2003. "The Labor Demand Curve Is Downward Sloping: Reexamining the Impact of Immigration on the Labor Market." *Quarterly Journal of Economics* 118(4): 1335–1374.

Borjas, George J., Jeffrey Grogger, and Gordon H. Hanson. September 2011. "Substitution Between Immigrants, Natives, and Skill Groups." NBER Working Paper 17461.

Borjas, George, and Lawrence Katz. 2007. "The Evolution of the Mexican-Born Workforce in the United States." In *The Evolution of the Mexican-Born Workforce in the United States*, ed. George J. Borjas, pp. 13–55. Chicago: University of Chicago Press.

Borjas, George, and Stephen Trejo. 1991. "Immigrant Participation in the Welfare System." *Industrial and Labor Relations Review* 44(2): 195–211.

Chojnicki, X., C. Defoort, C. Drapier, and Lionel Ragot. 2010. "Migrations et Protection Social: Etude Sure Les Liens et Les Impact de Court de Long Terme." Rapport pour la Drees-Mire, as summarized in OECD (2013).

Chojnicki, Xavier, F. Docquier, and Lionel Ragot. 2011. "Should the US Have Locked Heaven's Door? Reassessing the Benefits of Postwar Immigration." *Journal of Population Economics* 24: 317–359.

Clune, Michael S. 1998. "The Fiscal Impacts of Immigrants: A California Case Study." In *The Immigration Debate*, eds. James P. Smith and Barry Edmonston, pp. 120–182. National Academy Press: Washington, DC.

Collado, M. D., I. Iturbe-Ormaetxe, and G. Valera. 2004. "Quantifying the Impact of Immigration on the Spanish Welfare State." *International Tax and Public Finance* 11(3): 335–353.

Congressional Budget Office. 2007. "The Impact of Unauthorized Immigrants on the Budgets of State and Local Governments." A CBO Paper. December 2007.

Congressional Budget Office. 2013a. "S. 744 Border Security, Economic Opportunity, and Immigration Modernization Act." Congressional Budget Office Cost Estimate. June 18.

Congressional Budget Office. 2013b. "The Economic Impact of S. 744, the Border Security, Economic Opportunity, and Immigration Modernization Act." Congressional Budget Office. June 2013.

Cornelius, Wayne A., and Jessica M. Lewis, eds. 2007. *Impacts of Border Enforcement on Mexican Migration: The View from Sending Communities*. San Diego: University of California at San Diego, Center for Comparative Immigration Studies.

Cortés, Patricia, and José Tessada. 2011. "Low-Skilled Immigration and the Labor Supply of Highly Skilled Women." *American Economic Journal: Applied Economics* 3(3): 88–123.

Cully M. 2012. "More Than Additions to Population: The Economic and Fiscal Impact of Immigration." *Australian Economic Review* 45(3): 344–349.

Desai, Mihir A., Devesh Kapur, John McHale, and Keith Rogers. 2009. "The Fiscal Impact of High-Skilled Emigration: Flows of Indians to the U.S." *Journal of Development Economics* 88(1): 32–44.

Dixon, Peter B., and Maureen T. Rimmer. 2009. "Restriction or Legalization? Measuring the Economic Benefits of Immigration Reform." *Trade Policy Analysis* 40: 1–22. Cato Institute.

DuBard, C. Annette, and Mark W. Hassing. 2007. "Trends in Emergency Medicaid Expenditures for Recent and Undocumented Immigrants." *Journal of the American Medical Association* 297(10): 1085–1092.

Duleep, Harriet Orcutt. 1994. "Social Security and the Emigration of Immigrants." *Social Security Bulletin* 57(1): 37–52. Division of Economic Research, Office of Research and Statistics of the Social Security Administration.

Eisenhauer, Emily, Alex Angee, Cynthia Hernandez, and Yue Zhang. 2007. "Immigrants in Florida: Characteristics and Contribution." Research Institute on Social and Economic Policy, Miami, Florida. Florida International University.

Espenshade, Thomas J., and Vanessa E. King. 1994. "State and Local Fiscal Impacts of US Immigrants: Evidence from New Jersey." *Population Research and Policy Review* 13(3): 225–256.

Fairlie, Robert W. 2014. "Kauffman Index of Entrepreneurial Activity: 1996–2013." Ewing Marion Kauffman Foundation, Kansas City, Missouri.

Fehr, H., S. Jokisch, and L. Kotlikoff. 2004. "The Role of Immigration in Dealing with the Developed World's Demographic Transition." *Finanz Archiv* 60(3): 296–324.

Fehr, Hans, and Laurence Kotlikoff. 1999. "Generational Accounting in General Equilibrium." In *Generational Accounting around the World*, eds. Alan

Auerbach, Laurence Kotlikoff, and Willie Leibfritz. pp. 43–71. Chicago: University of Chicago Press.

Feinleib, Joel, and David Warner. 2005. "The Impact of Immigration on Social Security and the National Economy." Social Security Advisory Board, Issue Brief #1.

Fix, Michael, and Jeffrey Passel. 2002. "The Scope and Impact of Welfare Reform's Immigrant Provisions." Urban Institute, Discussion Paper 02–03.

Gans, Judith. 2007. "Immigrants in Arizona: Fiscal and Economic Impacts." Udall Center for Studies in Public Policy, the University of Arizona.

Garvey, Deborah L., and Thomas J. Espenshade. 1998. "Fiscal Impacts of Immigrant and Native Households: A New Jersey Case Study." In *The Immigration Debate*, eds. James P. Smith and Barry Edmonston, pp. 66–119. Washington, DC: National Academy Press.

Garvey, Deborah L., Thomas J. Espenshade, and James M. Scully. 2002. "Are Immigrants a Drain on the Public Fisc? State and Local Impacts in New Jersey." *Social Science Quarterly* 83(2): 537–553.

General Accounting Office. 1995. "Illegal Aliens: National Net Cost Estimate Vary Widely." GAO/HEHA, pp. 95–133. Washington, DC.

Goldman, Dana P., James P. Smith, and Neeraj Sood. 2006. "Immigrants and the Cost of Medical Care." *Journal of Health Affairs* 25(6): 1700–1711.

Griswold, Daniel T. 2012. "Immigration and the Welfare State." *Cato Journal* 32(1): 159–174.

Gustman, A., and Steinmeier T. 2000. "Social Security Benefits of Immigrants and the U.S. Born." In *Issues in the Economics of Immigration*, ed. George Borjas. pp. 309–350. Chicago: University of Chicago Press.

Hanson, Gordon H. 2012. "Immigration and Economic Growth." *Cato Journal* 32(1): 25–34.

Heet, Justin, Courtney Burkey, John Clark, and David G. Vanderstel. 2009. "The Impact of Immigration on Indiana." Sagamore Institute for Policy Research, Indianapolis, Indiana.

Hinojosa-Ojeda, Raul. 2012. "The Economic Benefits of Comprehensive Immigration Reform." *Cato Journal* 32(1): 175–199.

Kandel, William A. 2011. "Fiscal Impacts of the Foreign-Born Population." Congressional Research Service. October 19.

Kerr, Sari Pekkala, and William R. Kerr. 2011. "Economic Impacts of Immigration: A Survey." NBER Working Paper 16736.

Ku, Leighton, and Brian Bruen. 2013. "Poor Immigrants Use Public Benefits at a Lower Rate Than Poor Native-Born Citizens." Economic Development Bulletin No. 17. Cato Institute. March 4.

Lee, Ronald, and Timothy Miller. 1998. "The Current Fiscal Impact of Immigrants and Their Descendants: Beyond the Immigrant Household." In *The Immigration Debate*, eds. James P. Smith and Barry Edmonston, pp. 183–205. Washington, DC: National Academy Press.

Lee, Ronald, and Timothy Miller. 2000. "Immigration, Social Security, and Broader Fiscal Impacts." *American Economic Review* 90(2): 350–354.

Levine, Phillip B., and David J. Zimmerman. 1999. "An Empirical Analysis of the Welfare Magnet Debate Using the NLSY." *Journal of Population Economics* 12: 391–409.

Lewis, Ethan. 2010. "Immigration, Skill Mix, and Capital-Skill Complementarity." Dartmouth Working Paper.

Lewis, Ethan. 2011. "Immigrant-Native Substitutability: The Role of Language Abil-
    ity." NBER Working Paper 17609.
MaCurdy, Thomas, Thomas Nechyba, and Jay Bhattacharya. 1998. "An Economic
    Framework for Assessing the Fiscal Impacts of Immigration." In *The Immigra-
    tion Debate*, eds. James P. Smith and Barry Edmonston, pp. 13–65. Washing-
    ton, DC: National Academy Press.
Massey, Douglas S. 2011. "Chain Reaction: The Causes and Consequences of Ameri-
    ca's War on Immigrants." Institute for the Study of Labor (IZA). Julian Simon
    Lecture Series, No. VIII. Presented at the IZA Annual Migration Meeting.
    May 2011. Washington, DC: 29.
Mayr, K. 2005. "The Fiscal Impact of Immigrants in Austria: A Generational Ac-
    counting Analysis." *Empirica* 32: 181–216.
McKinnish, Terra. 2005. "Importing the Poor: Welfare Magnetism and Cross-
    Border Welfare Migration." *Journal of Human Resources* 40(1): 57–76.
Moscarolla, F. 2001. "The Effects of Immigration Inflows on the Sustainability of
    the Italian Welfare State." CERP Working Paper No. June 2001.
National Research Council. 1997. *The New Americans: Economic, Demographic, and
    Fiscal Effects of Immigration*, eds. James P. Smith and Barry Edmonston. Wash-
    ington, DC: National Academies Press.
Nowrasteh, Alex, and Sophie Cole. 2013. "Building a Wall around the Welfare State,
    Instead of the Country." Cato Institute Policy Analysis No. 732.
OECD. 2013. *International Migration Outlook 2013*. OECD Publishing, Paris, France.
Ortega, Alexander N., Hai Fang, Victor H. Perez, John A. Rizzo, Olivia Carter-
    Pokras, Steven P. Wallace, and Lillian Gelberg. 2007. "Health Care Access, Use
    of Services, and Experiences among Undocumented Mexicans and Other La-
    tinos." *Archives of Internal Medicine* 167.: 2354–2360.
Ottaviano, Gianmarco I. P., and Giovanni Peri. 2012. "Rethinking the Effect of Immi-
    gration on Wages." *Journal of the European Economic Association* 10(1): 152–197.
Peri, Giovanni, and Chad Sparber. 2009. "Task Specialization, Immigration, Wages."
    American Economic Journal: Applied Economics 1(3): 135–169.
Preston, Ian. 2013. "The Effect of Immigration on Public Finances." Centre for Re-
    search and Analysis of Migration, CDP no. 23/13.
Razin, Assaf, and Efraim Sadka. 2004. "Welfare Migration: Is the Net Fiscal Burden
    a Good Measure of Its Economic Impact on the Welfare of the Native Born
    Population?" NBER Working Paper 10682.
Rector, Robert, and Jason Richwine. 2013. "The Fiscal Cost of Unlawful Immigrants
    and Amnesty to the U.S. Taxpayer." Heritage Foundation. Special Report
    #133. Washington, DC.
Rothman, Eric. S., and Thomas J. Espenshade. 1992. "Fiscal Impacts of Immigration
    to the United States." *Population Index* 58(3): 381–415.
Rowthorn, E. 2008. "The Fiscal Impact of Immigration on the Advanced Econo-
    mies." *Oxford Review of Economic Policy* 24(3): 560–580.
Saiz, Albert. 2003. "The Impact of Immigration on American Cities." Federal Re-
    serve Bank of Philadelphia. Business Review, Fourth Quarter.
Saiz, Albert. 2007. "Immigration and Housing Rents in American Cities." *Journal of
    Urban Economics* 61(2): 345–371.
Schwartz, Karyn, and Samantha Artiga. 2007. "Health Insurance Coverage and
    Access to Care for Low-Income Non-Citizen Adults." Kaiser Commission on
    Medicaid and the Uninsured Policy Brief. The Henry J. Kaiser Family Founda-
    tion. Washington, DC.

Skinner, Curtis. 2012. "State Immigration Legislation and SNAP Take-Up among Immigrant Families with Children." *Journal of Economic Issues* 45(3): 661–681.

Social Security Administration. 2004. "The 2004 Annual Report of the Board of Trustees of the Federal Old-Age and Survivors Insurance and Disability Insurance Trust Funds." Communication from the Board of Trustees. http://www.ssa.gov/oact/tr/TR04/tr04.pdf.

Storesletten, K. 2000. "Sustaining Fiscal Policy through Immigration." *Journal of Political Economy* 108: 300–323.

Vigdor, Jacob. 2013. "Immigration and the Revival of American Cities: From Preserving Manufacturing Jobs to Strengthening the Housing Market." Partnership for a New American Economy. Washington, DC.

Zallman, Leah, Woolhandler, Steffie, Immelstein, David, David Bor, and Danny McCormick. 2013. "Immigrants Contributed an Estimated $115.2 Billion More to the Medicare Trust Fund Than They Took Out in 2002–2009." *Journal of Health Affairs* 32(6): 1153–1160.

CHAPTER 4

༄

The Civic and Cultural Assimilation
of Immigrants to the United States

JACOB VIGDOR

1 INTRODUCTION

In 2005, the guardian of a venerable American institution—a prime tourist destination and pride of many a Philadelphian—was moved to take action against a perceived cultural threat. Joey Vento, proprietor of Geno's Cheesesteaks at the corner of 9th Street and Passyunk Avenue, placed a sign in his shop window bearing a bald eagle, an American flag, and the words "This Is America; When Ordering 'Speak English.'" Vento, the grandson of Italian immigrants to the United States, renewed a concern that had been raised a century before, when his own ancestors arrived, and a century or more before that, as a nation of Protestant, English-speaking natives became home to growing numbers of Germans and Irish Catholics. The presence of newcomers has consistently raised concerns regarding threats to American cultural and civic institutions—the English language prominent among them.

The passage of time has proven many of these earlier worries unfounded. There is no significant German- or Italian-speaking minority in the United States. The erosion of cultural differences between earlier waves of immigrants and the English-speaking mainstream offers little comfort to critics of modern immigration. Roughly half of all immigrants to the United States in more recent years speak a single foreign language—Spanish. This is a stark contrast to the era of European immigrants, when those speaking German or Italian were joined by large numbers of migrants from smaller European countries speaking more obscure languages, as well as many from the United Kingdom and Ireland who spoke English.

Are today's immigrants exhibiting less progress toward the cultural and civic mainstream than their predecessors of earlier eras? This basic question was addressed at some length in my 2009 book *From Immigrants to Americans: The Rise and Fall of Fitting In.* The basic answer drew a distinction between immigrants from Mexico and nearby portions of Central America and those from all other parts of the world. On average, immigrants in recent decades learn English at more rapid rates than their predecessors of a century ago. Their progress towards US citizenship, a major civic assimilation indicator, is slower, but this is largely because changes to naturalization policy have extended the waiting periods for legal migrants. These averages obscure important variation across groups, as described above.

This chapter revisits and extends the analysis of *From Immigrants to Americans.* By virtue of its publication date, and the delays involved in releasing data on the immigrant population, that work did not account for what may ultimately represent a watershed moment in the history of immigration to the United States: the "Great Recession" of 2007–2009. After decades of continuous increase in the foreign-born population, the Great Recession brought immigration to a halt. Even in the recovery period that followed, immigration to the United States has not resumed its pre-recession trajectory. Migration from Mexico, in particular, has remained stagnant, while immigration from Asia has accelerated. The composition of newly arrived immigrants to the United States has been radically transformed. As will be shown below, newly arrived immigrants are better assimilated along multiple dimensions than their predecessors—even before accounting for the fact that immigrants are always least assimilated when they first arrive in the United States.

2   WHY ASSIMILATION MATTERS

Calls for immigrants to adopt the language and culture of the host country are often dismissed as xenophobic. The term "assimilation" has been rejected in some academic circles, for implying that one culture or set of norms is superior to all others and that immigrants ought to be judged by the degree to which they conform to it. In more recent years, however, a more nuanced pattern of support for assimilation, at least along certain key dimensions, has emerged (Alba and Nee 2005). In part, this stems from the recognition that members of any ethnic group need not abandon their own culture or norms when they familiarize themselves with those of another group. A non-native English speaker, for example, generally does not forget his or her native language upon learning English, and is free to use that native language at home or in public interactions with members of his own ethnic group. Sociologists have also recognized the concept of "segmented" assimilation, meaning that immigrants can fully accept the political or linguistic norms of their host society while maintaining a degree of distinctiveness along other dimensions (Zhou 1997). These other dimensions might include religious practice, consumption habits, or selection of children's extracurricular activities.

There is a sound economic rationale for promoting cultural assimilation (Lazear 1999). In competitive markets, transactions occur when buyers and sellers can mutually agree on a price for a good or service that leaves both parties better off. The process of arriving at a mutual agreement, however, depends critically on the ability of the parties to communicate with one another. The lack of a common language is an obvious barrier to communication. Other types of cultural differences might forestall mutually beneficial transactions as well. A seller might represent a culture where haggling over price is the norm, and therefore may set a price that is higher than what he or she is minimally willing to accept. A buyer accustomed to a norm of paying the list price might see this high price, assume that it is non-negotiable, and walk away from a potentially viable transaction.

Linguistic and cultural barriers threaten more than small-scale transactions in the marketplace. Most families seeking to purchase a home in the United States will be presented a settlement form created by the Federal Department of Housing and Urban Development (the HUD-1 form), available only in English. A young Spanish-speaking adult can read all about Bank of America's checking account options in her native language online, but can only apply to open an account in English.

These barriers to trade could conceivably be overcome with the assistance of a translator or facilitator. Such assistance is not typically costless, however, and must often be arranged in advance. As such, the barriers that exist when buyers and sellers cannot effectively communicate with one another can be likened to a tax on the transaction. Like any other tax, the theorized effect is to reduce the number of transactions below that which would occur in a perfectly functioning market, reducing social welfare in the process.

For any member of a multicultural society, there are incentives to familiarize oneself with the norms and language of cultures other than one's own. The incentives are rooted in the promise of being able to more frequently conduct successful transactions with representatives of the other cultures. These benefits must be weighed against the costs of acquiring this familiarity.

It is straightforward to show, in an economic model, that the incentives to bridge cultural gaps are not strong enough to attain the "optimal" level of multicultural understanding. The cause is a classic externality problem. When one actor in the economy bridges a cultural gap, that actor will engage in more transactions, which increase surplus for herself and for her trading partner. The actor internalizes the benefit to herself, but not to a partner.

From a public policy perspective, then, there is a positive role for government to promote the adoption of a common language and norms governing market transactions. The most cost-effective manner of promoting this commonality is to encourage members of minority linguistic or cultural groups to adopt the culture of the mainstream. This strategy is not rooted in any notion of the supremacy of one culture over another, but rather in simple mathematics. If our goal is to incentivize the adoption of a common language, society will spend the least on incentives if it offers them to those in the minority.

Just as there are strong economic returns associated with accepting common cultural norms and language, there are clear returns to members of different ethnic groups accepting common civic norms and institutions. At one extreme, the failure to support common civic norms and institutions can lead to violent conflict. The loss of life and destruction of property associated with violence constitutes a monumental economic cost. Although outright warfare between members of different ethnic groups might seem like a relic of a bygone era, or a phenomenon confined to developing countries today, the developed world has seen eruptions of ethnic violence in the not-too-distant past. Disaffected immigrant groups rioted in the suburbs of several French cities in 2005, and in Brussels the following year. Within the past decade, immigrants or the children of immigrants have been associated with violent incidents in Italy, the Netherlands, Spain, and the United Kingdom. Anti-immigrant protests have also turned violent in many countries.

The aversion of ethnic riots is not the only social benefit derived from immigrant acceptance of civic institutions. Governments bear the responsibility of providing public goods to the population, and the greater the proportion of residents sharing in the burden of providing those goods, the lower the cost to any one resident. National defense is the textbook example of a public good; the cost of providing defense is measured not only in terms of dollars but in service and sacrifice. On a more domestic level, government is charged with ensuring public safety. The burden of immigration on society is minimized when migrants exhibit a greater respect for law, reducing the strain on the criminal justice system.

Beyond these core responsibilities, governments in the developed world are also responsible for the redistribution and the provision of social welfare. The possibility that immigrants might disproportionately burden the social welfare system has long worried immigration opponents. In a sense, then, immigrants can support the civic functions of the state by being net contributors to the social welfare system.

3 PREVIOUS STUDIES OF ASSIMILATION

Social scientists have adopted a range of methods and measures to track the progress of immigrants and their children as they acclimate to a host society. Ethnographers have immersed themselves in enclave neighborhoods (Gans 1962; Margolis 2009). Sociologists have fielded large-scale surveys and have followed up with interviews (Kasinitz et al. 2008). Economists and others have used data from various sources to study patterns of English language adoption, intermarriage, and naturalization. Neither type of study is perfectly suited to draw generalizations regarding the process of assimilation. Studies of individual ethnic groups or cities may reveal patterns that are context-specific. Data analyses are commonly based on simple cross-sectional comparisons of immigrants in differing circumstances; true longitudinal research designs are difficult to undertake with a migrant population, as few data sets track individuals across national borders.[1] In spite of these limitations, the existing literature yields a set of consistent findings. First-generation immigrants in the United States make some degree of progress toward the cultural and civic mainstream. The children of immigrants become very difficult to distinguish from native-born Americans as adults.

Empirical evidence supports the modeling of second-language acquisition as a form of investment, where upfront costs are weighed against a future stream of benefits (Chiswick 2008). Economists Barry Chiswick

---

1. One prominent exception is the Mexican Migration Project, which aims to track a set of Mexican citizens as they move back and forth across the US border. See, for example, Espinosa and Massey (1997).

and Paul Miller, studying non-Anglophone immigrants in English-speaking nations, find that the process of learning English proceeds most rapidly when migrants are younger, belong to smaller linguistic groups, have a smaller family network to rely on, and lack access to sources of news in their native language (Chiswick and Miller 1996, 2001). The lack of a first-language network to acquire information increases the potential benefits of learning the host country language, and younger immigrants can look forward to a longer stream of benefits once they become multilingual. Most studies of immigrants and language ability use cross-sectional data, introducing the concern that apparent progress in learning the host country language might instead reflect selective return migration—the departure of immigrants who never speak English well. Espinosa and Massey (1997) use a longitudinal cross-national sample to show that migrants make real progress over time.

Intermarriage—the propensity to select a spouse outside one's own ethnic group—is often considered the ultimate form of cultural assimilation. In both recent and historical data, intermarriage is very uncommon among first-generation migrants (Drachsler 1920; Pagnini and Morgan 1990; Qian and Lichter 2001). Rates of marriage across ethnic groups increase dramatically in subsequent generations. When considering the cultural assimilation of the first generation, then, English ability is the dominant discriminating factor.

Just as the decision to learn English can be modeled as an investment decision, evidence supports the role of costs and benefits in the decision to become a naturalized citizen. The benefits of naturalization include eligibility for a range of career opportunities open only to citizens, the right to participate in government by voting or holding office, and immunity from future changes in immigration policy. The costs include preparing for the citizenship examination and in some cases relinquishing citizenship in one's country of birth. Multiple studies have established that immigrants naturalize more rapidly when the option of retaining birth citizenship is less attractive—because a migrant was born in a poor, oppressive, or war-torn country (Chiswick and Miller 2008; Jasso and Rosenzweig 1986). Immigrants born in nations recognizing dual citizenship are also more likely to become naturalized citizens (Chiswick and Miller 2008).

Once immigrants take the step of becoming citizens, additional questions arise regarding their political tendencies. As Bryan Caplan and Vipul Naik point out in Chapter 8 of this volume, immigrants responding to the General Social Survey (GSS) are on average more economically liberal—as measured by questions eliciting favorability toward social insurance programs and regulation—and socially conservative than the native-born.

The GSS does not necessarily capture a representative sample of the US immigrant population, as it administers surveys only in English. Including non-English speaking immigrants in the sample might accentuate the dimensions of difference between immigrants and natives.

Bearing in mind that assimilation is a process that plays out over time and in some cases across generations, one might hypothesize that the political differences between immigrants and natives dissipate over time. One study, also using the GSS, found increasing degrees of national attachment among immigrants who had spent more time in the United States (Huddy and Khatib 2007). Immigration may also invoke countervailing political preferences in the native-born population, as suggested in literature reviewed by Caplan and Naik (Chapter 8 of this volume). It is instructive to note that the significant expansion of the American welfare state that began with the New Deal and extended through the Great Society coincided with the period of least overall immigration to the United States, suggesting that the effect of immigration on natives' support for redistribution swamps the effect of adding foreign-born citizens to the roster of voters.

Prior studies of assimilation, in summary, have taught us much about how the process works in general, and suggest that conclusions about the process tend to concord across dimensions studied. This pattern supports the approach outlined below, which aggregates information along multiple dimensions to a set of summary index measures. The advantage of this approach is that summary measures can be computed with both recent and historical data, permitting a direct comparison of assimilation in the early twentieth and early twenty-first centuries—a perspective not represented in prior literature, with the exception of Perlmann's (2005) comparative analysis of Italians and Mexicans, which is of course limited to those ethnic groups.

4   MEASURING PAST AND PRESENT ASSIMILATION

The discussion above suggests several methods of assessing the degree of immigrant assimilation. Along cultural dimensions, one could assess immigrants' English-speaking ability, and perhaps devise a questionnaire to measure familiarity with American cultural and marketplace norms. A questionnaire could also help determine migrants' familiarity with American civic institutions, as well as asking questions about a range of civic behaviors from becoming a naturalized citizen to participating in elections, serving in the military, or holding an elected position of leadership in the community.

The challenge associated with drafting a new questionnaire to assess civic and cultural assimilation is that it is impossible to administer that questionnaire to immigrants of a decade ago, let alone a century. Without comparable information on past generations of immigrants, it is impossible to answer the question posed at the start of this chapter: whether today's immigrants progress toward the mainstream more or less rapidly than their predecessors. While there have been no systematic surveys collecting information on all the above-mentioned assimilation indicators over the past century, the United States Census provides an alternate source of information on certain indicators.

The Census, administered to the entire US population every 10 years since 1790, has always collected information on respondents' birthplace as well as information on year of arrival in the United States, citizenship, English-speaking ability, military service, and marital status. This last item can help determine whether an immigrant is intermarried, which has long been considered an indicator of cultural assimilation. The Census ceased collecting this detailed information following the 2000 enumeration, but in its wake the American Community Survey has provided data for a 1 percent sample of American households annually.

A simple method of assessing assimilation, then, is to track specific indicators such as English-speaking ability or naturalization rates over time. As a summary measure of cultural or civic assimilation, this chapter will present an assimilation index, which can be interpreted as the degree of distinction between the native- and foreign-born populations at any given point in time.

The assimilation index begins by using data on a random sample consisting of 50 percent natives and 50 percent immigrants. Using information on a series of indicators drawn from the Census, the data are used to estimate a statistical model that predicts whether an individual is foreign-born on the basis of the indicators. Some indicators, such as lack of citizenship, perfectly predict whether an individual is foreign-born. Not all citizens are native-born, however. When immigrants and natives are very distinct from one another, this statistical model will have strong predictive power—it will make very few errors in guessing whether an individual is born abroad. In cases where the model can perfectly predict where an individual was born, the assimilation index takes on a value of zero. As the two groups become more similar, the model will make errors more frequently. At the extreme, in a scenario where all immigrants were naturalized citizens, spoke English fluently, and approximated native behavior along other dimensions, the model would do no better than random guessing. In this case, the assimilation index would take on a value of 100.

The assimilation index can be computed for the entire foreign-born population, or for subsets of the population drawn along various lines. It is often instructive, for example, to consider the assimilation of members of specific immigrant groups, those living in certain metropolitan areas, or those who report arriving in the United States during a specific interval.

The index of cultural assimilation incorporates four data points on every individual represented in the data: their ability to speak English, their marital status and whether they are married to a native-born spouse, and the number of children in their household. The index of civic assimilation considers past or present military service and citizenship.

5   INDICATORS OF CIVIC ASSIMILATION

Figure 4.1 shows information on the civic assimilation of immigrants in the United States, tracking the civic assimilation index from 1980 through 2011 for five cohorts of immigrants: those arriving in the United States in the late 1970s, late 1980s, late 1990s, between 2001 and 2005, and between 2006 and 2010. Because the civic assimilation index relies largely on a measure of citizenship, and immigrants are automatically flagged as foreign-born when they are not citizens, this measure can be thought of roughly as measuring the rate of immigrant naturalization over time.

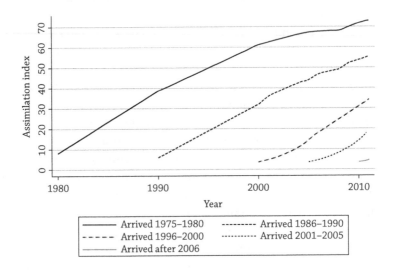

Figure 4.1
The Progress of Individual Cohorts: Civic
Source: The Manhattan Institute.

Across the board, successive waves of immigrants to the United States have exhibited low levels of civic assimilation upon arrival. This should not come as much of a surprise, since for the duration of this time period legal migrants have faced a minimum waiting period of five years before becoming naturalized citizens. The waiting period begins when an immigrant attains legal permanent residency—a green card. As wait times for green cards can themselves last more than a decade, the vast majority of immigrants observed one to five years after arrival are ineligible for citizenship.

Over time, the naturalization rate progresses. For those immigrants who had spent 30–35 years in the United States as of 2010, a clear majority had elected to become US citizens. This high rate of citizenship may in part reflect the impact of the Immigration Reform and Control Act of 1986 (IRCA), which would have awarded legal status to those members of this cohort who entered the country without it. It is important to note that the Census has never collected information regarding whether immigrants are in the country legally; as responses to the survey are self-reported and are not verified with any documentation, it is unclear whether a question about legal status would produce useful responses.

The next cohort of immigrants studied, who entered the country in the late 1980s, would not have been eligible for amnesty under IRCA. Nonetheless, recent data reveal that a majority of this cohort had elected to become citizens as of 2010. To complete the naturalization process, members of this cohort would have had to pass a civics examination. Members of this cohort born after 1960—the vast majority, as immigrants typically come to the United States as young adults—would have had to complete a separate examination assessing their English language abilities. Members of the cohort who arrived in the United States without legal status would be ineligible to become citizens. Taking these factors into consideration, it is clear that a strong majority of immigrants in this cohort who meet the eligibility requirements elect to complete the naturalization process. While acceptance of American civic institutions is not necessarily a requirement for naturalization, familiarity with those institutions is expected in the civics exam. Applicants who take the exam may be asked to name their US senator or representative, identify the office third in line for the presidency after the vice president (and the current holder of that office), name two cabinet positions, identify a power of government belonging to the states, and identify two ways that an American can participate in democracy. The required degree of familiarity with American civic institutions, in short, exceeds that of many native-born citizens. A recent

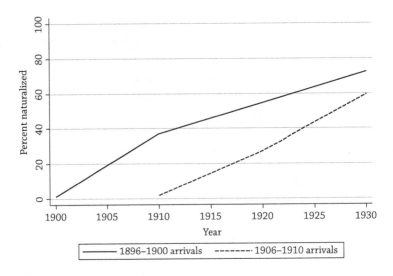

Figure 4.2
Naturalization of Immigrant Cohorts, 1900–1930
Source: Jacob L. Vigdor, *From Immigrants to Americans: The Rise and Fall of Fitting In* (Lanham, MD: Rowman & Littlefield, 2010).

Gallup poll, for example, revealed that only 35 percent of respondents could name their US representative.[2]

More recent cohorts of immigrants exhibit civic behavioral patterns that mimic their predecessors. Among those arriving in the late 1990s, for example, the civic assimilation index reached approximately 33 percent as of 2010, indicating that at least a third of the group had naturalized within 10–15 years of arrival. This closely matches the rate posted by the late 1980s cohort as of the 2000 Census. It falls somewhat below the figure seen in the late 1970s cohort, but the role of IRCA in enabling undocumented migrants to naturalize would be a plausible explanation for the difference. Immigrants entering the United States after 2000 have generated less naturalization data to date, but early indications are that their behavioral patterns will match those of their predecessors as well.

How do the naturalization rates of modern immigrants compare to those of the largely European immigrants who entered the United States during the late nineteenth and early twentieth centuries? Figure 4.2, drawn from *Immigrants to Americans*, shows that the 30-year naturalization rate of just over 70 percent exhibited by late 1970s migrants to the United States is nearly identical to the naturalization rate posted by late

2. The poll was conducted in May 2013. See http://www.gallup.com/poll/162362/americans-down-congress-own-representative.aspx.

1890s migrants as of the 1930 Census. While it is true that IRCA may have artificially boosted naturalization rates for this cohort, it should be noted that the migrants of the late 1890s entered under an open borders policy—so long as they were of European origin—and were eligible for citizenship within five years of entry. Moreover, the English language requirement for citizenship was not implemented until 1906, implying that many immigrants in this cohort would have been able to avoid linguistic barriers to naturalization. In terms of civic behavior, then, modern immigrants show behavior quite similar to those of earlier generations.

Although average rates of naturalization have remained remarkably steady over time, the average clearly does not apply to all groups. Undocumented immigrants are categorically prohibited from becoming naturalized citizens of the United States, and are thereby prevented from engaging in many other forms of civic behavior as well. To assess the prospects for future civic assimilation, it is necessary to contemplate the future course of illegal immigration to the United States, a topic of further discussion below.

6 INDICATORS OF CULTURAL ASSIMILATION

Figure 4.3 shows the progression of cultural assimilation for the same set of cohorts studied in the preceding section. Just as newly arrived immigrants are the least assimilated in terms of civic indicators, largely by law,

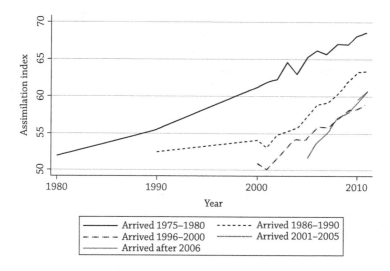

Figure 4.3
The Progress of Individual Cohorts: Cultural
Source: The Manhattan Institute.

cultural assimilation tends to start at a relatively low level and increase as immigrants spend more time in the United States.

Unlike civic assimilation, for which trends appear fairly stable across cohorts, there are important differences between immigrants arriving more than a decade ago and the most recent arrivals. For immigrants arriving in the late 1970s or late 1980s, progress toward cultural assimilation appears slow for the first decade before accelerating to some extent. The rate of cultural assimilation for late 1990s arrivals appears more rapid than that of earlier cohorts, and the progress of immigrants arriving between 2001 and 2005 is more rapid still; in fact the latter cohort actually overtakes the former right around the time of the 2008 "Great Recession." The migrants of the 2006–2010 period, first observed in 2010, show the same high level of cultural assimilation as their predecessors, above that of migrants who had arrived a decade earlier. The level of cultural assimilation displayed by today's newest migrants took the previous generation of migrants to the United States—those arriving 30 years earlier—nearly 20 years to achieve.

The dramatic rise in cultural assimilation among the most recent cohorts of immigrants reflects the change in immigration to the United States brought about by the Great Recession. The recession eroded job opportunities for workers in many sectors of the economy, but relatively low-skilled work in the construction and manufacturing sectors took a disproportionate hit. According to the Bureau of Labor Statistics, the number of jobs in the construction industry fell by more than one million in the decade between 2002 and 2012. Employment in the manufacturing sector fell by more than three million. These job losses are more dramatic in light of the fact that, from an official standpoint, the Great Recession occupied less than 20 percent of the decade.

The loss of employment opportunities in low-skilled sectors played a significant role in driving down the rate of net migration to the United States. Immigrants unable to find work opted to return to their homelands. Other potential migrants reacted to the lack of opportunity by electing not to arrive in the first place. Those migrants who persisted, or who chose to arrive in the wake of the recession, were drawn disproportionately from the more educated, higher-skilled segment of the workforce. These migrants are less reliant on available work in the low-skilled sector, and are more likely to become entrepreneurs. Immigrants overall have a higher business ownership rate than the native-born population, and start new businesses at more than twice the non-immigrant rate (Fairlie 2012).

The cultural assimilation of contemporary immigrants compares quite favorably, on average, to that of immigrants in the early twentieth century. Figures 4.4 and 4.5 track the English language ability of two cohorts

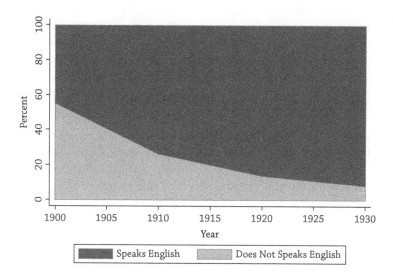

Figure 4.4
English Ability of 1896–1900 arrivals over Time
Source: Jacob L. Vigdor, *From Immigrants to Americans: The Rise and Fall of Fitting In* (Lanham, MD: Rowman
& Littlefield, 2010).

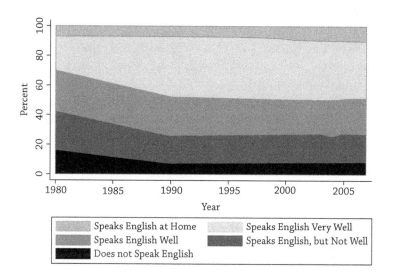

Figure 4.5
English Ability of 1975–1980 arrivals over Time
Source: Jacob L. Vigdor, *From Immigrants to Americans: The Rise and Fall of Fitting In* (Lanham, MD: Rowman
& Littlefield, 2010).

of immigrants to the United States for roughly 30 years each. The first cohort entered the country between 1896 and 1900. Over half these migrants were deemed unable to speak English by Census takers in the 1900 Census. Over time, the average language skills of immigrants in this cohort improved. Some portion of this improvement reflects learning; another component likely reflects return migration among those who had greater difficulty in adjusting to American society.

Comparing English ability over long periods using Census data is complicated by the fact that the method of assessing ability changed over time. Between 1930 and 1970, the Census had switched from using in-person enumerators to mail surveys. English ability was no longer assessed in person, for the most part, but was reported by respondents themselves. Moreover, language ability was no longer coded as a simple yes/no question. Instead, immigrants were permitted to rate their English ability on a five-point scale separating those who spoke English at home, at one extreme, from those who could not speak English at all in the other.

With these caveats in mind, the data show that the cohort of immigrants arriving in the late 1970s had much better English skills than their predecessors of the 1890s. Recalling that these migrants themselves would be upstaged by their successors arriving in the years after 2000, particularly after the onset of the Great Recession, it is reasonably safe to say that the English skills of newly arrived immigrants to the United States are better now than they have been at any point in at least one century, and possibly two.

Is this trend toward a more-assimilated immigrant population permanent? Five years after the recession's conclusion, there is no evidence of a resurgence of immigration from Mexico, the nation providing the highest share of low-skilled migrants to the United States for the past 50 years. The relatively weak American labor market helps to explain this trend, but economic and demographic factors in Mexico have contributed as well. World Bank data show that inflation-adjusted growth rate in per capita GDP in Mexico has doubled the rate in the United States over the past quarter-century. At the same time, Mexico's birth rate, the main driver of population growth, has plummeted to the point of parity with the United States. The World Bank projects that Mexico's population growth rate between 2000 and 2050 will be scarcely a quarter of the rate posted between 1950 and 2000. With economic growth bringing greater opportunity and a population slowdown implying fewer workers to compete for those opportunities, it may well be the case that the period of rapid Mexican migration to the United States is complete.

7   DO IMMIGRANTS STRENGTHEN OR WEAKEN AMERICAN INSTITUTIONS?

It is difficult to maintain the argument that the largely European immigration to the United States that occurred prior to the 1920s weakened American civic and cultural institutions. The children and grandchildren of Southern and Eastern European immigrants have blended into society, sometimes retaining vestiges of their ancestral cultural identity but showing no tangible signs of forming an underclass of disaffected Americans. The acceptance of cultural pluralism in American society permits individuals to celebrate their identity as, for example, Italian Americans or Polish Americans. In the United States, cultural identity is not bound up with nationality.

There is a strong contrast to this pattern visible in many European nations at present. From North Africans in France to Turks in Germany to Middle Eastern immigrants in Scandinavia, experiences in nations where ethnicity has long been tied to nationality have differed markedly. Figure 4.6 shows the result of an exercise using national Census data from nine nations to compute assimilation indices.

The indices consider a common set of factors observed in all data sets, encompassing civic, cultural, and economic factors. Only two nations in the set post assimilation values that exceed those in the United States. One is Canada, a nation that, like the United States, has long disassociated ethnicity from national identity. The second is Portugal, a special

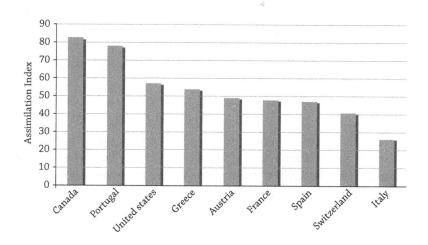

Figure 4.6
International Assimilation Index, 1999–2001
Source: The Manhattan Institute.

case, as many individuals coded as foreign-born individuals residing in that nation are ethnic Portuguese born in colonies such as Angola and Mozambique who returned to their native land when those colonies attained independence.

The greater assimilation of North American immigrants, relative to those in Europe, can be thought of as representing the existence of a unique cultural institution—immigration itself. In addition, variation in national policies undoubtedly plays a role. In the United States, for example, native-born children of immigrants—even undocumented ones—are entitled to citizenship. This is not the case in many European nations. The wait for citizenship, long as it is in the United States, can be far longer in Europe. Canada's standard three-year waiting period might help explain why its immigrants top the assimilation scale. And while economic assimilation is best thought of as a distinct dimension from the cultural and civic factors analyzed here, the greater rigidities brought about by European labor market regulations in many cases lock immigrants out of the labor market. In the United States, unemployment is significantly less common among immigrants than natives; in European countries the reverse is often true.

The notion that immigrants constitute a threat to cultural or civic institutions in Europe, but not the United States, is borne out with several additional observations. As noted above, any European nations have witnessed ethnically based rioting, either by immigrants motivated by their second-class status or by natives engaging in anti-immigrant demonstrations. Voters in European countries have reacted to immigrants' presence by passing referenda—such as Switzerland's notorious ban on minarets—that has never been seriously discussed in the United States.

As I argued in *From Immigrants to Americans*, there are two basic sources of motivation for migrants who choose to come to the United States. Some migrants leave their homeland to escape persecution or to pursue greater political freedom. This narrative of American history dates back to the Pilgrims and the Mayflower and extends fully to the present, with significant populations of Cuban and Vietnamese immigrants who fled rather than be subjected to communist regimes. Native reactions to these politically or religiously motivated migrants have typically been placid. These migrants pose little threat to American institutions because, at root, they chose this nation because they value its institutions—most obviously its commitment to political and religious freedom.

Economically motivated migrants, whose primary motivation is at least perceived as a desire to earn more money than they could at home, have long inspired greater worries in the native population. In recent times, Mexican and Central American immigrants fit the mold, but the

Irish immigrants escaping famine in the mid-nineteenth century and Eastern and Southern European immigrants of the early twentieth sparked a comparable, if not more virulent, backlash. Then as now, these immigrants raised concerns that their allegiance to American values and institutions was inherently weak, and that as permanent residents of society they might disrespect or actively work to undermine them.

With each prior worrisome immigration wave, concerns about lack of fealty to American institutions were coupled with a fear that the wave of migration would have no end. Economically motivated migrants have typically come from nations undergoing what is known as the demographic transition. In nations with a primitive public health infrastructure, mortality rates from infectious disease tend to be high, and families generally factor this high mortality risk into fertility decisions. As sanitation and health care infrastructure improve, mortality declines. When parents fail to anticipate or recognize these mortality decreases, maintaining high fertility rates, the result is a population explosion. The explosion usually corrects itself in time, as fertility rates drop.

The association of emigration with the demographic transition explains why every wave of European migration to the United States—from Ireland and Germany in the mid- to late nineteenth century, Scandinavia in the late nineteenth, and so forth—came to an organic end. Had immigration restrictions not been imposed in the 1920s, migration from Southern and Eastern Europe would have organically declined as well. Perhaps for this reason, the perceived threats posed to American institutions by economically motivated immigrants have consistently failed to materialize.

As noted above, the demographic transition in Mexico is now complete, as fertility rates have fallen dramatically over the past generation. In fact, the transition is now complete in virtually all parts of the world, with the exception of sub-Saharan Africa. African migration to the United States has increased in recent decades; however, the most common destination for African migrants is continental Europe rather than North America, for the simple reason that it is less costly to travel there.

Given these demographic trends, it would appear safe to conclude that the threat to American cultural and civic institutions posed by recent migrants to the United States, undocumented though many of them may be, is minimal. Like all waves of immigrants before them, these newcomers are dwindling in number, and in the long run they will all succumb. Their children, citizens when born here, will be educated in American schools and thereby socialized to understand and value American history, government, and culture, just as the children of European immigrants were in previous centuries.

8 ASSIMILATION AND IMMIGRATION REFORM

At this juncture of American history, congressional leaders are contemplating a series of immigration reform measures that might include improvements in border security, alterations to the number and type of visas issued each year, and most controversially a program of regularizing the immigration status of those who entered the country illegally. In mid-2013, the Senate passed a comprehensive immigration reform bill. Legislative efforts stalled in the House, where a Republican leadership sympathetic in many ways to the cause of immigration reform encountered opposition from more conservative members of the party.

The discussion above carries implications for each of the three major topics of debate in immigration reform. On the topic of border security, a review of demographic trends in Latin America suggests that the need for stricter enforcement will continue to dissipate as stronger economic conditions—and slower population growth—in Mexico and Central America reduce the incentive to emigrate. It is unclear whether improvements in border security can be reliably quantified—we can count the number of individuals apprehended, but by definition it is much more difficult to know how many cross the border undetected. In theory, stronger border security could result in stronger immigrant assimilation, as illegal immigrants tend to have fewer pre-existing economic or social ties. But in a world where illegal immigration dwindles for completely unrelated reasons, it is unclear whether border security truly stands to make a difference.

The question of altering the magnitude and composition of legal immigration flows carries very strong implications for assimilation and the support of American institutions. On the one hand, some US representatives have voiced support for expanded guest worker programs. By design, guest worker programs treat immigrants purely as workers, rather than potential civic or cultural contributors to American society. Assimilation is not expected of guest workers, who presumably will return to their native countries as the need for their temporary labor recedes. Guest worker programs would have key roles in the American economy filled by a class of residents without a political voice, and consequently with no stake in the preservation of American institutions.

At the other end of the spectrum, some voices in the immigration debate have called for an expansion in the number of visas and legal permanent residency slots, particularly for highly skilled workers. Skilled immigrants, most of whom originate in developed or rapidly developing countries, pose something of a conundrum in terms of assimilation. On the one hand, more educated immigrants tend to blend into American culture more easily. They typically arrive fluent in English, and possess a familiarity with cultural norms that in many cases was built through years of study at American universities. On the other, highly skilled immigrants often display lower degrees of civic assimilation. Immigrants from Canada and Europe tend to naturalize at low rates. The United States expects naturalized citizens to renounce their loyalty to other nations. For refugees escaping a despotic regime, this is typically not an issue. Among immigrants who would enjoy the benefits of a generous social welfare system upon return to their home country, incentives are more mixed. Skilled immigration may well be good for the American economy, but the implications for civic institutions and discourse are less clear. From the perspective of civic assimilation, visas and green cards based on family ties—often derided by those who hope to maximize the economic benefits of migration—might yield the strongest dividends.

Amnesty—and in particular offering undocumented immigrants a path to citizenship—could have a clear, direct impact on assimilation. As noted above, the amnesty offered by IRCA appears to have had exactly such an effect. By removing uncertainty regarding immigrants' future in the United States, amnesty would introduce incentives to undertake various forms of investment in American institutions, from learning English to voting and serving in the military.

The experience of IRCA, which most decidedly did not result in an end to illegal immigration in the United States, points out one possible concern with a renewed offer of amnesty. It could, in theory, embolden a new generation of undocumented immigrants, who would again foment concern regarding threats to American civic and cultural institutions. The most potent response, cognizant of economic and demographic trends in sending nations, would be "what new generation of undocumented immigrants?" Evidence suggests that the era of undocumented migration to the United States may in fact be coming to a close, whether we change our laws or not.

9   CONCLUSION

Fears that immigration threatens American cultural and civic institutions are not new; these fears predate the establishment of the nation itself. History has proven these institutions—the predominance of the English language, support of basic capitalist economic principles, and the American system of federal government—quite resilient. The ability of American institutions to withstand profound shifts in the nation's ethnic composition has contributed to the severing of ethnicity from national identity. The ability of American society to culturally and civically assimilate new ethnic groups is itself a form of institution.

While there are reasons to think of contemporary migration from Spanish-speaking nations as distinct from earlier waves of immigration, evidence does not support the notion that this wave of migration poses a true threat to the institutions that withstood those earlier waves. Basic indicators of assimilation, from naturalization to English ability, are if anything stronger now than they were a century ago. Moreover, just as earlier waves of migration came to an end once the sending countries had completed the demographic transition, there is evidence that the rate of migration from Mexico has exhibited what will be a permanent decline.

The worldview most conducive to supporting restrictions on immigration is one where the host country possesses finite wealth, and newcomers threaten to not only demand a share of that wealth but arrive in numbers sufficient to change the rules by which it is distributed. This worldview is difficult to reconcile with a reality where human capital has supplanted natural resources and physical capital as the most important determinant of wealth. It is even more difficult to reconcile with a reality where the civic institutions that incentivize the investments that produce capital are the very things that motivate immigrants to arrive in the first place.

REFERENCES

Alba, Richard, and Victor Nee. 2005. *Remaking the American Mainstream: Assimilation and Contemporary Immigration.* Cambridge, MA: Harvard University Press.

Chiswick, Barry. 2008. "The Economics of Language: An Introduction and Overview." IZA Discussion Paper #3568.

Chiswick, Barry, and Paul Miller. 1996. "Ethnic Networks and Language Proficiency among Immigrants." *Journal of Population Econo*mics 9: 19–35.

Chiswick, Barry, and Paul Miller. 2001. "A Model of Destination-Language Acquisition: Application to Male Immigrants in Canada." *Demography* 38: 391–409.

Chiswick, Barry, and Paul Miller. 2008. "Citizenship in the United States: The Roles of Immigrant Characteristics and Country of Origin." IZA Discussion Paper #3596.

Drachsler, Julius. 1920. *Democracy and Assimilation: The Blending of Immigrant Heritages in America.* New York: The Macmillan Company.

Espinosa, Kristin E., and Douglas S. Massey. 1997. "Determinants of English Proficiency among Mexican Migrants to the United States." *International Migration Review* 31: 28–50.

Fairlie, Robert W. 2012. "Immigrant Entrepreneurs and Small Business Owners, and Their Access to Financial Capital." Small Business Administration Office of Advocacy white paper.

Gans, Herbert. 1962. *The Urban Villagers: Group and Class in the Life of Italian-Americans*. New York: The Free Press.

Huddy, Leonie, and Nadia Khatib. 2007. "American Patriotism, National Identity, and Political Involvement." *American Journal of Political Science* 51: 63-77.

Jasso, Guillermina, and Mark Rosenzweig. 1986. "Family Reunification and the Immigration Multiplier: U.S. Immigration Law, Origin-Country Conditions, and the Reproduction of Immigrants." *Demography* 23(3): 291–311.

Kasinitz, Philip, John H. Mollenkopf, Mary C. Waters, and Jennifer Holdaway. 2008. *Inheriting the City: The Children of Immigrants Come of Age*. Cambridge, MA: Harvard University Press.

Lazear, Edward. 1999. "Culture and Language." *Journal of Political Economy* 107(6): S95–S126.

Margolis, Maxine L. 2009. *An Invisible Minority: Brazilians in New York City*. Gainesville: University Press of Florida.

Pagnini, Deanna, and S. Philip Morgan. 1990. "Intermarriage and Social Distance among U.S. Immigrants at the Turn of the Century." *American Journal of Sociology* 96(2): 405–432.

Perlmann, Joel. 2005. *Italians Then, Mexicans Now: Immigrant Origins and Second-Generation Progress, 1890 to 2000*. New York: Russell Sage Foundation.

Qian, Zhenchao, and Daniel Lichter. 2001. "Measuring Marital Assimilation: Intermarriage among Natives and Immigrants." *Social Science Research* 30: 289–312.

Vigdor, Jacob L. 2009. *From Immigrants to Americans: The Rise and Fall of Fitting In*. Lanham, MD: Rowman and Littlefield.

Zhou, Min. 1997. "Segmented Assimilation: Issues, Controversies, and Recent Research on the New Second Generation." *International Migration Review* 31(4): 975–1008.

CHAPTER 5

✧

Employment Visas

An International Comparison

ALEXANDRE PADILLA AND NICOLÁS CACHANOSKY

1   INTRODUCTION

This chapter compares and assesses the various labor-based immigration programs that OECD countries have adopted over the past 50 years.[1] These programs deserve our attention for several reasons. First, reforming these programs is often seen as one of the solutions to the current illegal immigration "problem" that has increasingly been at the center of the broader immigration debate (Ilias, Fennelly, and Federico 2008: 741). Second, US businesses regularly call for a reform of these programs, particularly the guest worker programs, because these programs are failing to solve the labor shortages these businesses face. For example, not only are high-skilled temporary guest worker programs (such as the H-1B visa program) so restrictive that businesses cannot hire the workers they need because of strict quotas, but also, as Slaughter (2014) argues, based on Bill Gates's 2008 testimony to Congress "that for every immigrant hired at technology companies, an average of five additional employees are added as well." Similarly, Theo Eicher's 2011 Microsoft Economic Impact Study (2013) of the United States and Washington State employment multiplier estimates that this inability to recruit foreign workers translates

1. The authors thank editor Benjamin Powell and the referees for valuable comments and suggestions to improve this chapter. The usual caveat applies.

into jobs not being created: "a new job is lost about every 43 seconds, around the clock, every single day that America is open for business" (Slaugther 2014).

US industries that rely heavily on low-skilled workers, such as the farming industry, also suffer from the restrictiveness of guest worker programs. In 2004, for example, only 30 percent of the Arizonian lettuce crop was harvested; the rest was left in the ground to rot. Losses amounted to nearly $1 billion (Powell and Gochenour 2013: 12). In 2011, in response to a GOP proposal to require farmers to check all new hires through E-Verify, a federal database run by the Department of Homeland Security devised to ferret out illegal immigrants, Bob Stallman, president of the American Farm Bureau Federation, stated that "the problem with that is our current system, without an alternative labor supply, means that we would lose those workers that are providing that $5 to $9 billion of production" (USDA Office of Communications 2011).[2] Other empirical evidence suggests that more low-skilled workers would also provide indirect benefits to the US economy and society. For example, Furtado and Hock (2010) find that "inflows of low skilled immigrants have made it easier for high skilled US born women to pursue careers without having to sacrifice family life," therefore leading to an increase of fertility of high-skilled native women in the United States. Similarly, Cortés and Tessada (2011) show that "by lowering the prices of services that are close substitutes of home production, low-skilled immigrants increase the labor supply of highly skilled native women."

Given the benefits that high-skilled and low-skilled workers provide in the present system where labor immigration, permanent and temporary, is strictly limited, it is important to analyze alternative permanent and guest worker programs to see what reforms could be implemented to reduce the losses associated with the current US immigration policies.

Section 2 presents some basic statistics on employment migration to give an empirical context of the immigration situation in OECD countries. Section 3 discusses the various migration policies as they relate to employment of low-skilled and high-skilled migrant workers. In section 4, we assess these policies. Section 5 provides concluding remarks.

2 EMPLOYMENT MIGRATION AROUND THE WORLD: STATISTICS

Before discussing the employment visa policies, a look at key indicators of migration and employment in OECD countries provides economic context

2. See also McKinley and Preston (2011).

Table 5.1 LIST OF COUNTRIES

Australia (AUS)	Finland (FIN)	Ireland (IRL)	New Zealand (NZL)	Switzerland (SWI)
Austria (AUT)	France (FRA)	Italy (ITA)	Norway (NOR)	United Kingdom (GRB)
Belgium (BEL)	Germany (GER)	Japan (JPN)	Portugal (PRT)	United States (USA)
Canada (CAN)	Greece (GRC)	Luxembourg (LUX)	Spain (SPA)	
Denmark (DNK)	Iceland (ICE)	Netherlands (NLD)	Sweden (SWE)	

and constraints to popular but inaccurate beliefs about migration. In this chapter we look at data and migration policy from the 23 OECD countries listed in Table 5.1.

2.1   Migration Stock and Flow

Figure 5.1 shows the average annual net migration rates (per thousand population) for the years 2005–2007 and 2008–2010. Some countries, like Netherlands, Denmark, Norway, Switzerland, and Luxembourg, have seen the net migration rates increase notably after the 2008 crisis. For other countries, like Portugal, Ireland, Spain, and Iceland, these rates have decreased notably. In Ireland and Iceland, their net migration rates for the period 2008–2010 reversed to negative values. These variations in net migration rates across countries are more likely due to variations on how each country was affected by the European crisis, rather than changes in immigration policies.

Table 5.2 shows the inflow of permanent immigrants from 2007 to 2011. There is a wide dispersion on the percentage change of permanent immigrants between 2007 and 2011. In some countries the inflow of immigrants has been reduced to almost half of the 2007 levels; other countries have seen important increases in the inflow of permanent immigrants. As a percent of the population, there are two distinct cases: Luxembourg with a high percentage of immigrants (3.7 percent) and Japan with a very low population of immigrants with respect to total population (almost 0 percent).

Figure 5.2 shows the permanent immigration by category of entry or of status change as percentage of total population. Italy, the United Kingdom, Canada, Spain, Australia, and New Zealand are the countries with the

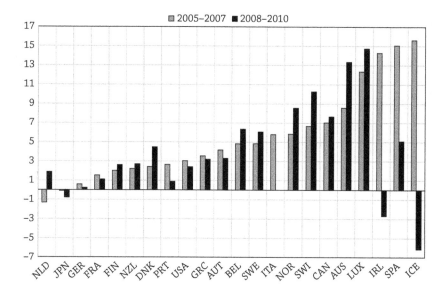

Figure 5.1
Average Annual Net Migration Rates (per Thousand Population), 2005–2007 and 2008–2010

largest percentage of worker immigrants. Free movement, that is, the ability of European Union citizens to move freely to another EU country, represents 45 percent of international migration in the European Economic Area (OECD 2013: 25).[3] On the other side of the spectrum, Japan, the United States, and Canada have zero percent "free movement" immigrants.

2.2 Immigrant Employment

Most countries have extended working opportunities for international students who have acquired a degree in their universities. Most countries have developed special programs to achieve that goal. One reason

3. This right of workers to move freely to another country of the European Union also extends to countries of the European Economic Area: Iceland, Liechtenstein, and Norway. However, workers from some EU countries such as Bulgaria and Romania may face restrictions when it comes to working in Iceland, Liechtenstein, and Norway. The EU-Switzerland agreement on the free movement of persons allows Swiss nationals to live and work in the EU and allows most EU citizens to work in Switzerland without a permit. However, some restrictions apply to nationals of Bulgaria, Croatia, and Romania, who need a permit in Switzerland. Similarly, some restrictions apply to Swiss nationals to work in Croatia (European Commission 2014a, 2014b).

Table 5.2 INFLOWS OF PERMANENT IMMIGRANTS INTO SELECTED OECD COUNTRIES, 2007–2011

Country	2007	2008	2009	2010	2011	% Change (2011/2008)	As % of Population (2011)
United States	1,052,400	1,107,100	1,130,200	1,041,900	1,061,400	0.9	0.3
Spain	691,900	409,600	334,100	300,000	349,300	-49.5	0.8
United Kingdom	343,300	317,300	352,700	388,000	321,200	-6.4	0.5
Italy	559,200	482,600	384,200	349,900	312,200	-44.2	0.5
Germany	232,800	228,300	201,500	222,500	290,800	24.9	0.4
Canada	236,800	247,200	252,200	280,700	248,700	5.0	0.7
Australia	191,900	205,900	221,000	208,500	219,500	14.4	1.0
France	184,500	192,200	182,100	196,300	211,300	14.5	0.3
Switzerland	122,200	139,100	114,800	115,000	124,300	1.7	1.6
Netherlands	80,600	90,600	89,500	95,600	105,600	31.0	0.6
Belgium	50,300	51,200	64,200	64,100	76,500	52.1	0.7
Sweden	74,400	71,000	71,500	65,600	71,700	-3.6	0.8
Norway	43,700	48,900	48,500	55,900	60,300	38.0	1.2
Japan	108,500	97,700	65,500	55,700	59,100	-45.5	0.0
Austria	47,100	49,500	45,700	45,900	58,400	24.0	0.7
New Zealand	51,700	51,200	47,500	48,500	44,500	-13.9	1.0
Denmark	30,300	45,600	38,400	42,400	41,300	36.3	0.7

Portugal	42,800	71,000	57,300	43,800	36,900	-13.8	0.3
Ireland	120,400	89,700	50,700	23,900	33,700	-72.0	0.8
Greece*	46,330	42,900	46,530	33,370	23,210	-49.9	0.2
Finland	17,500	19,900	18,100	18,200	20,400	16.6	0.4
Luxembourg*	15,770	16,800	14,640	15,810	19,110	21.2	3.7
Iceland*	9,320	7,470	3,390	2,990	2,750	-70.5	0.8

Source: OECD (2013).

Notes: Includes only foreign nationals; the inflows include status changes, namely persons in the country on a temporary status who obtained the right to stay on a longer-term basis. Series for some countries have been significantly revised. Settlement countries include Australia, Canada, New Zealand and the United States. Information on data for Israel: http://dx.doi.org/10.1787/888932315602. The * denotes national (non-standardized) statistics.

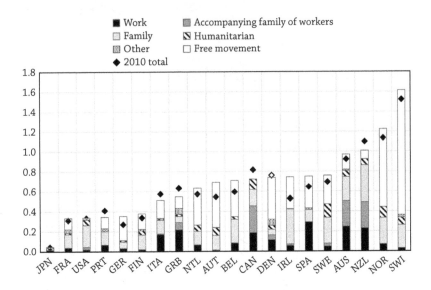

Figure 5.2
Permanent Immigration by Category of Entry or of Status Change into Selected OECD, 2011, and Total for 2010 (Percentage of Total Population)

could be that skilled foreign graduate immigrants boost innovation.[4] Figure 5.3 shows the maximum number of months an international student is allowed to stay in the country and look for work after graduation. The United States, though it does not offer an extension of the student visa, does offer foreign students, studying in or having graduated from a US university, the ability to work for 12 months through the "Optional Practical Training (OPT)" program. Even though the job does not have to be in academia, employment through the OPT program requires that the job must be directly related to the student's major area of study. Since the university is the petitioner of the student's visa, an OPT petition will require the university's approval rather than the employer's (US Citizenship and Immigration Services 2014c).[5] For most countries, the immigrant share of the labor force with post-secondary education is higher than the share of natives with post-secondary education (see Figure 5.4).

4. Hunt and Gauthier-Loiselle (2010: 31) show that skilled immigrants increase innovation in the United States. Particularly, they show that "immigrants patent at double the native rate, due to their disproportionately holding science and engineering degrees." They show that "a 1 percentage point increase in immigrant college graduates' population share increases patents per capita by 9–18 percent."
5. It should be noted that "[s]tudents who graduate with a qualified Science, Technology, Engineering or Mathematics (STEM) degree, and are currently in an approved post-completion OPT period based on a designated STEM degree may apply for a 17-month STEM extension of their post-completion OPT" (US Citizenship and Immigration Services 2014c).

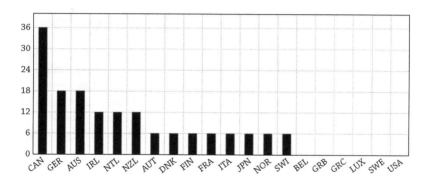

Figure 5.3
Maximum Duration of Job Search (Months) for Post-Secondary Schemes in Different OECD Countries

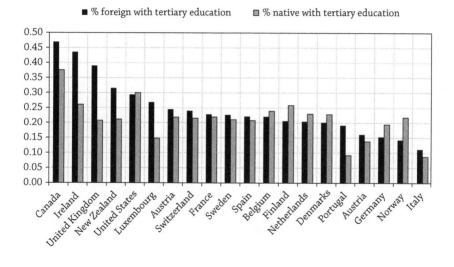

Figure 5.4
Country Share of Labor Force with Post-Secondary Education Attainment, 2005

At the turn of the twenty-first century, there was an increase in the employment of skilled immigrant labor (see Table 5.3). Some countries, like Belgium, Switzerland, Denmark, Ireland, Luxemburg, and Sweden, are close to having half of the migrant workers with post-secondary educations, and Switzerland and Luxemburg have at least half of the immigrant workers performing as managers, professionals, or associate professionals.

However, immigrants also face higher long-term unemployment rates than non-immigrants. Besides language barriers and extra legal costs

Table 5.3 SKILLED IMMIGRANT EMPLOYMENT AS PERCENT OF ALL
EMPLOYED IMMIGRANTS

	Employed Immigrants with Post-Secondary Education Having Arrived in Previous 10 Years		Employed Immigrants Working as Managers, Professionals, and Associate Professionals Having Arrived in Previous 10 Years	
	1995	2006	1995	2006
Austria	13.2	27.3	19.6	29.1
Belgium	45.3	43.3	40.0	36.8
Denmark	38.5	44.3	33.5	34.9
Finland	N/A	21.2	N/A	34.7
France	31.7	36.9	34.5	28.5
Germany	N/A	29.1	N/A	25.5
Greece	18.7	12.5	10.1	3.6
Ireland	56.1	49.2	35.4	25.6
Italy	23.5	12.5	18.8	8.6
Luxemburg	24.6	48.7	30.3	55.2
Netherlands	26.6	29.6	29.4	29.4
Norway	6.6	31.8	N/A	25.2
Portugal	16.6	15.9	20.7	9.6
Spain	39.5	23.9	31.8	8.1
Sweden	38.3	45.4	N/A	33.8
Switzerland	N/A	45.2	N/A	49.9
United Kingdom	N/A	N/A	46.2	38.6
United States	29.6	31.2	21.9	14.6

Source: Chaloff and Lemaitre (2009: 15). The designation "managers" excludes managers of small enterprises (ISCO 13), which covers small shopkeepers.

associated with hiring foreigners, immigrants lack work experience in the host country and do not have a local network as developed as that of the native population. Working restrictions for immigrants are one policy that contributes to their relatively high long-term unemployment rates.[6] Figure 5.5 shows long-term unemployment rates for 2012 for the total population and foreign-born workers. In most cases the long-term unemployment rate for immigrants is considerably higher than it is for the total population. In some cases it is more than twice as high, as in Belgium,

6. In the United States, for example, a working visa is attached to a job for a specific employer. Therefore, an immigrant worker wanting to work for a different employer would need to apply for a new working visa.

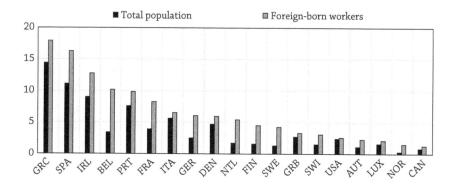

Figure 5.5
Long-Term Unemployment for Total Population and Foreign-Born Workers, 2012

Germany, the Netherlands, Finland, and Sweden. Only in Italy, the United Kingdom, the United States, and Luxembourg are the rates are similar.

3   POLICY BACKGROUND: EMPLOYMENT VISAS AROUND THE WORLD

Immigration laws as they apply to employment vary on two levels: the type of immigrants they target and the way they operate. First, immigration policies vary depending on whether they target low-skilled immigrants or high-skilled immigrants. Traditionally, immigration policies targeting high-skilled workers will attempt to attract them. On the other hand, immigration policies aiming at low-skilled workers tend to discourage entry except for some very limited and specific types of low-skilled workers.

There are two types of immigration systems: demand-driven or supply-driven (Chaloff and Lemaître 2009: 17). In demand-driven systems, employers who have identified foreigners with no right to work have to petition the immigration authorities for a work or a residence permit for the future employee.[7] Petitions from employers can be for temporary migration or permanent immigration. Usually, if permission is granted to the foreigner, he is only allowed to work for his employer and in some cases not more than a "certain amount of hours" on personal projects or for other employers. In demand-driven systems, the petitioner for the visa is the main employer of the immigrant.

7. As we will see below, obtaining such permit is not unconditional. The employer and worker must often meet some conditions of various sorts set by the immigration regulations.

In supply-driven systems, countries advertise that they are taking applications for immigration directly from potential foreign-born nationals who are interested in immigrating in the advertising country. Supply-driven system are typically merit-based point systems in which candidates for immigration are selected based on characteristics that are deemed to facilitate labor market integration, such as language proficiency, educational attainment, age, work experience, presence of family in the host country, the existence of a job offer, or holding a specific set of skills for occupations for which there is a shortage. Each characteristic is worth a certain amount of points. Candidates must exceed a minimum point threshold to be considered for admission (Chaloff and Lemaître 2009: 17). Typically, supply-driven systems are used for permanent immigration, while demand-driven systems are used for temporary migration.

It is important to note that immigration laws and policies are as complex, if not more complex, than tax codes. This section does not provide a detailed and exhaustive overview of all these laws and policies. Rather, it provides some general descriptions of their mechanisms and goals.

3.1   Immigration Policies and High-Skilled Migration

Most OECD countries have implemented various immigration policies targeting high-skilled workers (see Appendix 1 at the end of this chapter). However, while some countries like Canada and Australia have developed policies in which high-skilled immigration is part of an overall development strategy (Chaloff and Lemaître 2009: 30), in other countries like France, Norway, and the United States the approach to immigration has been one of protecting native workers while still permitting employers to meet their needs within limits.[8]

3.1.1   *Demand-Driven Systems*

In demand-driven systems, an employer who wants to hire a high-skilled foreign worker will petition the immigration authorities to allow the worker to migrate temporarily and, in some circumstances, to immigrate and become a permanent resident if the employer believes that the high-skilled worker will be a long-lasting member of the business. Most OECD

---

8. It is beyond the scope of this chapter to analyze the role that politics and private interest groups play behind this goal of protecting native workers. As we will see below, the added layer of proving that hiring a foreign worker is not displacing a native worker increases costs for employers to hire foreign workers.

countries, including the countries that use a point system, rely on employers petitioning for working visas for temporary migration. Traditionally, the goal of these working visas, particularly the temporary ones, is to meet skill shortages.

Most countries require employers to pass a labor market test to ensure that no native worker will be displaced by an immigrant. The characteristics of the labor market test vary across countries, depending on the role played by public employment services in matching workers with jobs. Not only are employers required to advertise the job vacancy for some period of time (the length of which varies, depending of the country), but in many European countries employers are also required to list the job opening in a public employment services' office. In some cases, the public employment services may refer candidates to the employer or may limit intervention to approving the request after the job has been advertised for a certain period of time. Other countries require employers to demonstrate that they attempted to fill the position before offering the job to a non-resident. Some countries, such as France and Norway, apply a discretionary consideration of the "added value" of hiring foreign workers in terms of added new skills or resources brought by these workers. In some countries, such as Denmark and Iceland, unions are directly involved, and any request for a working visa is submitted to the relevant union to confirm that there is a shortage and for approval (Chaloff and Lemaître 2009: 19–20).

Countries that require employers to submit to a labor market test also have developed a shortage occupation list. Employers who petition for working visas for an immigrant who will occupy a job listed on the shortage occupation list are exempt from advertising the position. These shortage occupation lists are often drafted regionally in collaboration with the public employment services, employers, and trade unions. France drafts its shortage occupation list using vacancy data. In the United States, the shortage occupation list, Schedule A, is very short. The current list includes physical therapists, professional nurses, sciences and arts, and performing arts (US Department of Labor 2013b).

Finally, some countries apply a quota limiting how many visas they will grant to employers. Australia, Austria, Italy, Norway,[9] Portugal, Switzerland, and the United States have quotas for their temporary migration programs.

9. In the case of Norway, even if the quota is full, employers can still petition for a permit following Norway's labor market test in which the Public Employment Service performs a labor market assessment (Chaloff and Lemaître 2009: 48).

In 2009, the European Union created the "EU Blue Card" Directive to attract high-skilled third-country nationals to come to Europe "to address labor shortages, [. . .] to sustain its competitiveness and economic growth" (Council of the European Union 2009: 17). Currently, Austria, Belgium, Bulgaria, Croatia, Cyprus, the Czech Republic, Estonia, Finland, France, Germany, Greece, Hungary, Italy, Latvia, Lithuania, Luxembourg, Malta, the Netherlands, Poland, Portugal, Romania, Slovakia, Slovenia, Spain, and Sweden have adopted the EU Blue Card Directive. The "EU Blue Card" is inspired by the US Permanent Residency Card, or "Green Card." It is a work permit that allows high-skilled non-EU citizens to reside and work in any country in the European Union (with the exception of Denmark, Ireland, and the United Kingdom) (Council of the European Union 2009: 21).[10]

Countries that have incorporated the EU Blue Card Directive into their domestic legislation have either substituted it for their previous immigration system or have added it on top of the existing system. Depending on the country, the employer must petition for the EU Blue Card Directive on the third-country national's behalf or, in other cases, the immigrant must petition for it. The EU Blue Card is valid for a period of one to four years. Applicants are notified within a period of 90 days after the application has been submitted whether their application has been accepted. In addition, some countries can put a quota on the number of admissions under the EU Blue Card Directive system.

There are several conditions the candidate must meet to qualify for an EU Blue Card. The candidate must produce a work contract or binding job offer with a salary of at least 1.5 times the average gross annual salary paid in the Member State concerned (for certain professions where there is a particular need for third-country workers, the Member States may lower the salary threshold to 1.2).[11] The candidate must have a valid travel document and a valid residence permit or a national long-term visa, and proof of health insurance. For licensed professions, documents must show that the third-country national meets the legal requirements, and for unlicensed professions, the documents must show the relevant higher

10. However, unlike the US Green Card, the EU Blue Card does not necessarily grant permanent residency. Application for permanent residency can be granted after five years of legal and continuous stay in the European Union. In order to fulfill the requirements of five years of legal and continuous stay, the EU Blue Card holder can accumulate periods of residence in different Member States (Council of the European Union 2009: 26).

11. For some countries, the employer can be required to make an offer more than 1.5 times the average salary, and in others it can be lower. In the Czech Republic, the benchmark is the average for the country and, in Finland, it has to be higher than the average for the country. In the Netherlands, the gross annual salary has to be at least EUR 60,000 (OECD 2013: 49).

professional qualifications. In addition, the applicant must not pose "a threat to public policy, public security, or public health" (Council of the European Union 2009: 22). The third-country national may also be required to provide his or her address in that Member State. The EU Blue Card may be withdrawn if the holder does not have sufficient resources to maintain himself or herself and family members without social assistance, or if he or she has been unemployed for more than three consecutive months or more than once during the period of validity of the card (Council of the European Union 2009: 24). After two years of legal employment, they may receive equal treatment with nationals with regard to access to any highly skilled employment. After 18 months of legal residence, they may move to another Member State to take another highly skilled job (subject to the limits set by the Member State on the number of non-nationals accepted) (European Union 2009).

Despite the attempt of the EU Blue Card Directive to make Europe a more attractive destination of highly skilled third-country foreign nationals, "the interests of the different institutional actors involved in the EU decision-making process and the associated inter-institutional struggles have considerably compromised the 'attractiveness' of the Blue Card Directive" (Eisele 2013: 22). The requirements for petitioners are prohibitive in terms of salary requirements, residency requirements before being able to move to another member state, or who qualifies as a highly skilled immigrant.

3.1.2 Supply-Driven Systems

In most supply-driven systems, the country advertises that it is accepting applications for immigration. Supply-driven systems are merit-based point systems in which applicants must meet a minimum threshold of points to be eligible. Eligibility depends on characteristics deemed desirable in terms of candidates' integration into the labor force and the society, such as language proficiency, educational attainment, age, work experience in the country, presence of family in the host country, the existence of a job offer, or being in an occupation for which there is a shortage (Chaloff and Lemaître 2009: 21–23). Unlike demand-driven systems, countries using the point system do not necessarily require the applicant to have a job offer to be eligible.[12] However, some countries, such as New Zealand

---

12. The United States does not rely on a point system, but under the EB-1 visa, permanent residency can be granted to "persons of extraordinary ability" of national or international renown without a job offer (Chaloff and Lemaître 2009: 22).

and Canada, give points to applicants who have a job offer in hand. Other countries, such as the United Kingdom and Canada, require that "arrivals have sufficient funds to support themselves during a certain period while looking for work" to avoid these immigrants becoming a fiscal burden (Chaloff and Lemaître 2009: 32). In Australia, new immigrants are ineligible to receive any social benefits for two years.

Since 2008, the United Kingdom, Denmark, the Netherlands, and Austria have introduced a points system into their supply-driven and their demand-driven systems to identify high-skilled workers. Japan and Korea have also introduced a point system into their immigration program for high-skilled workers. Unlike countries like Canada, Australia, and New Zealand, where the point system is primarily used for permanent residency, in these countries, being admitted under the point system does not automatically grant permanent residency. Denmark uses its point system to screen for high-skilled immigrants and grants a "Green Card" to those who qualify for six months to find a job either on the Job Card Scheme shortage list or a job paying at least 6,300 euros annually (Chaloff and Lemaître 2009: 21). In the United Kingdom, the Tier 1 high-skilled labor program is for an initial period of three years, which can be renewed. After five years of residence, the immigrant becomes eligible for permanent residency. In Japan, under the point system implemented in May 2012, "preferential treatment is given to university professors, academics and researchers, doctors and other professionals with highly specified knowledge or skills. It also favors corporate executives and managers" (OECD 2013: 266).

3.2   Immigration Policies and Low-Skilled Migration

Most countries' immigration policies have focused on limiting the entry of low-skilled workers, despite markets showing an increasing demand for low-skilled workers (OECD 2008: 133).[13] Historically, this was not always the case. From the 1940s until 1974, most OECD countries had guest worker programs for low-skilled workers to alleviate the upward pressure on low-skilled worker's wages resulting from domestic labor shortages created directly or indirectly by World War II. In Western Europe, the goal of these programs was "to help speed up reconstruction and to compensate in part for wartime manpower losses" (Castles 1986: 761–762). However,

---

13. However, as we will see below, in Europe there seems to be a return to recruiting low-skilled migrant workers to meet the market demand.

in Europe, these programs continued past the reconstruction period and lasted until the 1973–1974 oil crisis, which was the beginning of a period of economic stagnation and high unemployment. In the United States, the goal was "to replenish the United States' agricultural labor forces which had been absorbed by the Armed Forces and defense plants" (Martínez 1958: 1). Like similar programs in Europe, this guest worker program continued past World War II, lasting until 1964. Currently, in the United States, the guest worker program for low-skilled workers is extremely limited, while in European countries there has been a partial resurgence of guest worker programs for low-skilled workers (Castles 2006).

3.2.1   Guest Worker Programs Pre-1974

3.2.1.1   Europe

After World War II, Western European countries developed systems of temporary labor recruitment, first to replace the labor force lost to the war and to speed up reconstruction; then temporary migrant labor recruitment was used to meet the intense demand for unskilled labor that resulted from the rapid economic growth that these countries experienced until 1973. Between 1950 and 1973, 30 million foreign workers rotated in and out of West Germany, France, Great Britain, Switzerland, Belgium, the Netherlands, and Sweden (Massey and Liang 1989: 202). In countries such as Great Britain, West Germany, and France, the government and its immigration office had the monopoly on the recruiting, the mobility, and the working conditions of the migrant labor force (Castles 1986: 762). In other countries, such as Belgium and the Netherlands, the government recruited workers under bilateral agreements with Southern European countries such as Italy, Spain, and Portugal. However, in the Netherlands, employers were performing the actual recruitment of the workers. In Switzerland, employers also recruited foreign workers, but the government controlled the admission and conditions of residence (Castles 1986: 765–766). In order to ensure that the guest workers returned to their home country once their visas expired, "government policies sequestered guest workers from the native population, restricted their geographic and occupational mobility, and, more importantly, prevented or discouraged guest workers from bringing along family members" (Massey and Liang 1989: 202).[14]

---

14. In Great Britain, in the European Voluntary Worker program, which lasted until 1951, only single men and women were eligible to participate in the guest worker program, and they were rarely allowed to bring any dependents (Castles 1986: 762).

The 1973 oil crisis and the subsequent recession led Western European governments to ban the entry of guest workers except for seasonal workers and workers from the European Community (Castles 1986: 773). As a result, since the mid-1970s until the early 2000s, most low-skilled workers coming from countries outside the European Community entered European countries as illegal immigrants, family members, or asylum seekers (Castles 2006: 744). It was not until the early 2000s that European countries started to re-establish guest worker programs.

3.2.1.2   The US Bracero Program

The United States' entry into World War II, the mobilization of workers to support war efforts, and an increase in the demand for agricultural goods created a labor shortage for Southwestern farmers, particularly cotton growers.[15] This led to the creation of the Bracero program on August 14, 1942, through the discretionary authority of the Commissioner of Immigration, who waived the provision of the 1917 Immigration Act, which basically excluded labor contract with Mexican workers (Alston and Ferrie 1999: 107). This program was a bilateral program between the governments of the United States and Mexico. Initially, while the US employers recruited the Mexican agricultural workers, the contract was between the Mexican worker and the US government (Alston and Ferrie 1999: 107). The Mexican government was in charge of supervising the program, and Mexican workers were forbidden from making contracts in states where they were subject to discrimination (Alston and Ferrie 1999: 107). In 1943, the treaty between the United States and Mexico was given congressional approval and became Public Law 45. Under Public Law 45, the Bracero program allowed the US government to

---

15. Alston and Ferrie (1999: 101–103) argue that, in reality, the labor shortage may have been exaggerated and artificially maintained. According to Alston and Ferrie (1999: 106–107) it was more the result of wartime farm labor legislation and wartime programs, strongly supported by Southern farm interests, to prevent farm workers from moving out of the Southern states (where they were underemployed and paid low wages) to Southwestern states where there was a shortage of labor. Therefore, the Bracero program "by bringing Mexican workers into areas where domestic labor was scarce, this program greatly reduced the range of choices confronting farm workers in labor-surplus regions and made their migration less likely" (Alston and Ferrie 1999: 107). In other words, the political support by Southern farm interests was mainly due the fact that they feared Southwestern states would attract away their labor force and bid up wages (Alston and Ferrie 1999: 113).

admit guest agricultural workers from Central America, South America, and islands of the Caribbean. However, while the Bracero program was originally designed as a wartime measure, it was extended until December 31, 1947 (Alston and Ferrie 1999: 108). Between 1947 and 1951, the program fell somewhat into limbo. The admission of Mexican workers into the United States fell again under the 1917 Immigration Act and was regulated by several international agreements between 1947 and 1949. During that period of time, the US Employment Service was the agency in charge of issuing permission for Mexican workers to enter the United States. During that time, labor contracts were no longer between the Mexican worker and the US government, but between the employer and the Mexican worker (Alston and Ferrie 1999: 108). However, the Korean War led to another farm labor shortage and prompted the governments of the United States and Mexico to renew negotiations, which led to the institutionalization of the Bracero program through the passage of Public Law 78 on July 31, 1951. Public Law 78 was subsequently renewed six times with strong support from Southern state representatives, despite the fact that some of these states were not relying on Bracero workers (Alston and Ferrie 1999: 109).[16] Under the pressure of religious and labor organizations, Public Law 78 was finally defeated in 1963, putting an end to the Bracero program, which was terminated in 1964 (Massey and Liang 1989: 204).

Between 1942 and 1964, the Bracero program allowed for 4.5 million Mexican migrant workers to come to the United States on temporary visas not to exceed six months. The Mexican government recruited the workers who were sent to special camps on the US side of the border where US government agencies arranged for the employment, wages, working conditions, and transportation of these workers. In addition, "the braceros were limited in their geographic, social, and occupational mobility. They were confined to agricultural labor in southwestern states; and, as it was in Europe, they were not eligible to bring in their dependents" (Massey

16. Alston and Ferrie (1999: 112) argue that much of the support for the Bracero program was due to the fact that agricultural growers preferred Mexican labor to domestic labor, not because they were being paid less than domestic workers but rather because they were perceived as working harder than domestic workers. They argue that the braceros' willingness to work harder was most likely due to the fact "that the opportunity cost for Mexicans of losing their jobs in the United States was greater than that for domestic laborers" (Alston and Ferrie 1999: 112). In addition, even though Bracero labor was likely more expensive than illegal workers, braceros were more dependable than illegal Mexican workers and the transaction costs associated with negotiating with illegal workers prior to their arrival made hiring them more difficult (Alston and Ferrie 1999: 112).

and Liang 1989: 203–204).[17] Despite all these limitations, the Bracero program was very popular among Mexican workers because it represented an opportunity to earn higher wages than they would have received in Mexico, which allowed some of them purchase land in Mexico once they went back home (Alston and Ferrie 1999: 112).[18]

3.2.2   Contemporary Programs

Despite the reluctance of OECD countries to allow the entry of low-skilled temporary workers, in the past decade, some countries have introduced low-skilled migration programs (see Appendix 2 at the end of this chapter). All of these programs are employer driven, and entry is contingent on a job offer (OECD 2008: 133).

3.2.2.1   The United States

The United States has two guest worker programs for low-skilled workers: H-2A and H-2B. The H-2A program was created in 1952 to provide an adequate temporary supply of labor to the agriculture industry. Under the H-2A program, there is no limit on the number of foreign workers who can enter the country to fill these seasonal farm jobs. East Coast growers who did not rely on the Bracero program to find workers originally used this program. Under the program, petitioners must obtain a labor certification. Petitioners must demonstrate that there are not sufficient US workers who are able, willing, qualified, and available to do the temporary work, must offer pay high enough to counter any adverse wage effects on similarly employed US workers, must provide housing, and must cover one-way transportation costs (OECD 2008: 158).

In addition, H-2A petitions may only be approved for nationals of countries that the Secretary of Homeland Security has designated, with the concurrence of the Secretary of State, as eligible to participate in the H-2A

17. In 1943, the Bracero program was also expanded to the railroad industry because several American rail carriers reported suffering from severe labor shortage. By the end of 1944, more than 80,000 braceros were working for the railroad industry. This program was suspended in August 1945 but it was not until April 1946 that the last railroad braceros were returned to Mexico (Mandeel 2014: 172).

18. Alston and Ferrie (1999: 114) argue that the supply of braceros exceeding the demand led to a significant amount of bribing of Mexican authorities who oversaw the program. They estimate that bribery "amounted to at least $7.2 million in 1957. Aspiring braceros paid approximately 7 percent of their net incomes in bribes" (Alston and Ferrie 1999: 114).

program. The period of stay cannot exceed three years. A worker who has held an H-2A non-immigrant status for a total of three years must depart and remain outside the United States for an uninterrupted period of three months before seeking readmission as an H-2A non-immigrant. The migrant worker can bring his or her spouse and unmarried children under 21 years of age. They may seek admission in H-4 non-immigrant classification. However, family members are not eligible for employment in the United States while in H-4 status (US Citizenship and Immigration Services 2014b: 4). In 2012, 65,345 H-2A visas were issued (Wilson 2013).

Despite the fact that there is no cap for the H-2A program, it is largely unused because employers face burdensome requirements, such as proving that wages paid to foreign workers will not adversely affect native workers, providing housing, and covering one-way transportation costs (Powell and Gochenour 2013: 4). The H-2A program also mandates that the "employer must hire local workers even if they apply during the first half of the foreign worker's contract" (OECD 2008: 159, Annex Table II.A1.2). As a result, "only 5 percent of the U.S. agricultural labor force is currently employed under the H-2A program" (Powell and Gochenour 2013: 5).

The other guest worker program for low-skilled workers is the H-2B program, which is reserved for non-agriculture industry, particularly landscaping, cleaning, hospitality, and construction. The H-2B program is similar to the H-2A program in its requirements but, unlike the H-2A program, a quota is in place. "The H-2B cap set by Congress is 66,000 per fiscal year, with 33,000 to be allocated for employment beginning in the first half of the fiscal year (October 1–March 31) and 33,000 to be allocated for employment beginning in the second half of the fiscal year (April 1–September 30)" (US Citizenship and Immigration Services 2014a). The requirements under the H-2B program, such as ensuring that US workers are not adversely affected by the hiring of foreign workers, have discouraged many employers from using this program; in some cases, employers have been forced by the US Department of Labor to increase hourly wages by more than 50 percent (Sell 2011). As a result, while the number of H-2B VISAs is capped at 66,000 each year, "there was a 48% decrease overall in the number of H-2B temporary program positions requested in fiscal year 2010 compared with fiscal year 2009, and a 39% decrease in the number of positions certified over the previous fiscal year" (Sell 2011). Between 2009 and 2012, the number of positions certified has decreased from 154,489 in 2009 to 75,458 in 2012, which represents a 51 percent decrease in the number of position certified (US Department of Labor 2013a: 6).

3.2.2.2   Other OECD Countries

Since the early 2000s, European countries have had policies that allow employers to petition for temporary visas for low-skilled workers in some sectors of the economy or certain occupations, but in a limited manner. Most countries grant temporary working visas and demand that at the end of the period the workers return to their home country. To ensure compliance, particularly for visas related to seasonal work, countries give priority access, allowing employers to rehire the temporary workers they have hired in the past, and give priority access to these workers, who can go through a somewhat less burdensome bureaucratic process. These temporary workers who enjoy priority access also can be granted priority or exemption when the countries have capped their temporary migration programs (OECD 2008: 135).

The shortage lists discussed in the previous section for occupations can help on two levels. First, they can help employers to bypass the labor market test. Second, they can help lower-skilled workers to migrate to countries where otherwise only high-skilled workers are usually allowed.

Temporary labor migration in OECD countries decreased because of the economic crisis. Between 2006 and 2008, temporary labor migration was around 2.5 million workers. Following the crisis, temporary labor migration started to decline to reach 1.96 million workers in 2011 (OECD 2013: 26, Table 10.5). Data from 2006 on low-skilled workers show that, for the age group 25–34 years old, 29.6 percent of the low-skilled labor force is foreign born and 31.3 percent of the foreign-born labor force is low-skilled. Of the total working-age population (aged 15–64 years old), 20.7 percent of the low-skilled labor force is foreign born and 31.5 percent of the foreign-born labor force is low-skilled. In the United States, when looking at the total working-age population (15-64), foreign-born workers represent 38.7 percent of the low-skilled labor force, and 28.8 percent of the foreign-born labor force is low-educated. These numbers rise to 54.1 percent and 30.9 percent respectively for those aged 25–34 years old (OECD 2008: 128).

4   ASSESSING EMPLOYMENT VISAS AROUND THE WORLD

There are a number of ways in which the employment visa policies might be evaluated. One could study the makeup of the immigration population for each country and the skill level of incoming immigrants. For example, if more immigrants come to seek asylum or family reunification purposes as opposed to work, one could conclude that the immigration laws in terms of attracting workers are less effective than those countries where more immigrants come to work.[19] Another way to evaluate immigration policies would be to assess how effective these policies are in meeting their own goals. Assuming that several countries have the same objective of attracting high-skilled workers, one can compare which country attracts the most high-skilled immigrant workers.[20] If the immigration policy attempts to attract immigrants with specific skills, one can assess whether wages for these specific occupations that are in shortage declines as a result of an influx of immigrants occupying these jobs. A relative wage decline would indicate that the shortage had been relieved. One could also look at the prevalence of illegal immigrants. Most illegal immigrants come to take advantage of employment opportunities. A high number of illegal immigrants in the workforce indicates that the legal immigration procedure is failing to adequately meet employer needs. These last two criteria are particularly important. Because work visa programs are biased against low-skilled workers, some employers in need of lower-skilled workers are unable to legally hire them. These employers confront a choice between seeing their costs of doing business increase or hiring illegally.[21] Before we address some of the core requirements and goals of these policies and

19. It does not necessarily mean that some of these immigrants do not want to work. We mean that when comparing immigrating costs, they find it is easier to immigrate seeking asylum or marriage than immigrating through work. In addition, asylum and family reunification tend not to be subject to discretionary limits, so the incentives "to get married" with a native to immigrate are greater if it is easier to immigrate this way, as opposed to obtaining a job offer first and having the employer and potential employee bear additional costs in obtaining a visa or a permanent residency card.

20. Obviously, there are many factors that can explain why some people chose to immigrate to a specific country, as opposed to others such as geographic proximity, the attitude toward immigrants, the prevalence of immigrants of the same national origin in that country, the demand for their labor, and also the size of the welfare state and how easy it is to collect some of these benefits. Though, for the last variable, research shows that welfare generosity has little, if any, weight on deciding where immigrants elect to immigrate, except for those seeking asylum. See, for example, Zavodny (1999) and Kaushal (2005). Also one cannot ignore that the matching problem of employers-employees might be aggravated by non-immigration-related laws such as licensing. Therefore, in this case, the problem would not be the immigration laws but, rather, the licensing laws that do not recognize immigrants' education and training to practice some professions.

21. Hiring these workers illegally is not without costs for these businesses. One of these costs is that employers will have to pay these workers lower wages to account for the risks associated with hiring illegal workers, which in turn translates to lower productivity by these illegal workers (Rivera-Batiz 1999). But as long as the expected costs of hiring these workers illegally is less than the costs of not breaking the law, these employers will choose to hire these workers illegally.

assess how well these migration policies meet their goals, it is worth making a preliminary observation about the pretense of knowledge that policymakers exhibit when it comes to designing these working visa programs. While we can understand that policymakers, particularly elected officials, face political constraints and they are likely subject to the influence of various special interest groups,[22] we should ask ourselves why we should think that these policymakers are better than markets at determining where these labor shortages are. As we will see, their pretense of knowledge led these policymakers to put in place many restrictions and requirements into these visa programs that either are ineffective, fortunately, or turn into costly barriers to entry in the labor market that raise the costs for employers to use their local knowledge and to do business. Ultimately, because of these immigration policies, some gains from trade remain unrealized.

4.1 The Non-Neutrality of Immigration

Most immigration programs have one core requirement in common. Immigration, whether temporary or permanent, must not adversely affect the wages and working conditions of similarly employed native workers, even though the rationale for recruiting foreign workers is to prevent market forces from responding to a shortage of workers within the domestic labor market. Typically, when market forces are allowed to work, labor shortages cannot persist. Employers bid up wages until more people enter the workforce or until it becomes less costly to substitute capital for labor. This is not without consequences. Increasing costs of production means that fewer goods and services will be produced and that consumers will have to pay higher prices for what is produced.

Therefore, recruiting a foreign labor force is seen as an alternative mechanism to resolve these labor shortages and to prevent costs from rising without affecting the native labor force (Massey and Liang 1989: 201–202). Unfortunately, the assumption that immigration is neutral with regard to affecting the wages and working conditions of native workers is impossible to satisfy. The Bracero program experience shows that native workers were affected by immigration, as employers preferred hiring Bracero workers because of their willingness to accept lower wages in exchange for working and living in extremely poor conditions (Mandeel 2014: 178).

22. See note 8.

To further illustrate the case that immigration is not without an effect on native worker's wages, one can look at what happened to wages once the Bracero program was terminated. As Wise (1974) showed, after the Bracero program was terminated, wage rate increased by 67 percent and domestic employment increased by 262 percent in the production of winter melons, and wage rate increased by 12 percent and domestic employment increased by 51 percent in the production of strawberries in California. However, these benefits to native workers came at a cost. Overall production of winter melons in California fell by 23 percent, total employment decreased by 22 percent, acreage planted was reduced by 26 percent, and prices increased by 6 percent. Similarly, the production of strawberries in California dropped by 4 percent, prices increased by 11 percent, total employment fell by 16 percent, and acreage planted reduced by 15 percent. Similarly, the end of the Bracero program had a significant negative effect on the cultivation of white asparagus, which required four times more labor than tomatoes. Fifteen years after the program was terminated, "by 1979, asparagus acreage was only 55% of its postwar peak in 1959" (Mandeel 2014: 182). The end of the Bracero program also precipitated the mechanization of American farming (Mandeel 2014: 182).[23]

Similarly, Svorny (1991) shows that if the United States had not liberalized its immigration restrictions on the market for physician services from 1965 to 1976, physician earnings would have been 11 percent higher by 1971. On the other hand, she estimates that "the dollar value of the benefits to consumers from the 1965 liberalization of immigration restrictions reached 2.9 billion dollars by 1971 (in 1967 dollars)" (Svorny 1991: 331).

There is little doubt that immigration affects native workers despite the requirement from immigration authorities that immigration does not adversely affect natives' wages and working conditions. However, we cannot ignore the significant benefits associated with immigration in the form of increased production and lower prices. As Zachariadis (2012: 298) shows, "a 10% increase in the share of immigrant workers in total employment decreases the prices of final products by as much as 3%." The entire point of employment-based immigration is to get the net benefits associated with immigration (see Chapter 2 of this volume), but not everyone benefits equally from immigration, and some workers who directly

23. Lew and Cater (2008) show that the adoption of the tractor by farmers on the US Northern Great Plains is the direct result of the US immigration authority closing its border to European immigrants in the mid-1920s.

compete with immigrants lose, at least in the short run. The economic gains that an economy receives are impossible to realize without violating the neutrality requirements. Only the mismeasurement and poor enforcement of this absurd requirement allows these employment visa programs to secure economic gains for their respective citizens.

4.2   Comparing Migration Policies

Chaloff and Lemaître (2009: 30) compare policy choices for the highly skilled in 10 countries of the OECD and find that none of the policies that these countries have adopted or modified to attract high-skilled workers "actually supports immigration of the high skilled: there are no subsidies, no facilitation of the recognition of qualifications; no special job listings abroad." A true active immigration policy should work toward facilitating matching employers with foreign-born prospective employees, such as the job fairs in Australia or in the United Kingdom, and developing bilateral agreements between countries as opposed to raising barriers to entry (Chaloff and Lemaître 2009: 30).[24] Chaloff and Lemaître identify advantages and disadvantages to the supply-driven and demand-driven systems. The point-based systems were designed not to respond to shortages in the labor market but rather to meet a population target. The point-based systems was developed when cross-border recruitment via the Internet was not possible and, therefore, it made sense to invite people who had a set of highly desirable characteristics to immigrate even if they did not have any job offers. However, recent research has shown that new immigrants have difficulties finding jobs that match their skills, often due to sociodemographic factors such as socioeconomic status, language proficiency, previous work experience, and unfamiliarity with the local labor market, but also the fact that the domestic population's educational attainment increased (Chaloff and Lemaître 2009: 33; Frank 2013).

According to Chaloff and Lemaître (2009: 32), the advantages of demand-driven systems are that they tend "to ensure a close link between immigrant worker entries and labor market needs," and that the risks of the immigrant becoming a financial burden are significantly lower because the immigrant is immediately employed upon arrival. However, in demand-driven systems, the employers' decision to hire foreign-born workers can have external costs in the long run, particularly if they lose

24. Some countries do have bilateral agreements to bring temporary workers.

their job, if the candidates were wrongly chosen, if needs are overestimated, or if an economic downturn occurs (Chaloff and Lemaître 2009: 32). Chaloff and Lemaître's (2009: 42) main conclusions are that, in recent years, supply-driven and demand-driven systems are converging in terms of their objective of attracting high-skilled migrants. The main issue is that an increasing number of countries will have incoming labor force cohorts that are smaller than outgoing ones and, therefore, OECD countries will need to create more active recruiting policies rather "than just allowing for the possibility of granting permits to employers or to aspirant immigrants based on credentials."

4.3   How Well Do Countries Meet Their Objectives?

Given that most countries have more or less attempted to attract high-skilled workers, one way to assess their success in attracting highly skilled immigrants is to observe the participation of high-skilled immigrants in the labor force (see Figure 5.6). This information can be examined through three different ratios. First, of the immigrant population that enters the labor force, what percentage qualify as highly skilled? Second, from all highly skilled increases in the labor force, what is the percentage of immigrants? And third, from the change in total labor force, how much is explained by highly skilled immigrants?

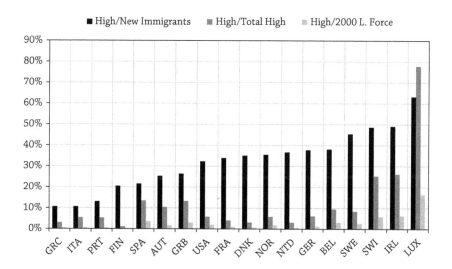

Figure 5.6
Contribution of High Education Level to the Growth in Labor Force 2000–2010.

In Greece, Italy, Portugal, Finland, Spain, Austria, and the United Kingdom, 25 percent or less of their immigrant population that entered the labor force between 2000 and 2010 qualify as highly skilled labor. Only Sweden, Switzerland, and Ireland are close to having highly skilled workers as 50 percent of their immigration, and tiny Luxemburg is the only country to exceed this threshold. In terms of highly skilled immigrants' contribution to the total highly skilled increase in the labor force, Spain, Austria, the United Kingdom, Switzerland, and Ireland show larger fractions of their increase attributed to immigration. In the case of Luxemburg, 80 percent of the increase in high-skilled labor force is explained by immigrants. Finally, Ireland, Switzerland, Spain, Belgium, and the United Kingdom are the countries where new highly skilled immigrants represent a larger share of total new labor force population (irrespective of skill level).

As an illustrative measure of success, Table 5.4 shows and ranks the countries in terms of the contribution of highly skilled immigration into the labor force through three ratios: (1) the share of highly skilled immigration to total immigration that joins the labor force, (2) the share of highly skilled immigration to total new highly skilled labor force, and (3) the share of new highly skilled immigration to the total labor force. All three ratios are for the period 2000–2010. We also built a simple average score based on the three rankings. We then rank the countries based on this average score. Measuring failure in immigration policy by examining illegal immigration is more difficult because information on illegal immigration is lacking and inaccurate due to the nature and status of these immigrants. Next to the rankings we show estimates (when available) of illegal immigration as a percentage of total population.[25] The table also shows if the listed countries have a quota and a shortage list as part of the immigration policy.

Table 5.4 indicates that there is no clear correlation discernible between quotas or shortage list with a high participation of highly skilled immigration in the labor force. In terms of attracting highly skilled immigrants into the labor force, the United States ranks 10 out of 18. But in terms of illegal immigration with respect to total population, the United States shows the highest value of all countries (for which there is data.) The United States has both quotas and shortage lists. The quota, in particular, is highly restrictive, falling considerably below the immigration applications (and potential immigrants who do not file an application due

25. Data are from 2008 for most countries except the Netherlands, which uses 2005 data because 2008 was unavailable. No years were available for the other countries.

Table 5.4 RANKING IN ATTRACTING HIGH-SKILL (HS) IMMIGRANTS INTO THE LABOR FORCE

Country	Ranking (High-Skill Imm. / New Immigrants)	Ranking (High-Skill Imm. / Total High-Skill)	Ranking (High-Skill Imm. / 2000 Labor Force)	Score	Score Ranking	Quota	Shortage list	Illegal Imm. (% of total population)
LUX	1	1	1	1.0	1	No	No	N/A
ICE	2	2	2	2.0	2	N/A	N/A	N/A
SWI	3	3	3	3.0	3	Yes	Yes	N/A
BEL	5	7	5	5.7	4	No	Yes	N/A
SWE	4	8	7	6.3	5	No	No	N/A
SPA	14	4	4	7.1	6	Yes*	Yes	0.72
GRB	12	5	6	7.7	7	No	Yes	1.03
GER	6	9	11	8.7	8	No	Yes*	0.37
NOR	8	10	9	9.0	9	Yes*	No	N/A
AUT	13	6	10	9.7	10	Yes	No	0.43
USA	11	11	8	10.0	11	Yes	Yes	3.80
FRA	10	14	12	12.0	12	No	Yes	0.17
DNK	9	15	13	12.3	13	No	Yes	N/A
NTD	7	17	14	12.7	14	No	No	0.54
ITA	17	12	15	14.7	15	Yes*	No	1.10
PRT	16	13	17	15.3	16	Yes	No	N/A
GRC	18	16	16	16.7	17	No	No	2.22
FIN	15	18	18	17.0	18	No	Yes	N/A

Source: Based on OECD (2012) and CLANDESTINO. Illegal immigration corresponds to year 2008, with the exception of the Netherlands (2005).
Note: Label "Yes*" in the quote column means that there are exceptions to the quota limit. See the Appendix 1 for more details.

to the unlikeliness of getting permission to immigrate). Spain has quotas and a shortage list, but it has a low ratio of illegal immigration to total population, which might be explained by the fact that Spain's quota system is flexible. Greece is the opposite. It has neither quotas nor a shortage list but has a high share of illegal immigration. This is likely due to the fact that Greece has weakened border control, characterized by a lack of enforcement resulting from the economic recession and budget restrictions (Stevis 2012). The illegal immigration ratio in Greece had been falling until it rose in 2007.[26] The United States, on the contrary, has a stable high share of illegal immigration.[27] The findings are certainly not conclusive, but the data suggest the possibility that quotas and shortage lists (which also work as quotas) have a positive impact on illegal immigration while not impacting high-skill immigration.

In assessing working visas for lower-skilled workers, countries that have developed a priority access system where employers get the opportunity to rehire immigrant workers (and these workers get priority) have enjoyed higher rates of compliance in terms of these temporary migrant workers returning to their home country after the season is over. In addition, these countries seem to experience proportionally less illegal immigration than other countries such as the United States that also have quotas for both high-skill and lower-skill immigration programs.[28]

5   CONCLUSION

This chapter has compared the various working visa policies in OECD countries. Typically, the purpose of working visas is to meet shortages in labor markets. However, our analysis shows that some of the requirements of these policies, such as ensuring that immigration does not adversely affect native workers, if they were fully satisfied, would virtually eliminate all the benefits of labor migration. In addition, when comparing working visa policies in OECD countries in their objective to reduce labor shortages, our analysis shows that working visa policies with quotas built in and the stringent requirements associated with recruiting low-skilled

26. Illegal immigration as percent of total population for Greece: 2004: 2.07%, 2005: 0.18%, 2006: 0.67%, 2007: 2.3%, 2008: 2.22%, 2009: 2.99%, 2010: 3.49%.

27. Illegal immigration as percent of total population for the United States: 2004: 3.2%, 2005: 3.5%, 2006: 3.9%, 2007: 3.9%, 2008: 3.8%, 2009: 3.5%, 2010: 3.8%.

28. We cannot ignore that the proximity of developing countries may be a factor in the pool of illegal immigrants.

workers are likely drivers of illegal immigration on which employers rely to meet their shortages in low-skilled workers.[29]

Illegal immigration is inevitable so long as there are restrictions on immigration while there are economic opportunities for immigrants in OECD countries. Therefore, at best, we can attempt to reduce illegal immigration by tweaking the incentives for employers and workers. For example, ending some of the requirements imposed on employers, such as the labor market test, would eliminate unnecessary costs imposed on businesses that already spend a significant amount of resources trying to recruit workers outside the country. In addition, programs giving priority access for temporary workers and developing bilateral agreements that allow employers to hire or rehire temporary workers more easily and to bypass the red tape have facilitated the recruitment of low-skilled migrants and have seen a high compliance rate when it comes to ensuring that the migrants leave the country at the end of their contract (OECD 2008: 135). Deferring a portion of some payment where "governments or employers defer payment of a share of guest-worker income and pay it with interest at the end of the contract period if the guest-workers leave" is also another possible mechanism to ensure that migrants return to their home country at the end of their contract (Schiff 2007: 4). Such a program exists in Taiwan, in the United Kingdom for migrants from the Baltics, and in the United States with Jamaican workers (Schiff 2007: 4).[30] Finally, countries like Greece, Israel, and Singapore have implemented a bond policy "where employers must buy a bond which they forfeit if their guest-worker employees overstay" (Schiff 2007: 4).

All these mechanisms can improve host countries' abilities to meet labor demand with foreign workers while reducing illegal immigration. The benefits associated with immigration, legal, and illegal, would be greater if many of the costly immigration policy requirements and their enforcement were abolished altogether.

---

29. It might be worth repeating what we wrote in footnote 17. One of the costs of illegal immigration is that, while illegal immigration contributes to reduce the labor shortage employers face, illegal workers are paid less than legal workers because employers transfer in part the costs of hiring them illegally to these illegal workers in the form of lower wages, and as a result, they will not be as productive workers as they would have been if they have been legally hired. Another reason that these illegal workers are not as productive is, often, it is very difficult for illegal workers to move out of poorly matched jobs (Kossoudji and Cobb-Clark 2002).

30. This program was also in place during "the US Bracero program where US employers were required to withhold 10 percent of Mexican workers' earning, deposit them in a Mexican fund, and pay them upon the workers' return to Mexico" (Schiff 2007: 4 n. 7). However, this provision was only in effect from 1942 to 1948 (Alston and Ferrie 1999: 114 n. 37).

REFERENCES

Alston, Lee J., and Joseph P. Ferrie. 1999. *Southern Paternalism and the American Welfare State: Economics, Politics, and Institutions in the South 1865–1965.* New York: Cambridge University Press.

Castles, Stephen. 1986. "The Guest-Worker in Western Europe: An Obituary." *International Migration Review* 20(4): 761–778.

Castles, Stephen. 2006. "Guestworkers in Europe: A Resurrection?" *International Migration Review* 40(4): 741–766.

Chaloff, Jonathan, and George Lemaître. 2009. "Managing Highly-Skilled Labour Migration: A Comparative Analysis of Migration Policies and Challenges in OECD Countries." Working Paper, OECD Social, Employment and Migration Working Papers. Paris: OECD Publishing.

Cortés, Patricia, and José Tessada. 2011. "Low-Skilled Immigration and the Labor Supply of Highly Skilled Women." *American Economic Journal: Applied Economics* 3(3): 88–123.

Council of the European Union. 2009. "Council Directive 2009/50/EC of 25 May 2009 on the Conditions of Entry and Residence of Third-Country Nationals for the Purposes of Highly Qualified Employment." *Official Journal of the European Union* 6: 17–29.

Eicher, Theo. 2013. "The 2011 Microsoft Economic Impact Study." http://assets. bizjournals.com/cms_media/pdf/msuwstudy.pdf?site=techflash.com.

Eisele, Katharina. 2013. "Why Come Here if I Can Go There? Assessing the 'Attractiveness' of the EU's Blue Card Directive for 'Highly Qualified' Immigrants." Working Paper, CEPS Paper in Liberty and Security.

European Commission. 2014a. "Free Movement: EU Nationals." European Commission. http://ec.europa.eu/social/main.jsp?catId=457&langId=en (accessed June 24, 2014).

European Commission. 2014b. "Non-EU nationals. 2014." European Commission. http://ec.europa.eu/social/main.jsp?catId=470&langId=en (accessed June 25, 2014).

European Union. 2009. "Entry and Residence of Highly Qualified Workers (EU Blue Card)." European Union. http://europa.eu/legislation_summaries/internal_market/living_and_working_in_the_internal_market/l14573_en.htm.

Frank, Kristyn. 2013. "Immigrant Employment Success in Canada: Examining the Rate of Obtaining a Job Match." *International Migration Review* 47(1): 76–105.

Furtado, Delia, and Heinrich Hock. 2010. "Low Skilled Immigration and Work-Fertility Tradeoffs among High Skilled US Natives." *American Economic Review* 100(2): 224–228.

Hunt, Jennifer, and Marjorlaine Gauthier-Loiselle. 2010. "How Much Does Immigration Boost Innovation?" *American Economic Journal: Macroeconomics* 2: 31–56.

Ilias, Shayerah, Katherine Fennelly, and Christopher M. Federico. 2008. "American Attitudes toward Guest Worker Policies." *International Migration Review* 42(4): 741–766.

Kaushal, Neeraj. 2005. "New Immigrants' Location Choices: Magnets Without Welfare." *Journal of Labor Economics* 23(1): 59–80.

Kossoudji, Sherrie A., and Deborah A. Cobb-Clark. 2002. "Coming Out of the Shadows: Learning about the Legal Status and Wages from the Legalized Population." *Journal of Labor Economics* 20(3): 598–628.

Lew, Byron, and Bruce Cater. 2008. "Farm Mechanization on an Otherwise 'Featureless' Plain: Tractor Adoption on the Northern Great Plains and Immigration Policy of the 1920s." Working Paper, Economics, Trent University.

Mandeel, Elizabeth W. 2014. "The Bracero Program 1942–1964." *American International Journal of Contemporary Research* 4(1): 171–184.

Martínez, Daniel. 1958. "The Impact of the Bracero Programs on a Southern California Mexican American Community: A Field Study of Cucamonga, California." A thesis presented to the General Faulty of The Claremont Graduate School. May 17.

Massey, Douglas S., and Zai Liang. 1989. "The Long-Term Consequences of a Temporary Worker Program: The US Bracero Experience." *Population Research and Policy Review* 8(3): 199–226.

McKinley, Jesse, and Julie Preston. 2011. "Farmers Oppose G. O. P. Bill on Immigration." *New York Times.* July 30. http://www.nytimes.com/2011/07/31/us/politics/31verify.html?pagewanted=all&_r=0.

OECD. 2008. "Management of Low-Skilled Labour Migration." In *International Migration Outlook 2008*, pp. 125–159. Paris: OECD Publication.

OECD. 2013. *International Migration Outlook 2013.* Paris: OECD Publishing.

Powell, Benjamin, and Zachary Gochenour. 2013. *Broken Borders: Government, Foreign-Born Workers, and the U.S. Economy.* Policy Report. Oakland, CA: The Independent Institute.

Rivera-Batiz, Francisco L. 1999. "Undocumented Workers in the Labor Market: An Analysis of the Earnings of Legal and Illegal Mexican Immigrants in the United States." *Journal of Population Economics* 12(1): 91–116.

Schiff, Maurice. 2007. "Optimal Immigration Policy: Permanent, Guest-Worker, or Mode IV?" Discussion Paper, Institute for the Study of Labor. Institute for the Study of Labor (IZA).

Sell, Mary. 2011. "Changes Make Guest-Worker Program More Costly for Employers." *USA Today.* November 6. http://usatoday30.usatoday.com/money/companies/regulation/story/2011-2011-06/immigration-guest-workers/51093080/1.

Slaughter, Matthew J. 2014. "How America Loses a Job Every 43 Seconds." *Wall Street Journal.* March 25. http://online.wsj.com/news/articles/SB10001424052702303802104579451122421049340.

Stevis, Matina. 2012. "Illegal Immigration Emerges as New Crisis for Greece—And EU." *Wall Street Journal.* September 15.

Svorny, Shirley. 1991. "Consumer Gains from Physician Immigration to the US: 1966–1971." *Applied Economics* 23: 331–337.

US Citizenship and Immigration Services. 2014a. "Cap Count for H-2B Nonimmigrants." US Citizenship and Immigration Services. June 18. http://www.uscis.gov/working-united-states/temporary-workers/h-2b-non-agricultural-workers/cap-count-h-2b-nonimmigrants.

US Citizenship and Immigration Services. 2014b. "H-2A Temporary Agricultural Workers." US Citizenship and Immigration Services. January 17. http://www.uscis.gov/working-united-states/temporary-workers/h-2a-agricultural-workers/h-2a-temporary-agricultural-workers.

US Citizenship and Immigration Services. 2014c. "Understanding F-1 OPT Require-
    ments." US Citizenship and Immigration Services. http://www.uscis.gov/eir/
    visa-guide/f-1-opt-optional-practical-training/understanding-f-1-opt-
    requirements (accessed November 28, 2014).

US Department of Labor. 2013a. "Annual Report October 1, 2011–September 30,
    2012." Report, US Department of Labor.

US Department of Labor. 2013b. "Permanent Labor Certification Details." US
    Department of Labor Employment and Training Administration. June 20.
    http://www.foreignlaborcert.doleta.gov/perm_detail.cfm#schedule.

USDA Office of Communications. 2011. "Media Conference Call on the Need for
    Comprehensive Immigration Reform Hosted by Tom Vilsack, Secretary,
    USDA and Bob Stallman, President, AFBF." US Department of Agriculture.
    May 25. http://www.usda.gov/wps/portal/usda/usdahome?contentid=2011/
    05/0222.xml&contentidonly=true.

Wilson, Jill H. 2013. "Immigration Facts: Temporary Foreign Workers." Brookings.
    June18.http://www.brookings.edu/research/reports/2013/06/18-temporary-
    workers-wilson.

Wise, Donald E. 1974. "The Effect of the Bracero on Agricultural Production in Cali-
    fornia." *Economic Inquiry* 12(4): 547–558.

Zachariadis, Mario. 2012. "Immigration and International Prices." *Journal of Inter-
    national Economics* 87: 298–311.

Zavodny, Madeline. 1999. "Determinants of Recent Immigrants' Locational
    Choices." *International Migration Review* 33(4): 1014–1030.

	Australia	Austria	Belgium
Permanent migration programs relevant for highly skilled workers **PTS: Point system**	• General Skilled Migration Program (GSM)—PTS • Employer Nomination Scheme (EN)—PTS • Regional Sponsored Migration Scheme (RSM)—PTS	• Permanent residence permit and unrestricted work permit (generally after 5 years of residence and fulfillment of the integration agreement) • EU-8 nationals after 1 year and third-country nationals with a key worker permit after 18 months can get an unlimited residence permit.	• A permit (generally after 4 years of continuous residence with a B permit over the last 10 years)
Main temporary migration programs relevant for highly skilled workers **#Y: maximum duration** **R: renewable** **LMT: labor market test**	• Temporary business long stay (457) 4YR	• Key workers permits • Restricted work permit 1YR LMT • Work permit 2YR LMT (52 weeks in employment over the last 14 months)	• B Permit 1YR LMT and limited to bilateral agreements (wage ≥ €33k no LMT and no condition on nationality. UE8 nationals with a job offer can get a Permit B without LMT) • "Professional Card" for Independent practice delivered by SPF Économie, 5 YR
Quota	Yes. Cap of 108,500 for 2007–2008. Queue spillover.	Yes	No

continued

Appendix 1. (CONTINUED)

	Australia	Austria	Belgium
Characteristics of the Labor Market Test	Shortage list occupations only. No LMT, although salary is verified.	No registered unemployed person is available and the employer respects applicable wages and labor law.	B permit issued if a worker cannot be found or trained "within a reasonable delay." Approval is within 30 days of application to the responsible labor office.
Shortage occupation list	SOL, Employer Nomination (ENSOL), MODL (bonus points for PR)	No	Yes
Foreign students can change status after the completion of their studies	Skill Independent (880), Australian Sponsored (881) & Designated Area Overseas Student (882)	Possible, but no specific program	Possible, but no specific program

	Canada	Czech Republic	Denmark
Permanent migration programs relevant for highly skilled workers **PTS: Point system**	• Skilled Worker Class (R 75)—PTS • Provincial Nominee Class (R 87)	• Permanent Residence (after 5 years of continuous residence with a Long-term Residence Permit; this is shortened to 2.5 YR for qualified workers and 1.5 YR for highly qualified—tertiary educated—workers).	• Permanent Residence permit (after 7 years)
Main temporary migration programs relevant for highly skilled workers **#Y: maximum duration** **R: renewable** **LMT: labor market test**	• Temporary Foreign Worker (R200) limited to the duration of employment, LMT except if included in Regional Lists of Occupations under Pressure • TN VISA 1YR (NAFTA)	• Long-term Residence Permit for the purpose of employment > 1YR LMT • Work Permit 1YR LMT • Project of Active Selection of Qualified Foreign Labor for young qualified foreigners (quicker access to a permanent resident status).	• Work Permit 1YR LMT • Job Card Scheme: 3 YR for occupations in the "positive list" or a job offer ≥ DKK 463k • Green Card: 6-month job-search permit issued on the basis of points for education, language, shortage list, experience, prior wages, experience, age. Must be converted to Job Card permit before expiry.
Quota	No (target of 129,000 to 142,000 in 2007 for Skilled Worker, Quebec Skilled Worker and Provincial Nominee)	No	No

continued

	Canada	Czech Republic	Denmark
Characteristics of the Labor Market Test	Temporary Foreign Worker: Labor market opinion, with demonstration of attempts to fill position (advertisements, etc., and public employment service), verification of prevailing wage, and conditions. The LMO also considers whether "employment of the foreign worker will directly create new jobs or retain jobs for Canadians." Trade union approval will accelerate the process. No LMO necessary for "Occupations under pressure." Permanent Migration: Arranged Employment Opinion for Skilled Workers provides additional points under the point system.	Employer must be authorized by Public Employment Service, and job is checked against registered unemployed for 30 days.	Danish Immigration Service consults the relevant trade union, except for shortage list occupations.
Shortage occupation list	Regional Lists of Occupations under Pressure (only for Temporary Foreign Workers)	No	Positive list of occupations. Generally master's level, in health, science, management, architecture/engineering, law, etc.
Foreign students can change status after the completion of their studies	Possible. The Post-Graduation Work Permit Program grants up to 3YR permit to work. This is important to acquire "Canadian Experience" for permanent residence.	Possible, accelerated access to Permanent Residence (2.5 or 1.5 YR depending on degree)	Possible. Automatic 6-month extension after graduation to seek work under Green Card terms. Study counts for permanent residence requirement.

	Finland	France	Germany
Permanent migration programs relevant for highly skilled workers **PTS: Point system**	• Permanent permit P (after 4 years with a A-permit)	• Residence permit (after 3 years for people with a permanent worker permit)	• Settlement permit (generally after 5 years of residence or immediately for highly qualified—researchers, university professors, those with a job offer over EUR 65.6K annually)
Main temporary migration programs relevant for highly skilled workers **#Y: maximum duration** **R: renewable** **LMT: labor market test**	• A-Permit 3YR LMT • B-Permit 1YR LMT	• Permanent worker permit • 1YR LMT: a job contract for unlimited duration is needed (Carte de Séjour Temporaire salarié) • Temporary work permit <1YR LMT (Autorisation Provisoire de Travail) • Card "Compétences et Talents" 3YR	• Temporarily restricted residence permit for the purpose of employment (1YR LMT) for people with a post-secondary qualifying education. It is subject to a local LMT and to Federal Employment Agency agreement. "Tolerated" foreigners with qualifications and experience in qualified jobs can obtain a residence permit.
Quota	No	No	No
Characteristics of the Labor Market Test	Employers or job applicants must apply for authorization from the Public Employment Service, which lists the job for 2–4 weeks, except for occupations on the regional shortage list. Local labor market authorities also check the skill level and that the job offer satisfies collective agreements.	Employer must publish position with the Public Employment Service, and submit application to the Departmental Labor, Employment and Vocational Training service for a discretionary review of professional qualifications, contract wage and conditions, the technological and commercial added value of the foreign worker, and the employer's guarantee of available housing.	Local labor market test, certain categories, and shortage areas provide exemption from vacancy listing. Graduates of German secondary schools abroad are exempt from LMT if they hold tertiary degrees.

continued

	Finland	France	Germany
Shortage occupation list	Regional list for each of 15 regions.	Since 2006 there is a shortage occupation list for nationals of new EU member states (LMT exemption); since 2007 a separate, shorter, list for third country nationals (access only for these occupations).	Possible; used only for engineers from new EU member states, although all tertiary educated EU citizens will have free access from 1/1/2009. The "Qualified Labor Shortage Monitoring" will also be expanded.
Foreign students can change status after the completion of their studies	Foreign students who earn a degree in Finland can apply for a work permit for a maximum of 6 months.	Student with a French master's degree, with the perspective to return in their origin country, can ask for 6 months permit to seek work in their field, and receive a permit exempt from the LMT. Other foreign students can change status under general rules.	Students are entitled to remain in Germany for up to one year after successfully completing their studies for the purpose of seeking employment. They are exempt from the LMT.

	Greece	Ireland	Italy
Permanent migration programs relevant for highly skilled workers PTS: Point system	• Residence permit—employment (1YR but may be indefinite after 10 years)	• Long-term residency permit (validity 5 years after 5 years of residence and unlimited duration after 10 years)	• Residence permit (possible after 5 years of legal stay)
Main temporary migration programs relevant for highly skilled workers #Y: maximum duration R: renewable LMT: labor market test	• A-permit 1YR LMT	• Green card permit 2YR (€30k < salary < €60k and shortage occupation list or all occupation with salary > €60k) • Work permit 1YR LMT (salary < €30k, occupation should not be included in the ineligible occupation list)	• Work permit 1YR LMT (fix term contract) • Work permit 2YR LMT (open end contract)
Quota	No	No	Yes (170,000 in 2007) with some exceptions (nurses, university professors, researchers, artists, etc.)
Characteristics of the Labor Market Test	Submission to the public employment service (OAED) for approval.	Advertisements in the national and/or local press, showing that the positions could not be filled from within the EEA	Listing with public employment service. Automatic approval even without response after 21-day listing.
Shortage occupation list	The Law 2910/01 introduced the possibility to respond to local needs in labor force by specialty, but in practice this has not been implemented	Shortage occupation list Ineligible occupation list	No, although quota contains separate subcategory for high-skilled and executives (1,000 in 2007).
Foreign students can change status after the completion of their studies	Possible, but no specific program	Students who completed a primary, master's, or doctorate degree may be permitted to remain in Ireland for 6 months to seek employment.	Yes, annual quota sets a maximum number of conversions of study permit to work permits (3,000 in 2007).

continued

	Japan	Korea	Luxembourg	Netherlands
Permanent migration programs relevant for highly skilled workers **PTS: Point system**	• Permanent resident (after 10 years of residence and still need a re-entry permit before leaving Japan)	• F-5: Approval by Ministry of Justice for employed people with approved salary level and: doctorate level in specific field; bachelor level/technology and 3YR; exceptional ability; E-5 or E-7 permit after 5YR	• Permit type C (after 5 years of residence)	• Permanent residence permit (after 5 years of residence)
Main temporary migration programs relevant for highly skilled workers **#Y: maximum duration** **R: renewable** **LMT: labor market test**	• Work VISA1 or 3 YR. Requires college degree or 10 years of professional experience.	• E-5 1YR LMT (Professional Employment—law, accounting, or certain medical area) • E-7 1YR LMT (Specially Designated Activities—information technology)	• Permit type A 1YR LMT (cannot change employer or occupation) • Permit type B 4YR LMT (cannot change occupation)	• Labor migrant work permit 3YR LMT non-renewable. In general people are required to take a civil immigration test in their home country (Applicants must be between the ages of 18–45) • Highly skilled migrant 5YR (wage ≥ €33. 3k for people under 30 or wage ≥ €45. 5k. No LMT and spouse can work)
Quota	No, although some bilateral agreements—not yet ratified—have addressed nurses (e. g., Philippines, Indonesia)	No	No	No

Characteristics of the Labor Market Test	None	Letter of recommendation of employment from the head of state administration or document proving the necessity of employment	Job must be submitted to the public employment service (ADEM). If no candidates are registered, the application may be approved	Centre for Work and Income must approve employer request, which must meet minimum wage to support entire accompanying family
Shortage occupation list	No	No	No	No, but in some cases the labor market test can be lifted for specific occupations or sectors
Foreign students can change status after the completion of their studies	Yes, graduating students are granted a 6-month Temporary Visitor permit to seek work	Possible, but no specific program	Possible, but no specific program	Yes, international students after graduating can stay for up to 3 months to seek a job

continued

Appendix 1. (CONTINUED)

	New Zealand	Norway	Poland
Permanent migration programs relevant for highly skilled workers PTS: Point system	• Skilled Migrant Category (SMC)—PTS	• Permanent residence permit (after 3 years with temporary permit)	• Settlement permit (after 5 years of residence)
Main temporary migration programs relevant for highly skilled workers	• Work to Residence policy: o Accredited employer (talent program) o Long Term Skill Shortage List • Work permits: LMT • Working holidays 1YR (work period ≤ 6 months)	• Skilled worker / specialist (SWS) 1YR Job seeker visa (generally 3 months)	• Work Permit 1YR LMT
#Y: maximum duration R: renewable LMT: labor market test			
Quota	No	Yes for skilled worker specialists (5,000 in 2007), but if the quota is full, it is still possible to grant a permit following LMT	No

Characteristics of the Labor Market Test	For work permits: The employer must make "a genuine attempt" to recruit suitable resident workers. The application is rejected if suitable workers are available in New Zealand, but not "prepared to do the work on the terms and conditions proposed by the employer," or if the employer could "readily train" residents to do the work. Exemption from LMT is the occupation is listed in the ISSL.	Employers are encouraged to request a labor market assessment (LMA) from the Public Employment Service (NAV) and enclose it with the application. Otherwise, the police contact NAV for an LMA. There is a quota for skilled workers and specialists; beyond this quota, prior LMA is required. Work permits are not granted if the post can be filled by domestic labor, and the position must require specific skills possessed by the candidate.	Regional employment service must authorize employer following publication with Public Employment Service and local media.
Shortage occupation list	Immediate Skill Shortage Lists (ISSL) Long Term Skill Shortage List (LTSL)	No	No
Foreign students can change status after the completion of their studies	Yes, people who have completed in New Zealand a 3-year course or a qualification that would qualify under Skilled Migration Category; may be granted a work permit for a maximum of 6 months to enable them to look for work	Possible, foreign students with a job offer after graduation may be granted a work permit for up to 1 year if they did not benefit from a grant from their origin country or a cooperation program.	Possible, but no specific program

continued

	Portugal	Slovak Republic	Spain
Permanent migration programs relevant for highly skilled workers **PTS: Point system**	• Permanent residence permit (after 5 or 8 years of residence depending whether the person is from PALOPS country—country with Portuguese as official language or not)	• Permanent residence permit (after 3 years of residence)	• Permanent residence permit (after 5 years of legal residence)
Main temporary migration programs relevant for highly skilled workers **#Y: maximum duration** **R: renewable**	• Work permit type II 1YR (to carry out a scientific research activity or an activity that requires highly qualified technical skills -including doctors and nurses) • Work permit type IV 1YR LMT (IEFP list)	• Work Permit 1YR LMT	• Work permit B type 1YR LMT (limited to specific activities and area; can be renewed for 2 years) • Work permit C type 3YR LMT (after B type permits; no restriction) • Permits D and E for self-employed
LMT: labor market test Quota	Yes, with some exceptions	No	Yes, only for anonymous hiring (contingent)
Characteristics of the Labor Market Test	30-day job listing requirement with the Public Employment Service. Possibility of an exclusion list where no authorization is granted, although this has not been used.	The Labor Office has 30 days to approve the request.	"Negative certification" is required for General Regime workers. Job must be listed with public employment service for 15 days, and employers must interview candidates sent by the Public Employment Service, although they are allowed to reject them. However, no LMT is applied for shortage list occupations.
Shortage occupation list	No	No	Regional shortage list (Catálogo de ocupaciones de difícil cobertura)
Foreign students can change status after the completion of their studies	Possible, but no specific program	Possible, but no specific program	Yes, foreign students can have a residence and a work permit after graduation if they have been in Spain for at least 3 years and did not benefit from a grant from their origin country or a cooperation program.

	Sweden	Switzerland	Turkey
Permanent migration programs relevant for highly skilled workers PTS: Point system	• Permanent Residence Permit (PUT)	• Settlement permit can be delivered after 5 years of residence for EFTA, USA, and Canadian nationals or 10 years for other countries	• Indefinite work and residence permit (after 8 years of legal residence and 6 years of legal employment)
Main temporary migration programs relevant for highly skilled workers #Y: maximum duration R: renewable LMT: labor market test	• Work Permit 5YR LMT	• Residence permit 1YR LMT (5YR for EEA nationals) • Short-term permit 1YR LMT once • Trainee exchange schemes with about 30 countries 18 months maximum	• Work permit 1YR LMT (can be renewed for up to 3 years after one year and then for up to 6 years). The first 3 years with no portability and, after three years, with employer mobility but not sector mobility
Quota	No	Yes, separate quotas for longer and short term. 7,000 (< 5YR) and 4,000 (< 1YR) (2008). EEA exemption.	No
Characteristics of the Labor Market Test	The Public Employment Service authorizes a work permit only if no Swedish, EU, or EEA workers are available or who can be trained "within a reasonable time" to fill the vacancy.	Priority is given to resident workers. 21 day required listing with Cantonal Public Employment Service, as well as EURES and other channels. Federal Office for Migration must also approve the request.	The public employment service has 4 weeks to find a suitable candidate in Turkey before approving the work permit application
Shortage occupation list	No	No	No
Foreign students can change status after the completion of their studies	No, as a general rule, a foreign student from outside the EU/EEA/Switzerland must leave after completing his/her studies.	Possible, but no specific program, although there is a quota exemption.	Possible, but there is no specific program

continued

Appendix 1. (CONTINUED)

	United Kingdom	United States
Permanent migration programs relevant for highly skilled workers **PTS: Point system**	Permanent residence—indefinite leave to remain (after 5 years of legal residence with a work permit)—PTS	• EB1 for those of "extraordinary ability"—no employer required • Employment based immigrant VISA EB1, EB2 or EB3—Green card (H1B VISA holders can ask for a green card after 6 years)
Main temporary migration programs relevant for highly skilled workers **#Y: maximum duration** **R: renewable** **LMT: labor market test**	• Tier 1 (General) High Skilled Worker 3YR (no job offer needed, points test covering age, qualification and field, prior wage, UK experience, sufficient funds and language requirement) • Tier 2 Skilled Worker 3YR Requires job offer, LMT (no LMT if occupation included the shortage occupation list), and points test covering qualifications, expected wages, language, sufficient funds.	• H1B visa 2YR maximum 6YR (specialty professional workers—bachelor's degree or more: includes doctors and registered nurses). LMT in some cases. H-1B1 for nationals of Chile and Singapore (special quota) • TN VISA 1YR (NAFTA), NAFTA occupation list includes most health professionals but physicians only for research and teaching activities • J1 VISA 3YR maximum 6YR (exchange visitor skill) generally must return for 2 years to its former country of permanent residence (except if eligible to J1 waiver) • L1 (intra-company transfer) 5–7YR maximum.
Quota	No	Yes for H1B (65,000). Permanent category quotas are EB1 (40,000), EB2 (40 000) and EB3 (40 000), although "recapture" occurs. No quota for TN, L1 or J1 VISA.

Characteristics of the Labor Market Test	The "Resident Labour Market Test" for Tier 2 requires employers to advertise for an EEA worker, submitting proof of advertisement within the past 6 months, information on applicants and selection process, and justification for not hiring applicants. The Shortage Occupation List provides an exemption from this test for specific occupations.	for EB2 and EB3—"permanent labor certification." A shortage list ("Schedule A") provides an exemption from certification. For H1B—Internal workplace listing only: 10 day posting at the workplace, or electronic distribution to employees, as well as to collective bargaining representative if relevant. Labor Condition Application is only for verification of prevailing wage. For "H1B-dependent employers" there is a LMT consisting in attestation of "non-displacement" of a U. S. worker within 3 months before and after request; "good faith" attempts to recruit U. S. workers and an offer of the job to a U. S. applicant who was equally or better qualified than an H-1B worker.
Shortage occupation list	Skill shortage occupation list	Yes "Schedule A" for permanent residence (EB2 and EB3). H-1B is available only for specified specialty professions.
Foreign students can change status after the completion of their studies	Non-EEA student who has obtained a degree level qualification may apply to switch into the relevant Tier without leaving the UK. The International Graduates Scheme allows graduates to stay up to 12 months for work, after which they must switch into a relevant Tier.	Yes, F1 VISAs allow graduates to stay for up to 12 months to pursue professional training (6 months for M1 VISA holders) Within the H1B program there is special quota (20,000) reserved for foreign students with a Master or PhD from US academic institutions

Source: Chaloff, J., and G. Lemaître (2009), "Managing Highly- Skilled Labor Migration: A Comparative Analysis of Migration Policies and Challenges in OECD Countries," OECD Social, Employment and Migration Working Papers, No. 79, OECD Publishing. http://dx.doi.org/10. 1787/2255053346577.

Appendix 2. TEMPORARY WORK PERMIT PROGRAMS FOR LOW-SKILLED WORKERS

Country	Program	Maximum Length of Stay Allowed	Guarantees Required	Sectors Involved	Number of Participants	Limits
Canada	SAWP	< 8 months	Labor market test; employer must pay transportation and housing (can deduct from salary)	Agriculture	18,000 (2006)	None
Canada	Temporary Foreign Worker Program C (intermediate and clerical)	< 2 years	Labor market test; cover all recruitment costs; help find suitable, affordable accommodation; pay full transportation costs from home country; provide medical coverage until the worker is eligible for provincial health insurance coverage	All sectors	34,000 (2006)	None
Canada	Temporary Foreign Worker Program D (elemental and laborers)	< 2 years	Labor market test; cover all recruitment costs; help find suitable, affordable accommodation; pay full transportation costs from home country; provide medical coverage until the worker is eligible for provincial health insurance coverage	All sectors	3,500 (2006)	None
France	Seasonal Agricultural	< 6 months/ annually for 3 years	Labor market test or shortage list; employers must guarantee housing	Agriculture	17,000 (2006)	None
Germany	Bilateral Agreements	< 8 months	Employers must provide housing (can deduct from salary)	Agriculture other temporary	290,000 (2006)	None

Country	Scheme	Duration	Requirements	Sector		
Italy	Seasonal Work	< 9 months	Demonstrate existence of (but not necessarily provide) housing; must pay repatriation costs for overstayers	Agriculture, tourism	64,540 (2006) (requests)	80,000 (2008)
Korea	Employment Permit System	3 years + 3 year renewal	Labor market test	All sectors	80,000 (2006)	Target 110,000 (2007)
New Zealand	Recognized Seasonal Employer	< 7 months	Labor market test; employer must demonstrate (but not necessarily provide) housing and pay half transportation costs; employer must pay repatriation costs for overstayers	Agriculture	5,000 (2007)	Quota of 5,000 (2007)
Spain	Contingent	< 9 months	Labor market test or shortage list	All temporary sectors	78,000 (2006)	None
United Kingdom	Seasonal Agricultural Worker Scheme (SAWS)	< 6 months	Employers must guarantee housing but can deduct costs	Agriculture	16,000 (2005)	Limited to Romanian/Bulgarian citizens from 01/01/08
United Kingdom	Sector Based Scheme	< 12 months	Employers must guarantee housing but can deduct costs	Food processing	3,500 (2007)	3,500 (2007); to be phased out

continued

Appendix 2. (CONTINUED)

United States	H-2A	Employer must pass labor certification test, pay at least enough to counter adverse wage effects, provide housing and cover one-way transportation costs	< 10 months	Agriculture	50,000 (2006)	None
United States	H-2B	Employer must pass labor certification test	< 10 months, renewable up to 3 years	Non-agriculture, especially landscaping, cleaning, hospitality, construction	200,000 (2006)	Capped at 66,000 entries annually

Source: OECD. "Management of Low-Skilled Labour Migration." In *International Migration Outlook 2008*, 125–159. OECD Publication (2008: 158).

Public Policy

CHAPTER 6

჻

Immigration Reform

A Modest Proposal

RICHARD K. VEDDER

1   INTRODUCTION

As stated in the earlier chapters of this book, the preponderance of
evidence suggests that immigration has been, on balance, good for
America.[1] Immigration is an integral part of the story of the nation, and
American economic exceptionalism has been propelled in part by the vitality that new infusions of human capital have bestowed on the nation. Yet it
is also true that anti-immigrant sentiments have been part of the American political landscape almost since the beginning, and that in modern
times, the magnitude of those sentiments became so powerful that restrictions were placed on movement to America, restrictions that after 1924
became particularly onerous. It is no accident that America's ascendency to
economic leadership in the world mostly came in a period before immigration restriction was an important feature of life in the United States. The
best international data suggest that the United States surpassed Great
Britain in terms of total output in the 1870s, and in terms of per capita
output in the first decade of the twentieth century—periods of high immigration and no important immigration restrictions (Maddison 2001).

1. This is a significantly revised and expanded version of a chapter of a short mon-
ograph on immigration prepared in 2012 for the George W. Bush Institute, whose
financial support is greatly acknowledged.

Although restrictions imposed on immigrants are probably, on balance, somewhat less onerous today than, say, half a century ago when Lyndon Johnson was president, they still keep hundreds of thousands of migrants from entering the nation each year. Yet the battles over modernizing and liberalizing immigration laws over the past decade suggest that it is probably politically utopian to call for a virtual end to all immigration restrictions except as they pertain to persons who are potential threats to national security, public health, or the rule of law. I believe what is needed is a policy that does at least eight things:

- Materially expands the flow of newcomers to American shores, giving the nation more of the economic vitality that young, hard-working immigrants have historically provided;
- Improves the average economic productivity of new immigrants and reduces economic and cultural problems of slow assimilation into American culture present among some immigrant arrivals;
- Does not discriminate overtly in favor of, or against, any person on the basis of nationality, race, gender, religion, or any other group characteristic, with the single exception of exclusion of persons perceived dangerous on national security or public health and safety grounds;
- Imposes no fiscal burden, short-term, on the American taxpayer, and, indeed, potentially provides some immediate help in dealing with the problems associated with large budget deficits, either by directly reducing those deficits or by offering relief to native-born taxpayers;
- Deals with and redefines the problem of immigration enforcement (unauthorized immigration);
- Provides encouragement, not barriers, to foreign students to remain in the United States upon completion of college degrees;
- Continues the American tradition of opening up itself to receive persons who are victims of political or religious persecution or extreme economic deprivation; and
- Lowers the bureaucratic, administrative, legal, and human psychic costs associated with enforcing the immigration laws.

2 A MARKET, NOT RULES-BASED, APPROACH TO IMMIGRATION

Basically, what I propose is a modification of an idea expressed publicly first by the late Professor Gary Becker (Becker 1987, 2011; Becker and Becker 1997) of the University of Chicago a long time ago, an idea I've endorsed for quite some time (Gallaway and Vedder 1997). More recently and comprehensively, the idea has received renewed attention (Orrenius and Zavodny 2010).[2] Rather than having immigrants selected on the basis of some administratively determined rules and after a long waiting period, allow market forces to primarily determine who can enter the United States. Immigration would not be determined on where you were from, how long have you been waiting to be admitted, who your family members living in the United States were, some bureaucrat's determination of your skill level, or other such criteria. There would be a price of admission—call it a visa fee—just as there are admission fees to join other associations of people, such as the American Association of Retired Persons (AARP), the Rotary Club, a homeowner's association, or a country club. The amount of the fee, however, rather than being administratively fixed, would vary with market conditions, similar to how the market for taxicab medallions (rights to drive a cab) varies in New York City. The federal government itself sometimes sells things in competitive markets, including a recent sell of airwaves to mobile broadband providers that netted a reported $34 billion (Redherring 2014).

Let me provide more specifics of what I propose. The exact numbers of immigrants admitted is obviously something that can be altered in an upward or downward fashion. The proposal below assumes a level of new immigrant inflows between 4 and 5 per 1,000 population annually, a considerably higher number than is currently coming in (even including undocumented immigrants), but still less than one-half the inflows, relative to population, observed at the peaks in the 1850s and 1900s. The allowable immigrant flows proposed are similar, however, in absolute numbers to those at the peak of immigration between 1905 and 1914.

Every day, sell 5,000 immigrant visas for permanent admission to the United States, probably via an electronic market setting, with visa prices determined by demand and supply conditions. The prices on any given day will be those that will lead to the sale of 5,000 visas (there can be multiple prices on any given day, similar to the stock market, because of intra-day variations in demand; for example, 10 visas could be sold each minute from 8:30 a.m. to 4:50 p.m. to achieve the 5,000 daily quota). Assuming 250 business days a year, the implication is that 1,250,000 visas will be sold annually.

A variant would be to alter the number of visas sold daily with labor market conditions. In times of low overall unemployment, when perceived

2. See also Hall, VanMetre, and Vedder (2012) for a discussion of this approach to immigration restriction.

labor shortages actually exist in some locations and/or occupations, the number of visas sold could be increased, and they could be reduced in recessionary periods when labor demand is smaller. For example, the number of daily visas sold could be reduced by 100 for each one-tenth of a percentage point the unemployment rate exceeds 7 percent, or increased by 100 for each one-tenth of a percent it is reduced below 6 percent. Thus if the unemployment rate were 8.1 percent, the number of visas sold would be 3,900 (5,000 minus 1,100 arising from the 1.1 percent increase in the unemployment rate above 7 percent); if the unemployment rate were 4.9 percent, the number of visas sold would be 6,100 (the 5,000 daily allocation plus 1,100 more for the 1.1 percentage points reduction in the unemployment rate below 6 percent). Implicit in this formula would be the temporary suspension of immigration completely if the unemployment rate were to go above 12 percent. The maximum immigration visa sales amount would probably be around 8,000 daily (2 million annually), happening only if unemployment rates fell to 3 percent.

How much money would be raised from visa sales? Since we have not had this market before, any estimate is just a guess. However, we do know that there are significant numbers of immigrants who spend $15,000, $20,000, or even more to attempt (with no certainty they will succeed) to facilitate entry into the United States (Zhang and Chin 2002). For example, there are reports that Latin American and especially Asian immigrants have paid sums this large to be smuggled into the United States, and many others who quite legally spend nearly that much to immigration lawyers to try to expedite admission or permanent residency in the United States under existing laws.

Suppose the government sold 1,250,000 visas annually at an average fee of $14,000 each. The US Treasury would receive $17.5 billion in new revenues. The use of those funds would be an issue for Congress and the president to decide, but several possibilities exist—reduce the annual budget deficit, dramatically increase funds for the enforcement of immigration laws, provide aid for government infrastructure improvements in areas heavily settled by new immigrants, and so on.

An idea that I think would make expanded immigration more popular with the American people would be to dedicate visa revenues to the reduction in individual income taxes. At this writing, individual income tax revenues are about $1.4 trillion annually. If individual taxpayers were given $17.5 billion in rebates proportionate to their income tax payments, their tax liability would fall by 1.25 percent. For a fairly typical taxpayer paying $10,000 annually in taxes, the tax liability would be reduced by $125 "from payment of immigrant visa fees." Negative attitudes toward immigration might materially decrease if taxpayers perceived they were receiving some direct financial benefit from the new influx of foreign-born persons. My guess is that the $14,000 visa fee estimate above is conservative. Suppose the true figure is $24,000. Visa fees would provide sizable ($30 billion) annual revenues to the Treasury, potentially offering a fairly consequential tax reduction (over 2 percent) in taxes, something that unquestionably would increase, albeit modestly, economic growth for fiscal reasons, in addition to the positive impact associated with large infusions of human capital.[3]

In keeping with one of the eight desired characteristics of immigrant law reform discussed above, it would probably be desirable to have a small additional quota for refugees from political or religious persecution, or for people whose very human existence is threatened by being caught up in civil or international wars. The need for refugee visas varies a good deal with political and military conditions. Moreover, overly liberal use of refugee visas could undermine the paid visa admission program. Perhaps one idea would be to allow a five-year moving average of refugee visas of 50,000 per year, with the president of the United States allowed to vary annual admissions from 0 to 100,000 within the parameters of the moving average maximum restriction. Obviously, that number could be increased or decreased as needed.

Finally, in addition to permanent visas, temporary short-term visas, especially for agricultural workers, might be included in immigration reform, allowing, say, 200,000 or so annually to enter the country for periods of a few months. Those visas could also be sold as most visas currently are, by payment of a fixed fee, or allocated using markets in a manner somewhat similar to that discussed for the permanent immigration visas that are the primary focus of this chapter. Some associate the rise in illegal immigration to the United States largely to the failure to have a rational guest worker program, with some also longing for a revival of the Bracero guest work program in effect during the 1950s and early 1960s (Fund 2006).

"Guest workers" are purely economic migrants who take temporary residence in the United States for employment. Some of the contentious issues associated with permanent immigration are avoided, such as those relating to cultural assimilation. Also, while it can be argued that some

---

3. The negative tax/economic growth relationship has been demonstrated in voluminous numbers of studies. Seven examples include Genetski and Chin 1978, Benson and Johnson 1986, Cashin 1985, Kartel and Mertens 2013, Gemmell, Kneller, and Sanz 2011, Romer and Romer 2010, and Reed 2008.

immigrants compete in the same labor markets with native-born Americans, most guest workers are doing very low wage agricultural labor in rural areas for which there is not a bountiful supply of native-born workers. To be sure, as with any international migration, there are enforcement issues: How do you assure that guest workers return home? There are innovative ways of dealing with that issue, such as having a bonding program that imposes significant financial costs on guest workers who fail to return home in a timely fashion. Thus, politically, the promotion of a market-based guest worker program has considerable appeal.

3   ADVANTAGES OF MARKET-BASED IMMIGRATION RESTRICTION

How would the proposed system be superior to the existing one? First of all, those admitted would almost certainly be individuals who, on average, have high levels of skills or productive potential. While there may be a few rich but lazy and unskilled immigrants who could buy their way into America, the ones likely to get high-paying skilled jobs in the United States are the ones most likely to benefit from the immigrant visas, and therefore the ones willing to pay more. An engineer from India with excellent prospects for a $60,000 job but who is making only $8,000 in India would probably gladly pay $20,000 or even more for a visa—the cost of the visa is less than five months of the earnings differential associated with moving to the United States. By contrast, the relatively illiterate agricultural worker who might move from a $3,000 annual income to a $15,000 yearly wage would find the potential income gain to be dramatically smaller, with the visit costing 20 months of the earnings differential, and thus would be far less likely to apply. In any case, he would have more trouble financing the transaction. However, those agricultural workers could still obtain entry under cheaper temporary guest worker visas, as discussed above.

One of the arguments by critics of immigration has been that the modern-day immigrants are dramatically less skilled and educated than the native-born American population, or than even earlier immigrants (Borjas 1999). It is true, as Table 6.1 shows, that contemporary American immigrants tend to hold more blue-collar jobs than native-born Americans, being much more represented in service jobs or in factory or construction work.

While recent data suggest that this trend is already changing somewhat, it is true that a large number of newcomers to Americans have severe deficiencies that make it difficult for them to assimilate rapidly and move

Table 6.1 OCCUPATIONAL MIX, NATIVE AND FOREIGN-BORN
AMERICANS, 2010

Occupational Category	Native-Born	Foreign-Born
Management, business, science, and arts	37.4%	28.6%
Service	16.6%	25.1%
Sales and office	26.4%	17.8%
Natural resources, construction, and maintenance	8.4%	13.0%
Production, transportation, and material moving	11.2%	15.5%

up the skill ladder to high-paying jobs. For example, a disproportionate number of immigrants have less than a high school education, as Table 6.2 shows.

The "pay to play" dimension of the proposed immigration policy would dramatically increase the mix toward those with higher skills and English language capabilities, thus increasing the immigrant-induced accumulation of human capital and entrepreneurial drive. Even now, immigrants play a disproportionate role in innovation. For example, I looked at the foreign-born concentration in the 10 states with the highest level of per capita patent activity, and compared it with that in the 10 states with the least per capita patent activity. The results, in Figure 6.1, are startling— the immigrant proportions were nearly twice as high in the states with high patent activity.

Similarly, work by the Kauffman Foundation verifies that their "entrepreneurial index" shows roughly double the incidence of entrepreneurship among immigrants compared with native-born Americans (Fairlie 2012). A market-based visa system should enhance this entrepreneurial instinct even more. It would, in short, increase US economic growth, and eliminate some of the gap between America's recent subpar economic performance and historical high growth norms.

Table 6.2 EDUCATIONAL ATTAINMENT OF NATIVE AND FOREIGN-BORN
AMERICANS, 2010

	Less Than High School Graduate	High School Graduate or Equivalency	Some College or Associate's Degree	Bachelor's Degree or Higher
Native	11.0%	29.7%	30.9%	28.4%
Foreign-born	31.7%	22.5%	18.8%	27.0%

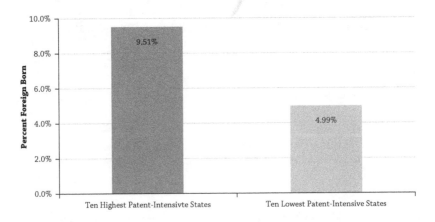

Figure 6.1
Patents and Immigration
Source: 2012 Statistical Abstract of the United States, author's calculations.

Moreover, American companies could gain some certainty over maintaining a skilled labor force. Under current law, there is uncertainty that
employers can obtain H-1 visas for skilled workers, given severe numerical limitations. By advancing funds to promising immigrants, they could
overcome the latter's financial problems of paying the fee, meanwhile getting quickly needed labor. This is a humane, modern-day version of so-
called indentured servitude, very popular in financing the passage to
America of many immigrants in colonial times. Employers in effect recap-
ture the cost of the visa by having workers sign, say, three-year contracts,
under which they are paid a modestly below market-level wage to compensate for the visa costs. So-called STEM (science, technology, engineering,
and math) skill shortages could be dealt with more efficiently and quickly
than under existing provisions such as the grossly inadequate and administratively cumbersome H-1 visa program.

In addition to potential employers directly financing visas, it might be
that new financial instruments would evolve. Human capital contracts,
also known as Income Share Agreements (ISAs), might be offered by entrepreneurial financial service firms, whereby the immigrant would agree
to pay the entrepreneur a share of earnings for a specific number of
years—for example, 10 percent of earnings for five years. This bears some
resemblance to higher education student loans where loan repayment is
income-based.

One group that would be particularly aided by a reformed immigration
law would be foreign students to the United States who, under current law,
are often forced to return to their native land. In some cases, they are

receiving higher education highly subsidized by American taxpayers, only to take their newly acquired human capital skills home—to compete with Americans. These foreign students have an American education, are familiar with the English language and American cultural traditions, and thus are likely to be highly viable candidates for jobs in the United States. The prospects of such jobs would allow them to acquire US immigrant visas. My guess is that banks and other financial service industries would start offering loans that would facilitate visa purchase by graduating foreign students, particularly where the graduating student has firm offers of a job contingent on receipt of a visa. Indeed, I suspect that employers themselves would offer visa payment as a fringe benefit, just as they offer new employees who are already US citizens help in paying tuition fees for graduate degrees.

The costs associated with migration to the United States today are vastly more than the transportation costs that historically were the largest barrier to international movement. As mentioned above, people spend thousands of dollars using immigration lawyers to negotiate the labyrinth of rules, laws, and so on, associated with moving to the United States. There are huge elements of uncertainty: Will my visa application be approved? When? Often the "when" question involves years of waiting. American embassies and consulates spend inordinate resources dealing with issues raised by potential migrants. The system is often unfair, costly, time-consuming, and always excessively bureaucratic. Most of that would be swept away under a market-based system. To be sure, some background checking of successful visa applicants would be necessary for national security reasons, but costs would be dramatically reduced for the applicant and the US government alike.

It is interesting that existing US immigration law, to a very limited extent, already recognizes that getting people with a high level of resources is particularly valuable to the nation. The EB-5 visa, dubbed the "millionaires' visa," permits entry into the United States for foreign investors agreeing to put at least $500,000 into creating or preserving a business with at least 10 jobs. Several hundred of these were issued annually for years, but now the number of applicants has grown dramatically; 7,641 EB-5 visas were issued, about 80 percent to wealthy Chinese investors, in fiscal year 2012, some of whom pay "EB-5 consultants" over $100,000 to facilitate the processing of the visa (Dawson 2013). A related investor visa, the E-2, attracts thousands annually, including over 3,000 from Mexico. Interestingly, other countries (most recently Australia) are imitating the US example regarding investor immigrants.

The H-1 visa is reserved for persons with talents and skills and is administered by the US Citizenship and Immigration Services (USCIS). In recent years, on average slightly over 100,000 of these visas have been issued annually, based on employer (not employee) application. The visas are not directly a path to citizenship. They are renewable for a finite time, and some H-1 visa holders at some point must return home for at least one year. They are strictly limited in number. In most recent years, the visa quota for the year is used up very early. Inadequate as it is, the H-1 visa system is a small but still tangible acknowledgement that "skills matter," and that immigration is a way of meeting critical labor needs.

Thus my suggestion of financial and/or productivity criteria for admission is not a new idea, and the idea of skills-based immigration admission is well established (if inadequately so) in the law. Nearly 100 years ago, the literacy test imposed by the 1917 Immigration Act was designed to attract immigrants who assimilated more readily and were likely to be more productive. On average, the literate persons admitted were probably financially better off than the illiterate individuals excluded from migrating. So the concept that financial resources can facilitate immigration to the United States is not a new one in this modern era of immigration restriction.

A final advantage of the market-based approach is that it provides the nation a vital metric measuring the attractiveness of the United States. A rise in visa prices signifies market judgments that the United States has significant and increasing occupational and other advantages over other nations, while a price decline would indicate the opposite effect. Politicians, social scientists, and others would be able to assess in much more accurate ways than at the present the "bottom line" question: Is the United States becoming a more or less attractive place to live? I could see changing visa prices becoming a measure that presidential candidates use in electoral campaigns, and that policymakers use in identifying problems or solutions dealing with perceived deficiencies in the quality of American life.

4 CRITICISMS OF THE MARKET-BASED APPROACH

Yet there will be many objections to a market-based approach. Some object to immigration generally, of course, and favor a protectionist stance with respect to both the inflow of goods as well as human capital; Pat Buchanan (1998) exemplifies this perspective, in modern times, but protectionism was even common in the private utterances of the Founding Fathers (Eckes 1995). But even strong supporters of immigration might argue that my proposal discriminates against poor deserving immigrants. In one sense, that is quite true, in the sense that those with resources have advantages in life over those without them: Rolls Royce ownership, for example, is highly concentrated among high net worth individuals. But only a limited number of immigrants are going to be admitted to our shores, given the skepticism of Americans about unrestricted immigration—some persons are going to be turned away. Why is using financial criteria more "unfair" or "discriminatory" than rationing admission on other criteria, including, in some cases, where the immigrant is from? Why should some aspiring Americans be given preferences because of familial connections (under the family provisions of existing law), while others are not? While fairness is a subjective, normative concept, my sense is that it is more equitable to discriminate on the basis of financial considerations than on such things as family backgrounds or nationality of birth.

Others might observe that since Latin American immigrants tend to be less educated and skilled, this proposal would reduce the proportion of immigrants coming from those areas. Probably this is true, but that does necessarily mean a large reduction in the absolute *number* of immigrants from those areas, since the fall in the "market share" of, say, Mexican immigrants could well be offset by an increase in the size of the immigrant pool. If, for example, the Mexican immigrant market share were to fall from 25 to 15 percent while total US immigration rose from 800,000 to 1,400,000 annually, the absolute number of Mexican immigrants admitted annually would actually rise slightly, going from 200,000 to 210,000.[4]

Yet even if Mexican immigration (or that from other relatively low-income Latin American countries) were to decline, it means that an immigrant from, say, China or India substitutes within the aggregate numerical limit for one from Mexico or, say, Honduras. On "fairness" grounds, why is Mexican immigration to be preferred to Chinese immigration? Moreover, if certain individuals or groups want to promote, say, Mexican immigration, they can do so by assisting prospective immigrants in paying their admission fee.

Moreover, a shift in immigrant composition somewhat away from those from the Western Hemisphere south of the United States toward those living elsewhere might actually reduce immigrant-induced public policy tensions and improve public attitudes toward immigration. For example, a major issue in several Southern and Western states has been the

4. Of course, a large portion of Mexican immigration to the United States has been illegal, and changing rules of legal immigration could also impact that flow as well. It is noteworthy, however, that the general consensus is that there have been essentially no net inflows of illegal Mexican immigrants since 2008.

attempt, most notably seen in Arizona, to crack down on immigration of those entering the United States illegally from our southern border, a group that has been dominated by Mexican and Latin American cohorts. To that subject we now turn.

5 POLICIES REGARDING UNAUTHORIZED IMMIGRANTS: PAST AND FUTURE

Without question, the most difficult issue in immigration policy is dealing with persons who have entered, or will in the future enter, the United States illegally. A centerpiece of American economic exceptionalism has been that the nation has been governed by rules—laws—that most Americans automatically accept. Voluntary acceptance of laws is a hallmark of prosperous nations, and disrespect for laws is commonplace in poor countries. It is universally agreed in prosperous nations like the United States that those who break the rules must be punished, with the major disagreement usually being over the severity of punishment, although there is also occasional debate whether some existing laws are really necessary or appropriate, such as laws restricting the use of marijuana.

The "law and order" side of me believes that all laws must be enforced until changed through constitutionally sanctioned procedures, typically a vote of Congress and the signature of the president (or an override of a presidential veto). If people can enter the United States without regard for the laws, it creates three large problems. First, of course, is that the flouting of laws has an adverse impact with respect to the maintenance of overall law and order, a bulwark of American capitalism and democracy. Second, it undermines attempts to shape through public policy the magnitude and nature of immigration to the United States. Third, illegal immigration creates unfairness and inequities—lawful persons wait in line (current policy) or pay large visa fees (proposed policy), while those breaking the laws avoid these costs and inconveniences.

For all of these reasons, even persons with highly pro-immigrant sympathies should proceed with caution in endorsing blanket amnesties for those living in the United States in violation of immigration laws.[5] Some

5. The stunning defeat of House Majority Leader Eric Cantor in a June 2014 Republican primary was largely attributable to Cantor's support of a path to citizenship for illegal immigrants, which his opponent opposed. While a majority of Americans seem willing to consider legalizing undocumented immigrants, there is a significant minority who feel very strongly that immigration laws should be enforced rather strictly.

sanctions for unauthorized immigration to the United States seem in order so that respect for the rule of law is maintained.

That said, however, there are real problems about taking draconian approaches to immigration enforcement. First of all, the 10–12 million unauthorized immigrants in the United States are now an important part of the nation's human capital stock and perform many jobs for which native-born Americans seem to be disinterested in filling, at least at current wage rates. As an economist, I would argue that "disinterest" would change if wages rose sharply for these positions, which is what would probably happen if we had mass deportations of immigrants.

Second, many of these illegal immigrants have spent years in the United States and have children who, under the US Constitution, are US citizens. There would be horrendous issues of equity and arguably legality about deporting US citizens who themselves are minors who have instigated no crimes.

Third, the laws broken in general were highly flawed and showed no regard for the positive economic impact that immigration has had on the US economy. A massive crackdown on unauthorized immigrants living in the United States would no doubt lead to output and income reductions and a fall in the nation's output. It would be disruptive even for legal immigrants. The stores selling goods to undocumented immigrants, for example, would see sharp sales declines, leading to business failures and the laying off of workers—most of whom are legal residents of the United States and, indeed, in many cases, native-born US citizens.

The most important previous attempt to deal with the unauthorized immigrant problem was the 1986 immigration law, in which full amnesty was granted to a large number of previously illegal immigrants (those residing in the United States more than five years). If a similar law were adopted now, it would seemingly make a mockery of immigration laws, implying that those breaking the laws can go scot free of punishment if they simply stay hidden long enough until another amnesty occurs, perhaps 25 years from now.

Having a large number of residents hiding from authorities and concealing their identity for long time periods poses all sorts of problems for a functioning democracy. Of paramount importance is that illegal residency probably often leads to exploitation of that illegal status by unscrupulous employers, as these individuals are highly constrained in offering their labor services to others. We have "another America," one where labor markets are more akin to those in feudal times where serfdom prevailed, if not the overt slavery of early America.

But this is not the only issue. Should illegal immigrants be eligible for government benefits? How do we assure that they pay taxes and other acts associated with residency, if they do not even have legitimate Social Security numbers? Should the children of illegal immigrants born in the United States be treated differently from the children of those immigrants born in their country of origin? The problems that illegal immigration poses are many. Reducing or eliminating it thus seems highly desirable.

At this writing, public opinion polls show that a majority of Americans now are generally supportive of allowing illegal immigrants to stay in the country, but are divided on details, such as whether these individuals should be able to become citizens or merely permanent resident aliens, whether they should be required to know English, and so on (Pew Research Center 2013). A 2012 Rasmussen poll found that most (73 percent) agree with President Barack Obama's proposal that those brought to the United States as children (under 16) and who have graduated from high school or have served in the military and have no criminal record should be allowed to get a legal work permit (Rasmussen Report 2012). However, a majority (63 percent) oppose giving driver's licenses or public benefits even to these persons.

An alternative approach to amnesty for existing undocumented immigrants more appealing from a law and order perspective, but accepts the reality that these residents contribute importantly to the nation's resources. Under this scenario, a law is passed making it a misdemeanor crime to live in the United States illegally, but allows such individuals who come forth and confess to their guilt an opportunity to both pay for their "crime" and acquire a path to legal status.

There are a variety of ways that this move toward ultimate decriminalization of undocumented immigrants could occur. Here is one example, assuming that the visa system discussed above was implemented for legal migrants. Have illegal immigrants to the United States who present themselves to authorities pay a fine of $1,000 each. Let them also borrow from private lenders (my preference), or even the US government itself, the money to buy, at current market prices, visas that give them the same rights as other purchasers of visas have—including a path to citizenship. Allow the lender to garnish the wages of the individual until the loan is paid off. If a federal program, set interest rates on the loan at a relatively low level, but well above what the US Treasury pays on long-term obligations to cover the costs of the lending program. In order to maintain a large flow of new immigrants who otherwise would be crowded out by visa applications from existing illegal immigrants, it would be probably necessary for a significant transition period to increase the number of visas issued beyond the 5,000 or so a day proposed above.

Suppose an immigrant from Mexico living illegally in the United States comes clean. He or she would pay $1,000 as a fine immediately, and then would borrow, say, $14,000 to cover the cost of the visa, paying 5 percent interest ($700 a year in interest payments). Suppose he or she were making $15,000 a year as an illegal migrant. With a secure legal status, he or she likely would make more, since the worker now could sell his or her services competitively in labor markets and employers would be more willing to hire this now legal immigrant, as they would not face the possibility of being criminally charged themselves for employing illegal workers. With increased competition for his or her services, work income might easily rise to $20,000 a year. If he or she pays 10 percent of that income for loan repayment, disposable income would still rise about 20 percent from what it otherwise would have been, and the US government within nine years or so would be fully paid with interest. The government comes out ahead (it has collected the visa fee and will collect more taxes in the future), and so does the immigrant. The economy gains since the immigrant can now go above ground in the labor market and likely do more productive work. Moreover, the immigrant becomes eligible for the government social safety net, the right to seek citizenship, and participate in the democratic process through voting and ultimately perhaps even running for office. It would dramatically speed up assimilation into American society, which would help all Americans.

To be sure, some illegal immigrants no doubt would turn down that deal. Regrettably, we would have to punish this group more harshly than in the past. First, employer sanctions for employing illegal immigrants perhaps would have to rise. Second, we might have to bite the bullet and put large numbers of arrested illegal immigrants into makeshift work camp/corrections sites for a period of, say, three to six months. My guess is that if we round up, say, one million unauthorized immigrants who refuse the visa offer and also fine their employers several thousand dollars per worker (maybe even the price of a visa sold under the market-based auction system) and imprison the immigrants for three months and then return them to their home country for some time period, the recidivism rate would be *dramatically* lower than under current policy, particularly if the penalty for second offenses is greater than the already much increased first offense penalty. Moreover, the cost of the incarceration could easily be completely covered by employer fines, and from revenues from the sale of visas under the new immigration policy. Suppose five million illegal immigrants came clean, paid $1,000 fines (netting the US Treasury $5 billion), and purchased visas at $14,000 each—that is $70 billion, a significant multiple of what is spent annually on border enforcement.

From opinion polls, we know that Americans feel more charitably toward illegal immigrants who entered the States as children under the tutelage of their parents. These individuals themselves did not willfully break US laws. Arguably, the financial penalties for obtaining legal status could be set considerably lower for these individuals relative to their parents, who willfully disobeyed US immigration laws. Similarly, we grant various kinds of benefits to those who serve in the US Armed Forces, including in some previous periods in history a quick path to US citizenship. It would make sense, perhaps, to excuse $500 of fines and visa fee payment for each month served in the military, roughly consistent to the college scholarship assistance provided to native-born Americans under the G.I. Bill. In most cases, this would lower the cost of a visa for veterans to zero or near zero (it is a mystery to me how illegal immigrants currently serve in the Armed Forces, but apparently it happens).

With regard to unauthorized adult immigration occurring after a new immigration law is introduced, there is no question that we need to impose real penalties of a very significant magnitude so that intended immigration objectives are realized, the rule of law is maintained, and unfairness to legal purchasers of visas is minimized. That must include significant employer penalties as well as at least some jail time (or the equivalent) for the illegal workers themselves. Currently, crime pays for many with respect to immigration laws; we must make it so crime does not pay.

This conceivably could lead to all sorts of changes. If fines to employers and risks to employees become too great, more and more employers will simply help workers buy visas from the beginning. The cost of the illegal path to American employment would rise sharply relative to the previously largely unavailable legal path, leading to a very sharp decrease in new incidences of illegal migration. Even now, there has been a virtual cessation of net illegal inflows from Mexico since 2008. My sense is that the illegal immigrant problem would diminish, probably fairly quickly, toward zero in a world of liberalized market-based migrant inflows.

To be sure, any change in immigration laws are going to have varying impacts. While generally beneficial, it is possible that the new market-based approach would change the occupational mix of immigrants, possibly raising the cost of employing workers and a subsequent decline in competitiveness in some industries, such as the production of fruits and vegetables, but in the long run it should lead to a more efficient and equitable allocation of resources and treatment of employees. Should a second guest worker visa program be established in addition to a market-based visa for permanent residency, the potential negative effects should be minimal on agriculture from changes in immigration law. On the whole, the availability of a larger, more productive immigrant workforce should increase the competitiveness of the United States in the world economy, stimulating economic growth and entrepreneurship, particularly since immigrants tend to be more work- and innovation-intensive than the American population as a whole.

Some of the provisions above may seem somewhat harsh toward immigrants. I think, however, that in the long run, a policy similar to that suggested above is desirable because it will dramatically reduce political opposition to liberalization of the immigration laws. There is a wide subset of the population who, while contemptuous and even angry about illegal immigration, are basically accepting the principle that our nation should open its doors to newcomers from abroad.

The proposal stated above can be tweaked or changed in a variety of ways. If it were up to me, I would sell a larger number of visas annually—say 1,500,000 instead of 1,250,000. I think it is certainly advantageous economically and probably salable politically. The revenue effects are uncertain, largely dependent on the price elasticity of demand for visas. The trade-off between visa magnitudes and probability of political success, however, are real, and actual visa magnitudes have to be governed by that reality. Personally, I would be relatively lenient in penalties imposed on those who illegally came into America at a young age, or who served in the nation's armed services. Law enforcement should be effective and meaningful, but also compassionate and fair. Again, some political trade-offs may be necessary—fortunately, these are policy options that have room for flexibility and compromise.

6 ALTERNATIVE APPROACHES TO LIBERALIZED RESTRICTION

6.1 Market-Based Alternatives

One big and valid objection to the market-based visa proposal above is that it is hard to sell politically. An alternative that would achieve a large portion of the gains of the proposal outlined above would be to maintain the current immigration law with its myriad of provisions, mostly favoring family preferences, but then add on a new visa, with perhaps 400,000 or so sold annually, using the market-based approach described above. This would end or dramatically reduce opposition from those liking or benefiting from particular provisions of the current law, including those anticipating bringing in relatives under the family preference provisions.

Additionally, immigration lawyers, potentially a strong lobbying group, might feel threatened by the initial market-based proposal that might largely eliminate the need for their services, but would view any system that still requires their legal expertise as acceptable.

The "add-on" visa system would achieve the objective of increasing the magnitude of immigrants, and at least partially achieve the goal of having an immigrant population even more economically productive than the existing immigrant stock. Moreover, to further stifle opposition, trigger mechanisms could be implemented that would reduce, or even eliminate, the sale of visas in periods of economic stress. For example, the number of visas sold could equal 400,000 annually in any period when the unemployment rate is in the range 5–6.5 percent, but be reduced by 20,000 on an annual basis for each 0.1 percentage point unemployment rises above 6.5 percent. With unemployment rates above 8.5 percent, the visa sale program would be suspended. On the other hand, if unemployment fell to 4 percent, visa sales would be increased to a 600,000 annual rate. Alternative labor market indicators (e.g., the employment-population ratio) could be used as a trigger mechanism instead of or in addition to the aggregate unemployment rate.

A second market-based approach has gained favor in recent years (even with Gary Becker), namely instituting what might be called an immigrant tariff, allowing anyone paying the tariff (tax) admittance to the United States, assuming he or she is not a national security or health risk. This approach creates an element of certainty—any person contemplating a visa purchase knows precisely what the costs will be—and is superior to the original proposal on that ground. It should be administratively simple to administer—issuing a visa upon payment of the tariff would be little more difficult than issuing a passport.

Yet from my perspective the tariff approach has some disadvantages. First, of all, what should the initial price (tariff) be? We really do not know with any certitude what the demand curve for admission to the United States looks like. If the price is set extremely high, the gain in the number of immigrants over current levels could be too small; if it is set very low, the number of immigrant inflows might exceed what is politically acceptable, leading to a rationing system that departs from the market ideal. Moreover, the tariff approach does not provide what I view as an extremely valuable metric—an objective estimate of the relative attractiveness of the United States. Still, on the whole, this approach is much superior to existing immigrant allocation procedures, and, again, could be implemented either in lieu of existing policies or as a supplement to other ways of determining immigrant admissions.

Could visas sold under either the pure market or tariff approach be resold by the initial purchaser? I think, politically, the answer should probably be no. Aside from concerns that speculative financial transactions into the right to migrate appear unseemly and inappropriate to some, resalable visas could open the door for political lobbying for setting immigration limits based on the narrow interests of small groups of individuals—existing visa holders. Immigration lobbying already is immense, with more than 1,000 lobbyists registered to lobby on immigration matters, and the American Immigration Lawyers Association was one of the top 25 lobbying groups in 2014, spending directly over $75,000 (OpenSecrets.org 2014).

6.2 Non-Market-Based Alternatives

It is possible, of course, to improve immigration policy somewhat within the context of a rules-based law administered by government bureaucrats. We could move to a more skills and vocationally based policy within the current bureaucratic framework. We could, for example, triple the number of H-1 visas issued annually, bringing perhaps 200,000 more skilled immigrants to the United States annually, a vast improvement over current law. However, I view this as a far less attractive option, since evidence has shown us time and time again that market-based resource allocation decisions almost always bring superior results to those given to us by centralized government bureaucracies. Moreover, the volume of immigration is likely to still be too low. While diminishing returns likely do set in with respect to increased immigration at some point, I suspect that fairly large increments to immigrant flows are on balance welfare enhancing. Moreover, a market-based approach could be *revenue enhancing* for the government, while most alternative approaches are more likely to have negative, not positive, budgetary consequences in the short run.

Canada has used a points system that rewards attributes that likely would lead to an economically more productive population. For example, using a Canadian-style system, we might agree to admit annually the 1,250,000 persons who have the highest number of points. Suppose the maximum number of points attainable is 100, and that 1.25 million apply with 84.2 points or more. Those individuals whose score is 84.2 points or more would be admitted, while those with fewer numbers of points would not. Perhaps the application would include an English literacy test on which those unable to perform at all well would get 0 points, those who show some English comprehension but not a lot would get 5 points, those with fairly high levels would get 10 points, while those with obvious high levels of proficiency would get 15 points (it could be refined to a continuous variable with a wide number of possible scores). Arguably, an oral examination would be part of the test. Education can be factored in: graduates of colleges with advanced professional and technical degrees might get 15 points, those with bachelor degrees 10 points, and those with high school diplomas or the equivalent would get 5 points. Similarly, points could be awarded for previous work experience, for involvement in certain fields of employment (e.g., computer programming, engineering), and so on. Close relatives of those with high scores could get a few points credit for their relative's high score, although that sends one down the slippery slope of making immigration allocation decisions based on family background rather than considerations of individual merit.

The points system has some modest advantages over existing procedures, but is definitely highly flawed in my judgment. A graduate of Oxford University is likely to be more productive than a graduate of an obscure school in Asia or Africa that has no academic distinction, but both graduates get 15 points. Five years working as a professor at a German university arguably suggests higher productivity potential than five years doing manual agricultural labor in Latin America or Asia, but the point system has difficulty allowing for that distinction. Any points system is going to suffer from deficiencies such as these, and attempts to remedy them through an extremely elaborate procedure robs the approach of its simplicity and low administrative cost.

By contrast, with a rationing system based on price, these nuances in individual training and background are taken into account. If an American company desperately wants someone with some peculiar skill that is not fully appreciated by the points system, it can use its money and take a chance on the individual by paying for his or her visa. If someone wants to buy his way into the country as well as bring in a wife who is not likely to work and two young children, he can do so, but he will have to pay for that privilege. Most likely, under practices followed throughout history, the breadwinner would enter first, and with the passage of time use his or her earnings to buy passage into the country for relatives.

7 A COMPASSIONATE, MUTUALLY BENEFICIAL, PRO-GROWTH IMMIGRATION POLICY

The United States is a nation of immigrants that has become truly economically exceptional in part because its vitality as a nation has been constantly renewed and strengthened by new eager human resources entering the country. This was or is true in the 1600s, the 1800s, and the 2000s. Fears of immigrants, present throughout history, have led us into a century of restricting inflows, a move that on balance has had adverse effects on the American economy. We need to start to reduce those restrictions, at the same time recognizing that immigration fears make unlimited immigration politically infeasible.

In opening up immigration, we should seek that the increase in immigrants be bright, disciplined, educated, and likely productive workers who will assimilate readily into American culture. If immigration is rationed on the basis of price (the cost of a visa), it is virtually certain that the persons who would most likely buy visas are those with favorable economic characteristics, such as good English language facility and high educational attainment, since productive persons are also those with access to financial resources. A market-based immigration policy is administratively easier to run, likely would produce an even more relatively productive immigrant population, and treats persons neutrally with respect to race, gender, religion, nationality, and so on. It would promote economic growth and help us maintain our leadership in some fields, such as high technology and scientific endeavors. It would actually reduce the fiscal stress on Washington. It would improve the lives of more of our planet's citizens. In short, it is a win-win policy for native-born Americans, for immigrants themselves, and for future generations who will benefit from the economic prosperity unleashed by the human capital resources of our immigrant population.

REFERENCES

Becker, Gary S. 1987. "A Radical Proposal to Improve Immigration Policy." Mimeo.
Becker, Gary S. 2011. "Gary Becker's Immigration Plan." http://modeledbehavior.com/2011/04/13/gary-beckers-immigration-plan.
Becker, Gary S., and Becker G. N. 1997. *The Economics of Life: From Baseball to Affirmative Action to Immigration, How Real World Issues Affect our Everyday Life.* Columbus, OH: McGraw-Hill.
Benson, Bruce L., and Ronald N. Johnson. 1986. "The Lagged Impact of State and Local Taxes on Economic Activity and Political Behavior." *Economic Inquiry* 24(3): 389–402.
Borjas, George J. 1999. *Heaven's Door: Immigration Policy and the American Economy.* Princeton, NJ: Princeton University Press.
Buchanan, Patrick J. 1998. *The Great Betrayal: How American Sovereignty and Social Justice Are Being Sacrificed to the Gods of the Global Economy.* New York: Little, Brown.

Dawson, Kelly Chung. 2013. "In Immigration Debate, Millionaire's Visa under the Radar." *China Daily.* May 4. http://chinadaily.comcn/epaper/2013–2005/01/content_16465519.html.

Eckes, Alfred, E., Jr. 1995. *Opening America's Market: U.S. Foreign Trade Policy since 1776.* Chapel Hill: University of North Carolina Press.

Fairlie, Robert W. 2012. *Kauffman Index of Entrepreneurial Activity, 1996–2011.* Kansas City, MO: Kauffman Foundation.

Fund, John. 2006. "Cross Country: Bring Back the Braceros." *Wall Street Journal,* July 27: A13.

Gallaway, Lowell, and Richard Vedder. 1997. "Charging Our Way to Better Immigrants." *USA Today.* January 30: A13A.

Gemmell, Normal, Bichara Kneller, and Ismael Sanz. 2011. "The Timing and Persistence of Fiscal Policy Impacts on Growth: Evidence from OECD Countries." *Economic Journal* 121(550): F33–F58.

Genetsk, Robert L., and Young D. Chin. 1978. "The Impact of State and Local Taxes on Economic Growth." Chicago: Harris Bank.

Hall, Joshua C., Benjamin VanMetre, and Richard Vedder. 2012. "U.S. Immigration Policy in the Twentieth-Century: A Market Based Approach." *Cato Journal* 32(1): 201–220.

Maddison, Angus. 2001. *The World Economy: A Millennial Perspective.* Paris: Organisation for Economic Co-Operation and Development.

OpenSecrets.org. 2014. "Lobbying Spending Database." www.opensecrets.org/lobby/issue/obs.php?=IMM.

Orrenius, Pia M., and Madeline Zavodny. 2010. *Besides the Golden Door: U.S. Immigration Reform in a New Era of Globalization.* Washington, DC: AEI Books.

Pew Research Center. 2013. "Immigration: Key Data Points from Pew Research." September 24. http://www.pewresearch.org/key-data-points/immigration-tip-sheet-on-u-s-public/opinion.

Rasmussen Report. 2012. August 20. http://www.rasmussenreports.com.

Redherring.com. 2014. "FCC's Mobile Broadband Spectrum Auction Hits Reported $34 bn." November 25. http://www.redherring.com/mobile-fccs-mobile-broadband-spectrum-auction-hits-reported-34bn/.

Reed, Robert. 2008. "The Robust Relationship Between Taxes and U.S. State Income Growth." *National Tax Journal* 51(1): 57–80.

Zhang, Sheldon X., and Ko-lin Chin. 2002. *The Social Organization of Chinese Human Smuggling: A Cross National Study.* San Diego, CA: San Diego State University.

CHAPTER 7

cᴠɔ

Immigration's Future

A Pathway to Legalization and Assimilation

HERBERT LONDON

1   INTRODUCTION

Immigration policy is somewhat like taxes: reform, to the extent you can get it, is based on expectation. A tax designed to cool an overheated economy or a currency that is fading fast may be different from a tax policy designed to stimulate economic growth. Policies are a reflection of perceived need. The same is true of immigration.

There are several value propositions in play when it comes to immigration, albeit one overarching principle that I advocate: a grand bargain that includes some form of legality for long-established, nonviolent illegals in exchange for an end to mass legal immigration. This is a compromise that makes sense for many on both sides of the political aisle—although common sense and immigration policy are not always compatible. Nonetheless, my position is stated up front so that it is not caught in the fog of background evidence.

My stance has been adopted because the flood of immigrants, more than one million a year, puts enormous pressure on the already fragile process of assimilation. Providing a fast track for current illegals who have not committed crimes, who pay their taxes and have been residing here for years, is merely a sensible, albeit hardly ideal, solution to the immigration morass. Moreover, the number that fall into this category is about 6 million, making the adjustment difficult, but not insuperable.

2   WHAT TO DO WITH THE CURRENT ILLEGAL IMMIGRANTS?

Proponents of "amnesty"—and I am not one—demand "enforcement first," even though employment-verification and exit tracking systems have not been implemented to anyone's satisfaction. In 1986, amnesty was granted, but enforcement failed. If an enforcement regimen leads to millions of illegals being displaced, it would be disruptive and ultimately unacceptable. It is essential that enforcement precede any plan for leniency, but a policy based on preventing new illegals should not stand in contradistinction to a policy on illegals residing here.

The immigration statistics, particularly on undocumented immigrants, paint a generally grim picture, with some exceptions. Pew Research Center's Hispanic Trends Project has estimated that from 2005 to 2010, 1.4 million Mexicans, including many born in the United States, left this country. During the same period, 1.4 million "new" Mexicans entered the United States (most illegally), resulting in a net migration of zero (Passel, Cohn, and Gonzalez-Barrera 2012).

In the context of immigration, "amnesty" is any condition that permits illegals to remain legally. If we account for those without criminal convictions, plus those who came before the age of 10 and grew up here, there are about 6 million in this category, or half the current illegal population eligible for amnesty. (This number is an extrapolation based on those illegal immigrants residing in the United States who have not committed a felony offense.)

Amnesty beneficiaries, in my judgment, should get Green Cards and an opportunity to pursue citizenship, but there must be milestones on the road to citizenship. To offset the "amnesty" provisions, immigration should be cut in half from the present 1.1 million coming to the United States annually. Cuts to legal immigration can offset the effect of amnesty since empirical evidence suggests high levels of legal immigration produce high levels of illegal immigration (Passel 2005). Legal immigration creates the networks and connections that make illegal immigration possible.

A lower level of overall immigration would tighten the labor market, ease pressure on welfare, health, and education systems, and it might promote assimilation, which is lagging in any case. But it is especially important for the absorption of the "soon-to-be amnestied" illegal population.

3 SHOULD THERE BE COMPREHENSIVE REFORM?

The absurd conceit behind comprehensive immigration reform is that several entirely separate issues are conflated. While the illegal issue in the United States is related to immigration limits, there are other questions that must be addressed: Does the country benefit from welcoming more English-speaking skilled professionals, or should it invite low-skill-level immigrants who fill jobs at the bottom of the economic ladder? Clint Bolick and Jeb Bush contend that there are jobs Americans will not pursue and, as a consequence, we should liberalize the opportunity for temporary laborers (Bush and Bolick 2013: 82). Yet, it should also be noted that only 30 percent of this unauthorized immigrant population is proficient in English, and are not easily assimilable, as the evidence that follows indicates (Stoney and Batalova 2013).

It should also be noted that there is only one occupation in the United States of the kind noted by Bolick and Bush (agriculture) where the majority of workers are illegal immigrants. The other categories present a different pattern (see Table 7.1).

Advocates of comprehensive immigration reform, such as Robert Lynch and Patrick Oakford of the Center for American Progress, contend that the wages of unauthorized immigrants would increase by as much as 15.1 percent if they were granted legal status (Lynch and Oakford 2013). However, they noted that 22 percent of all adults without a high school diploma came from the ranks of the unauthorized, even though they represent 4 percent of the US adult population. Similarly, Gianmarco Ottaviano and Giovanni Peri maintain that a substantial increase in legal immigration increased the wages of native-born workers by 0.6 percent (Ottaviano and Peri 2006: 30). They also found that new immigration would reduce the wages of existing immigrants by 6 percent. This

Table 7.1. PERCENTAGE OF NATIVE-BORN
LABORERS IN SELECTED OCCUPATIONS

Maids and housekeepers	51 percent native born
Taxi drivers	58 percent native born
Meat processors	63 percent native born
Groundskeepers	64 percent native born
Construction	66 percent native born
Porters	72 percent native born
Janitors	73 percent native born

Source: Camarota and Zeigler (2009).

conclusion is consistent with a 2011 comprehensive immigration analysis by Kavier Chojnicki, Frederic Docquier, and Lionel Ragot, which showed that postwar immigration benefited all US natives, but that the benefits would have been more profound had the United States pursued a selective, skills-based immigration policy.

It is precisely in this unskilled worker category that immigrant dreams are shattered. Recent studies indicate that incarceration rates for second-generation Mexican American and Caribbean American men are as high as incarceration rates for African American men, while adolescent child-bearing and dropout rates for members of these communities are higher than they are for black Americans (Haller, Portes, and Lynch 2011: 20). These are arguments that militate against "easy" assimilation.

While Jacob Vigor in "The Civic and Cultural Assimilation of Immigrants to the United States" (chapter 3) points to the effective assimilation of some immigrant groups, he overlooks, in my opinion, why the recent migration from Latin America and South America is different. The evidence that follows suggests second-generation immigrants are going "backward." Instead of embracing their adopted home, they are encouraged to be multiculturalists, retaining loyalty to the "mother country" or to ethnic identification. This, as I see it, is attributed in large part to a dramatic ideological shift in American attitudes that has as its consequence a reduced demand and desire for patriotic assimilation.

This argument, made by John J. Miller in *The Unmaking of Americans* (1998), offers one more reason that legalizing the unauthorized population, decreasing unskilled immigration, and increasing, by degree, skilled immigration may be complementary strategies. The sheer number of a particular ethnic group often militates against easy assimilation. Highly skilled immigrants, however, tend to have more diverse attitudes than unskilled counterparts and, as a consequence, find assimilation somewhat easier. By increasing the number of skilled immigrants who are likely to consume fewer public services than their unskilled counterparts, the nation's ability to assist the native-born poor and existing stock of less skilled immigrants is given a boost.

Not all commentators on immigration regard these facts with fear. Michael Barone, in *Shaping Our Nation* (2013), argues that we have grown unnecessarily alarmist about immigration policy. From this strain of analysis emerges an appreciation of American durability. As he sees it, American society is founded on mass migration, with immigration as a source of turbulence and creativity. There is nothing new about challenging waves of anti-establishment immigrants destabilizing the status quo.

Although it is probably too early to generalize, the drop-off in Mexican immigration after the recession of 2007–2008 may be comparable to the sudden decline in German and Irish newcomers in the 1890s. If Barone is right that Mexican immigration has peaked—a point not generally embraced by immigration analysts—the pressure for comprehensive policy reform has probably diminished.

4 HIGH-SKILLED IMMIGRANTS

On one matter there appears to be consensus, at least if one relies on cliché-driven arguments. Just as there is a belief that low-skilled immigration should be reduced, there are many who believe that high-skilled immigration should be increased. Alex Nowrasteh of the Cato Institute calls skilled immigration "the new common ground in the reform debate." However, most holders of H-1B work visas are college educated, presumably here to fill gaps in specialized occupations.[1] It is almost impolitic to observe that the H-1B program is manipulated by government and hardly in the hands of a free labor market. However, the employment picture for recent college graduates has grown bleak. The unemployment rate for Americans in their twenties is at 8.8 percent, up from 5.7 percent in 2007. Underemployment stood at 18.8 percent, almost double what it was five years ago. And a Congressional Budget Office (CBO) report said that, by 2024, Obamacare would eliminate or reduce full-time jobs for the equivalent of 2.5 million Americans (CBO Report 2014: 13).

The Obama administration itself argued in court filings for an H-1B visa fraud case that "in January of 2009, the total number of workers employed in the information technology occupation under the H-1B program substantially exceeded the 241,000 unemployed U.S. citizen workers within the same occupation" (Thibodeau 2009). If H-1B workers outnumber unemployed techies, and if companies that outsource tech jobs overseas are gobbling up these visas, fears about domestic employment may not be unfounded.

Robert Bennett, a former US senator from Utah, said, "Once it's clear [the visa bill] is going to get through, everybody signs up so nobody can be in the position of being accused of being against high tech" (Matloff 2003: 13). In fact, as he notes, H-1B visa holders frequently do not have more advanced skills than what is available in the domestic market. And there

---

1. H-1B requirements can be found at http://www.uscis.gov/eir/visa-guide/h-1b-specialty-occupation/understanding-h-1b-requirements.

is scant evidence of a tech labor shortage, although industry sources refer to a 100,000-person shortfall (Matloff 2003: 73). Norm Matloff, professor of computer science at the University of California, Davis, argues, "The H-1B work visa is fundamentally about cheap, de facto indentured labor" (Matloff 2003: 3). He goes on to note, "The vast majority of H-1B's, including those hired for U.S. universities, are ordinary people doing ordinary work, not the best and brightest" (Matloff 2008). They are simply paid less through a "prevailing wage rate," a mechanism riddled with holes.[2]

By contrast, Matthew Slaughter, professor at the Tuck School of Business, contends that the cap of 85,000 on H-1B visas impedes economic development (Slaughter 2014). He argues that an estimated 100,000 jobs lost directly because H-1B visa application were denied has resulted in a loss of an additional 400,000 jobs "not created at immigrant-hiring" companies. Leaving aside the view that this arithmetic is based on assumptions, the analysis does not take into account domestic techies who could fill these positions.

Obviously, this H-1B issue is a debatable proposition, but it is subordinate to the issue of mass, low-skilled immigration that dominates the present debate. Whether H-1B is to be reduced or increased by 10 percent can be argued either way. In the end, its influence on the larger immigration issue is *de minimis*. As long as "family unification" has been the linchpin of immigration policy since the 1920s, the waves of unskilled workers have imperiled the nation's social service system and dramatically affected the normal digestion of employees into the workplace.

5   THE PROBLEMS OF MASS LOW-SKILLED MIGRATION

While Michael Barone offers historical context for the economic turbulence associated with immigration in the past, it is my judgment that present conditions are magnified by the inability of even second-generation immigrants to assimilate and by a reversal in government sentiment that once relied on mediating structures to promote integration. While the evidence that demonstrates these assertions is not dispositive, it is persuasive.

Fifty percent of unauthorized immigrant children and 60 percent of immigrant adults have no health insurance (Passel 2005: 35). As a consequence, they rely on emergency facilities, clinics, health centers, or public hospitals for treatment.

---

2. The requirements can be found at http://www.uscis.gov/eir/visa-guide/h-1b-specialty-occupation/understanding-h-1b-requirements.

Unauthorized immigrants who are minors require more educational service than do native-born children because of a lack of English proficiency (CBO Report 2007: 2).

The CBO reviewed measured costs associated with services to unauthorized immigrants and concluded that these costs range from a few million dollars in states with small unauthorized populations to tens of billions in California, Texas, Illinois, New York, Florida, and New Jersey (CBO Report 2007: 3). The costs were concentrated in programs that comprise a large percentage of total state spending, mainly healthcare, education, and law enforcement.

In 2010 (the last year of formal statistics on this matter), the average unlawful immigrant household received $24,721 in government benefits and services while paying $10,334 in taxes, an average fiscal deficit of $14,000 per household (Rector and Richwine 2013). In Chapter 3 of this volume, Alex Nowrasteh makes a case for the "unambiguous and large" fiscal impact of taxes provided by new immigrants. But, as I see it, this case must be evaluated against a backdrop of additional expenses in education, social services, and criminally related matters created by the illegal immigrant population. The net effect on the US budget is not "unambiguous." Even CBO estimates are judgments based on approximations. Although I am persuaded that the $14,000 net fiscal cost per immigrant family, after tax revenue is taken into account, is close to reality, that too is an estimate—not a clearly determined number.

Under current law, unlawful immigrant households in the aggregate produce an annual deficit of $54.5 billion (Rector and Richwine 2013). In 2010, 36 percent of immigrant-headed households used at least one major welfare program (primarily food stamps and Medicaid), compared to 23 percent of native households (Camarota 2012).

The US Census Bureau released figures showing that average per pupil funding from all revenue sources is $12,200. Although this number does not disaggregate the school-age children of illegal immigrants, multiplying $12,200 by the 3.8 million students with illegal immigrant parents yields a total of about $46.4 billion, a sum not included in social service expenditure (Izumi 2010).

The 18th Street Gang and the Mara Salvatrucha (MS-13) are gangs largely composed of illegal immigrants. Recent Department of Justice reports indicate that the availability of methamphetamines is due to the proliferation of Hispanic gangs. According to the FBI, MS-13 is the fastest growing and most violent of these gangs; their motto is "Mata, Viola, Controla" or "Kill, Rape, Control." There are estimated to be 12,000 hardcore members in the United States and as many as 300,000 across Latin America (Feere and Vaughan 2008).

While it is impossible to quantify precisely the influence of illegal immigration on crime, every local law enforcement officer in a recent survey, including Dallas, Fairfax County in Virginia, and Chicago, contends that the city or county's murder rate declined between 20 to 32 percent with the reduction of alien immigration (Feere and Vaughan 2008).

In 2012, approximately 52 percent of the 40 million foreign-born persons were "limited English Proficient" (LEP), practically the same percentage as those in 2000. Fifty-nine percent of the LEP elementary school children were born in the United States to immigrant parents, one sign that second-generation assimilation is not working as well as many assume (Batalova and Lee 2012).

Of adult immigrants (25 to 65), 28 percent have not completed a high school diploma, compared to 7 percent of natives. Mexican immigrant teenagers have the highest school dropout rate among all immigrant groups (Soifer 2009).

"The Social Security Administration *assumes* that about half of unauthorized immigrants pay Social Security taxes" (CBO Report 2007: 6). In fact, "most of the estimates that the CBO reviewed did not include costs associated with children who were born to unauthorized immigrants in the United States because those children are U.S. citizens" (CBO Report 2007: 7). If those children had been included in the estimates, their financial impact—particularly on education—would have been demonstrably higher. Moreover, as the CBO readily admits ". . . the scope and analytical methods of studies vary, and the reports do not provide detailed or consistent enough data to allow for a reliable assessment of the aggregate national effect of unauthorized immigrants on state and local budgets" (CBO Report 2007: 3). Yet the CBO characterizes the fiscal influence of illegals as "likely modest" (CBO Report 2007: 3).

The number of immigrants naturalized has decreased by 17 percent from 2009 to 2010, even though the number of people entering the country was relatively constant during this two-year period, a fact that suggests even lawful immigrants do not necessarily want to embrace US citizenship (Batalova and Lee 2012). Of the approximately 12 million illegals residing in the United States, 8.5 million are eligible to establish a pathway to naturalization, but do not do so for a variety of undisclosed reasons.

Some analysts contend that a portion of the illegal immigrant population avoids assimilation for fear of being reported or deported. That may be true, but the literature on the subject is entirely anecdotal and the extent of the fear is speculative.

6 AN ASSESSMENT OF MASS IMMIGRATION
AND THE FREE MARKET

When all of the data on this issue of immigration are assembled, I am left with a basic yet intractable enigma. I am an emotional, free marketeer; even when I realize free markets do not work perfectly, they are invariably the best option available on the policy front. I advocated free market principles when I ran for office and continue to espouse the virtues of a free market today. Why then do I not embrace an open immigration policy? After all, the success of wave after wave of immigrants, despite turbulence, provides some empirical evidence for liberalization.

The *Wall Street Journal* editorial page, whose views I usually agree with, argues for "open borders" (Riley 2008). "The case for open borders is a case for moving immigration policy in a more market oriented direction. The workers at the plants were coming to this country to work. Why not let them come legally?" It was also noted that ". . . the reason they [illegal immigrants] were breaking the law is because we have a policy in which too many immigrants are chasing too few visas" (Riley 2008). Yet I stand at the barricades opposed to my free market allies because I am persuaded that open borders are a threat to the free market we both admire.

As I see it, the free market is kept vibrant by a series of cultural imperatives. It is not only the law of supply and demand that keeps it functioning, but a religious, philosophical, and political position that I often refer to as "the burden of freedom." The market works in an ecology that includes the Protestant Ethic, the rule of law, notions of personal responsibility, risk taking, trust, and individualism. A free market remains free when mediating structures such as schools, churches, families, and associations perpetuate the requisite cultural ideals.

In the great wave of European immigration from 1880 to 1924, elites were generally united in advocating Teddy Roosevelt's admonition that people who come to our shores should be "Americanized." By that, Roosevelt meant that immigrants should obey our laws, embrace our customs, learn our ways, and speak our language. Assimilation was not an option; it was a necessity for living here. That was the standard, notwithstanding a tolerance for filial piety. You can love the mother of your birthplace as well as the mother of your adopted home.

It is not clear when this view changed. Nat Glazer and Pat Moynihan did refer to the growing influence of cultural pluralism in *Beyond the Melting Pot* (1970), but even they could not imagine a nation separated by cultural islands in which assimilation even for the second generation is not encouraged.

The 1920s immigration acts, as already noted, which relied on family unification and mass immigration, led directly to a fundamental shift on the part of the immigrant population coming here as well as the elites who welcomed them. Rather than emphasize the unique, idiosyncratic virtues of America, elitists assumed that we should allow new immigrants to retain the culture of the past, which, in far too many instances, was a culture "bound to unfreedom": namely, dependency, government control, and group identification.

To accommodate the new immigrants, among other reasons, elites created or altered an institutional apparatus that challenges the very essence of a free market in the form of affirmative action, "disparate impact" decisions, racial and ethnic government grants, and race- and ethnicity-based university admissions policy. The size and scope of government activity needed to bolster the status of new immigrants is mind numbing. But most significantly, this activity is designed ostensibly to challenge the 1964 Civil Rights Act, which suggested that race and ethnicity should be neither a handicap nor an advantage. Immigration policy is now basically organized around government-conferred privilege. All things being equal—and they rarely are—a Mexican American has an advantage over a native-born American in most job applications and in admission to colleges and universities.

Nevertheless, there is overwhelming evidence suggesting that Americanization, or what I would call patriotic assimilation, is not proceeding well, certainly not in the manner Mr. Barone predicted. The Alejandro Portes and Ruben Rumbaut longitudinal study—arguably the most comprehensive of its kind—reports that children of immigrants are not "assimilating," but are "selectively acculturating" (Portes and Rumbaut 2001: 274). That is to say, many learn some English, but identify themselves "increasingly" with their parents' birth nation (Mexico, El Salvador, etc.) instead of the United States. In their report, Portes and Rumbaut (2011) indicate that, in one Los Angeles high school populated by Hispanics, freshmen students were asked if they wanted to be Americans. The response was overwhelmingly positive. However, when this same question was asked of the same students when they became seniors, only a tiny fraction answered affirmatively.

The Pew Hispanic Survey taken seven months after 9/11, when patriotic sentiments were running high, shows the same pattern (Taylor et al. 2012). Only 34 percent of Latinos (who are American citizens) considered themselves Americans first. Forty-two percent identified with the old country first, and 24 percent considered themselves as pan ethnic, as "Latino" or "Hispanic" first. Even among the third generation, Hispanics who have held American citizenship for 80 years or more, 41 percent consider their primary identity as either the family's country of origin or Latino-Hispanic identity.

In its conclusion, the Portes-Rumbaut study notes: "we should have seen an increase over time in the proportion of youths identifying themselves as American, with or without a hyphen, and a decrease in the proportion retaining an attachment to a foreign national identity. But . . . the results . . . point in exactly the opposite direction" (Portes and Rumbaut 2001: 157). Patriotic assimilation is decreasing and "foreign national identities command the strongest level of allegiance and attachment" (Portes and Rumbaut 2001: 158).

As the Hudson Institute study on "America's Patriotic Assimilation System Is Broken" by John Fonte and Althea Nagai indicates, "A large 'patriotic gap' exists between native born citizens and immigrant citizens on issues of patriotic attachment and civic knowledge. Despite what some believe, native born citizens have a much higher degree of patriotic attachment to the U.S. than naturalized citizens" (Fonte and Nagai 2013: 1).

It strikes me as obvious that you cannot seriously discuss immigration policy without comprehensive assimilation reform. And in considering the latter, it must be noted that, since the 1970s (nothing precise about the date), American elites have altered the de facto assimilation position from Americanization (or patriotic integration) to a multiculturalism that emphasizes ethnic group consciousness at the expense of American common culture. Not only are we sending immigrants the wrong message, in my opinion, but the message we do send has a deleterious effect on the free market and its attendant cultural imperatives.

Ultimately, multiculturalism insinuated itself into federal bureaucratic practices and court decisions that are difficult to undo. But it may be possible to challenge multicultural education, bilingual education, and even dual citizenship. As I see it, Americanization is a moral issue that defines the character of citizenship and for what a constitutional republic stands.

Surely, any debate about immigration should incorporate assimilation into the analysis. My opening plea for a "grand bargain" is an offer to combine compassion with hard-headed realism, recognizing that many illegal immigrants who have resided in the United States as taxpayers and law-abiding residents deserve a chance for a pathway to citizenship. Nonetheless, I do not have illusions about the difficulty involved in integration as long as elites uphold a standard of multiculturalism. Thus I also believe that this "grand bargain" must cut current levels of legal immigration in half in order to better assimilate immigrants into traditional American values, recognizing, at the same time, the evidence which suggests that assimilation, as presently understood, is not working effectively.

REFERENCES

Barone, Michael. 2013. *Shaping Our Nation: How Surges of Migration Transformed America and Its Politics*. New York: Crown Publishing Group.

Batalova, Jeanne, and Alicia Lee. 2012. "Frequently Requested Statistics on Immigrants and Immigration in the United States." Migration Policy Institute.

Bush, Jeb, and Clint Bolick. 2013. *Immigration Wars: Forging an American Solution*. New York: Simon & Schuster.

Camarota, Steven A. 2012. "Immigrants in the United States: A Profile of America's Foreign-Born Population." Center for Immigration Studies. http://www.cis.org/sites/cis.org/files/articles/2012/immigrants-in-the-united-states-2012.pdf.

Camarota, Steven A., and Karen Zeigler. 2009. "Jobs Americans Won't Do? A Detailed Look at Immigrant Employment by Occupation." Center for Immigration Studies. http://cis.org/illegalImmigration-employment.

Chojnicki, Xavier, Frédéric Docquier, and Lionel Ragot. 2011. "Should the US Have Locked Heaven's Door?" *Journal of Population Economics* 24(1): 317–359.

Congressional Budget Office. 2007. "The Impact of Unauthorized Immigrants on the Budgets of State and Local Governments." No. 2500. Washington, DC.

Congressional Budget Office. 2014. "The Slow Recovery of the Labor Market." No. 4837. Washington, DC.

Feere, Jon, and Jessica Vaughan. 2008. "Taking Back the Streets: ICE and Local Law Enforcement Target Immigrant Gangs." Center for Immigration Studies. http://cis.org/ImmigrantGangs.

Fonte, John, and Althea Nagai. 2013. *America's Patriotic Assimilation System Is Broken*. Culture and Society Briefing Paper. Washington, DC: Hudson Institute.

Glazer, Nathan, and Daniel P. Moynihan. 1970. *Beyond the Melting Pot*. Joint Center for Urban Studies of The Massachusetts Institute of Technology and the President and Fellows of Harvard University. Cambridge, MA: MIT Press.

Izumi, Lance T. 2010. "Educating Illegal Immigrants Is Costly." *Atlanta Journal-Constitution*. August 17.

Lynch, Robert, and Patrick Oakford. 2013. "The Economic Effects of Granting Legal Status and Citizenship to Undocumented Immigrants." Center for American Progress. https://www.americanprogress.org/issues/immigration/report/2013/03/20/57351/the-economic-effects-of-granting-legal-status-and-citizenship-to-undocumented-immigrants/.

Matloff, Norman. 2003. "On the Need for Reform of the H-1B Non-immigrant Work Visa in Computer-related Occupations." *University of Michigan Journal of Law Reform* 36(4): 815–914.

Matloff, Norman. 2008. "H-1Bs: Still Not the Best and the Brightest." Center for Immigration Studies.

Miller, John. 1998. *The Unmaking of Americans*. New York: The Free Press.

Ottaviano, Gianmarco I. P., and Giovanni Peri. 2006. "Rethinking the Effects of Immigration on Wages." Technical paper no. 12497. NBER Working Paper Series. Cambridge: National Bureau of Economic Research.

Passel, Jeffrey S. 2005. "Unauthorized Migrants: Numbers and Characteristics." Pew Hispanic Center Hispanic Trends. http://www.pewhispanic.org/2005/06/14/unauthorized-migrants/.

Passel, Jeffrey S., D'Vera Cohn, and Ana Gonzalez-Barrera. 2012. "Net Migration from Mexico Falls to Zero-and Perhaps Less." Pew Research Center Hispanic Trends. http://www.pewhispanic.org/2012/04/23/net-migration-from-mexico-falls-to-zero-and-perhaps-less/.

Haller, William, Alejandro Portes, and Scott M. Lynch. 2011. "Dreams Fulfilled and Shattered: Determinants of Segmented Assimilation in the Second Generation." *Social Forces* 89(3): 733–762.

Portes, Alejandro, and Rubén G. Rumbaut. 2001. *Legacies: The Story of the Immigrant Second Generation*. Berkeley: University of California Press.

Rector, Robert, and Jason Richwine. 2013. "The Fiscal Cost of Unlawful Immigrants and Amnesty to the U.S. Taxpayer." The Heritage Foundation. http://www.heritage.org/research/reports/2013/05/the-fiscal-cost-of-unlawful-immigrants-and-amnesty-to-the-us-taxpayer.

Riley, Jason L. 2008. "A Welcome, Not a Wall." *Wall Street Journal*. May 16.

Slaughter, Matthew J. 2014. "How America Loses a Job Every 43 Seconds." *Wall Street Journal*. March 25.

Soifer, Don. 2009. "The Value of English Proficiency to the United States Economy." Lexington Institute. http://lexingtoninstitute.org/the-value-of-english-proficiency-to-the-united-states-economy/.

Stoney, Sierra, and Jeanne Batalova. 2013. "Mexican Immigrants in the United States." Migration Policy Institute. http://www.migrationpolicy.org/article/mexican-immigrants-united-states.

Taylor, Paul, Mark Hugo Lopez, Jessica Martinez, and Gabriel Velasco. 2012. "When Labels Don't Fit: Hispanics and Their Views of Identity." Pew Research Center Hispanic Trends. http://www.pewhispanic.org/2012/04/04/when-labels-dont-fit-hispanics-and-their-views-of-identity/.

Thibodeau, Patrick. 2009. "U.S.: H-1B Workers Outnumber Unemployed Techies." *Computerworld*. May 26.

CHAPTER 8

ᴄᐯᴖ

A Radical Case for Open Borders

BRYAN CAPLAN AND VIPUL NAIK

1   INTRODUCTION

S uppose you get laid off in Oklahoma.[1] Local opportunities are sparse,
so you find a job in California, rent a new place, and go. *Voilà*, your
move is done. You need not get permission from a government official or
convince anybody that your presence is a net positive for California.[2]
That's because the member states of the United States have *open borders*.

This chapter argues in favor of *global* open borders. In an open borders
world, you don't need permission to move from Lahore to London or Mon-
treal to Mumbai any more than you need permission to move from Oklahoma to California. The case for open borders is universal: it applies to the
United States, Australia, Japan, India, China, Germany, and all other
countries. For the most part, though, we focus on the modern United
States, with occasional discussion of other countries and earlier eras. Our

1. We thank Zachary Gochenour and Nathaniel Bechhofer for excellent research
assistance, Alex Nowrasteh, Carl Shulman, Hansjoerg Walther, and seminar partici-
pants at Texas Tech for helpful suggestions, and the Public Choice Center, Mercatus
Center, and Free Market Institute for financial support.
2. California actually adopted an anti-Okie law, but it was struck down in 1941;
original newspaper available online: "Anti-Okie Law Ruled Void," November 24,
1941. *The Tuscaloosa News*, http://news.google.com/newspapers?nid=1817&dat=19
411124&id=qdQ-AAAAIBAJ&sjid=uUwMAAAAIBAJ&pg=33024023575. See also
the memoir "The Difference Between an Illegal Immigrant and Me" by Robert Higgs,
published 20 February 20, 2008, available online at http://www.independent.org/
newsroom/article.asp?id=2126.

American focus is partly a matter of convenience; data and social science on US immigration are relatively abundant. But given its long history of near-open borders, and its ongoing role as the world's leading superpower, the US case is also especially relevant and enlightening.

2   THE WORLD IS FAR FROM OPEN BORDERS

How far are we today from open borders? Very. Let's look at the question from three angles: the letter of the law, how much migrants sacrifice to evade the law, and how many people want to move but cannot. Precisely because the world today is remote from open borders, all numbers are crude guesses. But they help us appreciate the radical nature of open borders, or, more precisely, the radical extent to which closed borders distort global society and destroy freedom and economic value.

Let's begin with the law. By First World standards, US immigration laws are fairly liberal. Still, the only routes for legal immigration are family reunification, high skill, refugee or asylum status, and the diversity lottery. Typical family reunification wait times run 7–12 years, and around two decades for Mexicans.[3] Employment-based visa requirements are stringent: to apply, you need extraordinary ability, distinguished accomplishment that requires at least a postgraduate degree, sponsorship by a US multinational, or $500,000 to invest.[4] High-skilled workers can also try for a non-immigrant H-1B visa that allows a transition to permanent residency. This category is so competitive that the annual application quota normally fills in 10 days.[5] The United States grants refugee or asylum status to about 50,000 people a year, with a 2012 ceiling of 76,000.[6]

---

3. "Immigrant Numbers for October 2013," *Visa Bulletin* 61, p. 2, October 2013, available online at http://travel.state.gov/content/dam/visas/Bulletins/visabulletin_october2013.pdf.

4. See US Department of State Bureau of Consular Affairs, "Employment-Based Immigrant Visa," accessed 1 May 2014. http://travel.state.gov/content/visas/english/immigrate/types/employment.html.

5. For the most recent figures, see United States Citizenship and Immigration Services, "USCIS Reaches FY 2015 H-1B Cap," 10 April 2014, http://www.uscis.gov/news/uscis-reaches-fy-2015-h-1b-cap-0.

6. Daniel Martin and James Yankay, "Refugees and Asylees: 2012," Office of Immigration Statistics, April 2013 http://www.dhs.gov/publication/refugees-and-asylees-2012. For a more detailed discussion of the various humanitarian statuses (temporary and long-term) offered by the US government, see Michelangelo Landgrave, "A Survey of the United States Humanitarian Migrant Statuses," *Open Borders: The Case*, 14 May 2014, http://openborders.info/blog/a-survey-of-the-united-states-humanitarian-migrant-statuses/.

Winning the diversity lottery, finally, is as improbable as it sounds: in 2008, 13.6 million people applied for 50,000 slots.[7] In addition, some low-skilled workers get H-2A and H-2B visas, but these are hard to get, quick to expire, and cannot be converted to long-term residency.

In sum, the United States offers no path for the typical world resident to move long term, and few options for temporary work. Even temporary visits are hard to arrange, because applicants are, as a matter of US policy, denied if they fail to convince their consular officer that they do *not* intend to migrate long term.[8] As a result, many prospective migrants cross borders illegally or overstay temporary visas. The United States currently has 11–13 million illegal immigrants, about a third of its foreign-born population and about 4 percent of the total population.[9]

How much do these laws matter? Look at the black market prices that poor migrants eagerly pay to hop to the border. Smuggler fees from Mexico to the United States are now about $4,000—four years' income for a typical farm laborer in Mexico.[10] Prices for more distant countries are predictably higher. A median-income Indian would need to save all his income for over a decade to pay the $60,000 that smugglers currently charge for illegal transport to the United States.[11] High though they are, fees *under*estimate foreigners' commitment to moving. Migrants along the Mexico-United States border brave a difficult trek through a hot

7. US Department of State Bureau of Consular Affairs, "DV 2013—Selected Entrants," accessed 1 May 2014, http://travel.state.gov/content/visas/english/immigrate/diversity-visa/dv2013-slected-entrants.html. The number of applicants for the Diversity Visa is misleadingly low because countries that have sent more than 50,000 immigrants to the United States in the previous five years are ineligible for the program. This rule excludes would-be immigrants from populous countries like India and China, as well as countries with strong historic ties such as the United Kingdom and Mexico.

8. See "Calculation of the Adjusted Visa Refusal Rate for Tourist and Business Travelers Under the Guidelines of the Visa Waiver Program," US State Department, http://travel.state.gov/content/dam/visas/Statistics/Non-Immigrant-Statistics/refusalratelanguage.pdf. For discussion on the challenges in the US system, specifically the doctrine of consular nonreviewability, see Dobkin (2009).

9. Jeffrey Passel, D'Vera Cohn, and Ana Gonzalez-Barrera, "Population Decline of Unauthorized Immigrants Stalls, May Have Reversed," Pew Research Hispanic Trends Project, 23 September 2013, p. 6. Available online at http://www.pewhispanic.org/2013/09/23/population-decline-of-unauthorized-immigrants-stalls-may-have-reversed/.

10. Economic Research Service/USDA (2001), "Hired Farm Labor: Comparing the U.S. and Mexico." *Agricultural Outlook*, p. 15, reports a Mexican daily wage of $3.60, about $1,000 a year for a five-day work-week.

11. Havocscope, "Prices Charged by Human Smugglers," accessed 1 May 2014, http://www.havocscope.com/black-market-prices/human-smuggling-fees/.

desert, migrants from Africa to Europe sail on rickety boats, and border-crossers to South Africa risk getting eaten by lions.[12]

Where do poor unskilled migrants find the money to pay these huge smuggling fees? Short answer: many of them don't, which is why we see much less migration than we would under open borders. Those who do manage to pay the fees rely on family savings over long time periods, help from family members already in the destination country, and loans that they pay back with higher earnings after they've successfully migrated. Due to the underground nature of the whole operation, local criminals play an important role in enforcing the repayment of loans.[13] After full deregulation, smuggling fees and the attendant dangers would all but disappear. How many people would choose to relocate? Gallup has conducted world-wide polls since 2010 asking adults whether they would move to another country immediately if allowed. Over 600 million adults—14 percent of the world adult population—wish to permanently move to another country. Over a billion want to seek temporary work abroad.[14] For comparison, 232 million people currently live outside their country of birth.[15] The United States is the first-choice destination for over 100 million adults.[16] Gallup has used these polls to estimate population gain and loss for each country if everyone migrated to their first-choice destination. The effects are huge: Haiti would lose half its population. Australia, Singapore, and New Zealand's would more than double. Even the United States, the world's third most populous country, would see population increase by 60 percent.[17]

12. See BBC News, "Italy Boat Sinking: Hundreds Feared Dead off Lampedusa," 3 October 2013 http://www.bbc.co.uk/news/world-europe-24380247 for one of many stories of refugee boats sinking and ending in tragedy. See Bob Frump, *The Man-Eaters of Eden: Life and Death in Krueger National Park* (Guilford, CT: Lyons Press, 2006), pp. 132–136, for the risks that border-crossers to South Africa face from lions.

13. Patrick Radden Keefe, *The Snakehead: An Epic Tale of the Chinatown Underworld and the American Dream*, New York: Anchor, 2010, pp. 44–46.

14. Neil Esipova and Julie Ray, "More Adults Would Move for Temporary Work Than Permanently," Gallup World, 9 March 2012 http://www.gallup.com/poll/153182/Adults-Move-Temporary-Work-Permanently.aspx.

15. Phillip Connor, D'Vera Cohn, and Ana Gonzalez-Barrera, "Changing Patterns of Global Migration and Remittances," Pew Research Center, 17 December 2013, p. 4, http://www.pewsocialtrends.org/files/2013/12/global-migration-final_12–2013.pdf.

16. John Clifton, "More Than 100 Million Worldwide Dream of a Life in the U.S.," Gallup World, 21 March 2013, http://www.gallup.com/poll/161435/100-million-worldwide-dream-life.aspx.

17. Neil Esipova, Rajesh Srinivasan, and Julie Rayand, "Potential Net Migration Could Change Countries," Gallup World, 6 November 2009, http://www.gallup.com/poll/124193/potential-net-migration-change-developed-nations.aspx and Neil Esipova, Rajesh Srinivasan, and Julie Rayand, "Potential Net Migration Index Declines in Many Countries," Gallup World, 17 January 2014, http://www.gallup.com/poll/166796/potential-net-migration-index-declines-countries.aspx.

This does not mean that 200 million immigrants would arrive tomorrow if the United States opened its border today. Migrants face a series of bottlenecks. Markets need time to respond to the vast increase in demand for transportation, housing, and jobs. The more enduring bottlenecks, though, are cultural and linguistic. Spain is a more popular migrant destination than Germany because of the global Spanish-speaking population, and Saudi Arabia is a top choice for potential migrants because of its religious importance for Muslims worldwide. Even under open borders, people rarely move to a new country *unless* that country already has a substantial "diaspora"—a subculture that shares their culture and language.

How do diasporas work?[18] Migration rates between culturally and linguistically disjoint regions start low. Over time, though, buzz builds— and migration snowballs. The first wave sends good news: "We're prospering." The second wave sends better news: "We're prospering, and we're starting to have our own community." The third wave sends better news still: "We're prospering, and our community is flourishing." When the United States opened its border with Puerto Rico in 1904, for instance, the flow was almost invisible. Between 1900 and 1910, Puerto Rico's net emigration was only two thousand souls. Yet decade by decade, Puerto Ricans kept coming—and stateside Puerto Ricans felt increasingly at home. By 2000, there were more Puerto Ricans in the United States than there were in Puerto Rico.[19]

As of 2010, 29 percent of foreign-born Americans hailed from Mexico, 24 percent from the rest of Latin America, 28 percent from Asia, 12 percent from Europe, 4 percent from Africa, 2 percent from North America, and 1 percent from elsewhere.[20] The most reasonable forecast, then, is that open borders would swiftly lead to a large increase in Latin American—and especially Mexican—immigration. Their diasporas—and families eager to help—are already here. In the medium term, we should expect the initially smaller diasporas of populous China and India to swell. Given the tiny African immigrant population, and their cultural

18. See Collier (2013), pp. 27–56, for a detailed treatment of diaspora dynamics and its implications for migration flows.

19. See Carmen Whalen, "Colonialism, Citizenship, and the Making of the Puerto Rican Diaspora: An Introduction," in Carmen Whalen and Víctor Vázquez-Hernández, eds., *The Puerto Rican Diaspora: Historical Perspectives* (Philadelphia, PA: Temple University Press, 2008), p. 2, available online at http://www.temple.edu/tempress/chapters_1400/1523_ch1.pdf.

20. See Elizabeth Grieco, Yesenia Acosta, G. Patricia de la Cruz, Christine Gambino, Thomas Gryn, Luke Larsen, Edward Trevelyan, and Nathan Walters, "The Foreign-Born Population in the United States: 2010," US Census Bureau, May 2012, p. 2, http://www.census.gov/prod/2012pubs/acs-19.pdf.

and linguistic distance from African Americans, migration from Africa's rapidly growing population will probably start out very low—but end up very high.

Until the 1920s, the United States retained nearly open borders. Few dispute that mass migration played a key role in America's nineteenth-century economic miracle. Some even argue that near-free migration outweighed, and thus masked, the negative effects of late nineteenth-century trade restrictions.[21] Synergies continued in the early twentieth century: mass manufacturing industries, such as Detroit's auto industry, benefited from a large and mobile population, including many recent migrants and children of migrants.[22]

Still, by modern standards, migration during the open borders era remained moderate. The peak foreign-born proportion in 1910 was 15 percent, comparable to 13 percent today.[23] If the American border were reopened, we should expect larger, faster changes—diaspora dynamics notwithstanding. Transportation is far cheaper and safer, making long-distance migration practical for the poorest and most remote populations. Communication is vastly better, allowing migrants to keep in touch with friends and family—and word of opportunities to spread far and wide. Culture has globalized. Hundreds of millions of prospective migrants are "pre-assimilated"—fluent in English and avid consumers of American periodicals, television, and movies. The bottom line is that open borders could easily double the US population in a matter of decades.

3   HOW OPEN BORDERS WOULD CHANGE THE WORLD

For all its radicalism, open borders' main effects are fairly well understood. Open borders would dramatically increase global production. It would drastically reduce global poverty and global inequality. At the same time, open borders would make the remaining poverty and inequality much more visible for current residents of the First World. On other

21. See Cecil Bohanon and T. Norman Van Cott, "Tariffs, Immigration, and Economic Insulation: A New View of the U.S. Post-Civil War Era," *Independent Review* 9(2005): 529–542, available at http://www.independent.org/pdf/tir/tir_09_4_4_bohanon.pdf.

22. See Southeast Michigan Council of Governments (2002), "Historical Population and Employment by Minor Civil Division, Southeast Michigan," http://library.semcog.org/InmagicGenie/DocumentFolder/HistoricalPopulationSEMI.pdf.

23. See Grieco et al. (2012), and "Table 1: Nativity of the Population and Place of Birth of the Native Population: 1850–1990," US Census Bureau, 9 May 1999, https://www.census.gov/population/www/documentation/twps0029/tab01.html.

important dimensions—especially budgets, politics, and crime—we should expect no more than moderate changes for good or ill. Let us consider each effect in turn.

3.1   Effect on Global Production

Why does the average American earn so much more than the average Nigerian? Part of the reason is that the average American worker has better skills. The rest of the reason, though, is that the American economy makes *better use* of whatever skills a worker happens to have. Researchers who disentangle these two effects find that the latter accounts for almost all of the global pay gap: being *in* America is much more important than *being* American. Moving unskilled workers from Mexico to the United States raises their pay by about 150 percent. Moving unskilled workers from Nigeria to the United States raises their pay by over 1,000 percent.[24] The productivity gain is most visible in agriculture or manufacturing: an unskilled Mexican farmer grows far more food in America than in Mexico. But the gain is equally real in services. A Mexican barber produces more economic value in America because affluent Americans are willing to pay much more for haircuts than poor Mexicans.

Once you grasp the massive effect of location on worker productivity, the economic case for open borders swiftly follows. Global living standards depend on global production. Immigration restrictions trap labor in unproductive locations, stunting output. Open borders, in contrast, let everyone on earth move wherever their labor is most productive. Making Nigerians stay in Nigeria is as economically senseless as making farmers plant in Antarctica.

Open borders will thus grow the world economy. By how much? The most serious review of the academic evidence concludes that unrestricted migration would roughly *double* global GDP, with estimates of the gain ranging from +67 percent to +147 percent.[25] In other words, existing regulations stunt the world's output at roughly *half* its free-migration level. These magnitudes are staggering, but hardly surprising. Labor is the world's most valuable commodity—yet thanks to strict immigration regulation, most of it goes to waste.

24. Clemens, Montenegro, and Pritchett (2008) introduce the concept and estimate the value of the "place premium" to quantify the effect of location on worker productivity and earnings. For place premium estimates, see p. 11.
25. Clemens (2011).

What would this wealth explosion look like? Destination countries for migrants would experience frenetic economic growth—a First World version of the sustained booms that China and India enjoyed in recent decades. Hundreds of millions of Chinese and Indians have already moved in response to rising urban wages. China's urbanization rate rose from 18 percent in 1976 to 52 percent today. Massive migration has turned villages into towns and towns into megacities. By 2025, China will have a *billion* people living in cities, with 23 cities of over five million and 221 cities of over one million (compared to 35 such cities in Europe).[26] India's 2001 census estimated that 191 million people—19 percent of the country—were long-distance internal migrants.[27] India's urban population will soar from 340 million in 2008 to 590 million in 2030.[28]

The flip side is that origin countries will swiftly depopulate. Over a generation or two, poor countries could easily lose half their people—and more than half of their most skilled and ambitious workers. But this is no more tragic than poor villagers exiting the backwaters of China and India. Development is ultimately about people, not places.[29]

And non-migrants benefit, too. Remittances—which already far exceed the flow of foreign aid—start coming home almost immediately.[30] Before long, successful immigrants start using their newfound business connections to develop their mother countries.[31] Puerto Rico provides an excellent illustration. Over half of Puerto Ricans live abroad, but Puerto Ricans who stayed behind now enjoy a First World standard of living.[32]

26. Jonathan Woetzel, Lenny Mendonca, Janamitra Devan, Stefano Negri, Yangmei Hu, Luke Jordan, Xiujun Li, Alexander Maasry, Geoff Tsen, and Flora Yu, "Preparing for China's Urban Billion," McKinsey Global Institute, March 2009, http://www.mckinsey.com/insights/urbanization/preparing_for_urban_billion_in_china.

27. See Rameez Abbas and Divya Varma, "Internal Labor Migration in India Raises Integration Challenges for Migrants," Migration Policy Institute, 3 March 2014, http://www.migrationpolicy.org/article/internal-labor-migration-india-raises-integration-challenges-migrants.

28. Shirish Sankhe, Ireena Vittal, Richard Dobbs, Ajit Mohan, Ankur Gulati, Jonathan Ablett, Shishir Gupta, Alex Kim, Sudipto Paul, Aditya Sanghvi, and Gurpreet Sethy, "India's Urban Awakening: Building Inclusive Cities, Sustaining Economic Growth," McKinsey Global Institute, April 2010, http://www.mckinsey.com/insights/urbanization/urban_awakening_in_india.

29. We owe this adage to Michael Clemens.

30. See Dean Yang, "Migrant Remittances," *Journal of Economic Perspectives* (2011): 129–152.

31. Guest (2011) includes many examples of such businesses.

32. The World Bank, http://data.worldbank.org/indicator/NY.GDP.PCAP.CD/countries/PR?display=graph, estimates the nominal GDP per capita in Puerto Rico at $27,000, comparable to Spain. Note that the case of Puerto Rico is somewhat unusual in that Puerto Rico not only got open borders with the mainland United States but was also governed by US institutions.

In the short run, open borders would massively reduce the capital/labor ratio in destination countries, and raise it in origin countries. The First World would see a large expansion in the low-skilled service sector, including childcare, cleaning, and driving, and a switch to more labor-intensive farming and construction. The United States could also easily become a hub for the sort of labor-intensive manufacturing currently done in China, with natives taking on higher-paying supervisory roles.

Over the long run, as usual, we should expect capital accumulation to rise with labor supply.[33] How long would workers have to wait for "the long run" to arrive? The Israeli experience is instructive despite its peculiarities. The Law of Return, valid since 1950, grants every Jew the right to settle in Israel.[34] Israel's 1989 population was 4.6 million. Between 1990 and 1997, 700,000 immigrants from the Soviet Union showed up—about half during a two-year period. In the short run, this seemed to depress native wages about 5 percent. Yet by 1997, native wages were back at their expected pre-immigration level.[35]

How will the oversize fruits of open borders be distributed? Researchers often focus on the change in the capital/labor ratio, and conclude that open borders enrich First World capital and Third World labor at the expense of Third World capital and First World labor. Estimates of the size of the effect on First World labor are small; according to Kerr and Kerr's state-of-the-art literature survey, a 10 percentage-point increase in the immigrant share of the labor force reduces native wages by a mere 1 percent.[36] Furthermore, the net effect for First World workers is unclear because labor is not their only asset. Immigration sharply increases real estate prices, so any home-owning worker would enjoy a massive capital gain.[37] Furthermore, every worker with a retirement fund is, in part, a capitalist.

More sophisticated analysts point out that immigration can raise First World wages, too. In the real world, there are many distinct kinds of labor. Native workers suffer when immigrants have *competing* skills, but gain when immigrants have *complementary* skills. This chapter's authors, for

33. See Barro and Sala-i-Martin (2003).

34. "Law of Return 5710–1950," Israel Ministry of Foreign Affairs, http://www.mfa.gov.il/MFA/MFA-Archive/1950–1959/Pages/Law%20of%20Return%205710–1950.aspx.

35. See Legrain (2007), pp. 133–135.

36. From Kerr and Kerr (2011), p. 14.

37. In the United States, housing prices and rents rise by roughly 1 percent when immigration raises a city's population by 1 percent (Saiz 2007, 2003). Gonzalez and Ortega (2009) find an even larger effect for Spain. The US home-ownership rate is about 66 percent, so the benefits of appreciation would be widely dispersed.

example, are both PhDs. When foreign PhDs enter the US labor market, we suffer. The immigration of waiters, in contrast, enriches us. We are waiters' *customers*, not their competitors.

Under open borders, immigrant and native skill sets will drastically diverge. Compared to natives, most prospective immigrants are very poorly educated. Rather than losing their jobs to immigrants, natives will likely become their supervisors and managers. Between 1980 and 2000, US immigrants tended to be either low-skilled or high-skilled. Even relatively pessimistic economists confirm the expected result: immigration hurt low-skilled and high-skilled natives, but raised wages for *mid*-skilled natives.[38] Other observers note that formal education is a crude measure of skill. Most obviously, natives speak better English than equally educated foreigners. Accounting for these subtleties, recent immigration seems to slightly *raise* average natives' wages.[39] Some development economists worry that liberalizing migration retards the Third World's economic growth and political reform by siphoning off their best and brightest citizens. But this "brain drain" is largely an artifact of current skill-based immigration policies. Under open borders, ditch diggers are as free to migrate as computer programmers. Even under the status quo, though, so-called brain drain has offsetting benefits for those left behind. Skilled immigrants often return with valuable skills, investment capital, and business connections. Furthermore, opportunities for high-skilled emigration spur skill acquisition. Empirically, such incentives look strong enough to make the average *non*-migrant more skillful.[40]

Migration doesn't just make migrants more productive; it makes them more *innovative*. Silicon Valley is a breeding ground for world-changing technology. If Silicon Valley's immigrants had stayed home, it is hard to see how they could have created more than a fraction of what they did in the United States.[41] Since new ideas anywhere now rapidly help people everywhere, moving the best and brightest to centers of global innovation indirectly enriches source countries, too. Analyses of innovation in the nineteenth-century United States paint similar conclusions.[42]

38. See Borjas and Katz (2005).
39. Ottaviano and Peri (2012).
40. See Docquier and Rapoport (2012).
41. See, for instance, Saxenian (1999) and Catherine Rampell, "Immigration and Entrepreneurship," *New York Times* Economix Blog, 1 July 2013, http://economix. blogs.nytimes.com/2013/07/01/immigration-and-entrepreneurship/.
42. See Khan and Sokoloff (1993).

3.2   Effect on Global Poverty and Inequality

Rural-to-urban migration *within* China, India, and other low-income countries has not just been a key pillar of expanding per-capita output. Migration-fueled growth has also sharply reduced global poverty and global inequality. Sala-i-Martin (2006) uses international data to construct the World Income Distribution for 1970–2000.[43] During this period, the share of the world living in poverty drastically fell. Raising the poverty line naturally raises measured poverty, but the fact of decline is robust.[44] Subsequent research confirms that these beneficent trends are continuing.[45] Open borders could well cast the decisive blow against human poverty, even if the estimate of the impact of open borders on global production is significantly overstated.[46]

Migration-fueled economic growth around the world has also steadily reduced global inequality. In 1970–2000, the World Income Distribution became more equal by eight distinct metrics.[47] How is this possible given the sharp rise in inequality within countries? Simple: in the modern world, about two-thirds of global inequality reflects inequality *between* countries rather within them.[48]

Economically speaking, open borders are familiar rural-to-urban migration writ large. When poor people relocate from low-productivity to high-productivity areas, they simultaneously enrich the world, escape poverty, and equalize the income distribution. The key difference: open borders will lead to larger, quicker progress than traditional rural-to-urban migration because international gaps dwarf *intra*national gaps. Due to diaspora dynamics, we should not expect international inequality to vanish overnight. But given the enormity of the wage gains that migrants experience, progress will start strong and steadily accelerate.

3.3   Effect on the Visibility of Poverty and Inequality

Migrating to a rich country is a great way to escape absolute poverty. When low-skilled immigrants arrive, however, most will remain *relatively*

43. Sala-i-Martin (2006).

44. Sala-i-Martin (2006), pp. 372–375.

45. Chandy and Gertz (2011), pp. 3–4.

46. See Carl Shulman, "How Migration Liberalization Might Eliminate Most Absolute Poverty," 27 May 2014, http://reflectivedisequilibrium.blogspot.com/2014/05/how-migration-liberalization-might.html.

47. Sala-i-Martin (2006), pp. 383–386.

48. For further discussion, see Milanovic (2012a, 2012b).

poor by the standards of their new country. Given expected flows, most natives will soon encounter relatively poor foreigners on a daily basis.[49]

The visibility of poverty and inequality is likely to be unsettling, particularly if government policies restrict newly arrived migrants' access to the welfare state. The shift to labor-intensive occupations will make developed countries look more primitive. Shantytowns may emerge. Some natives will react by helping migrants learn the language, find jobs, and adjust to their new societies. Others will resent new arrivals and pine for the good old days when low-skilled immigration was but a trickle. Before long, however, most natives will, like the Third World middle class, simply learn to tolerate the sight of poverty and inequality. From immigrants' point of view, callous natives are preferable to narcissistic altruists who minimize their feelings of pity by keeping poor foreigners out of the country.

3.4   Effect on the Budget

Immigration's fiscal effects are uncertain in sign, moderate in size, and small compared to the economic effects.[50] Overall, the net fiscal gain from migration is near zero for OECD countries, with estimates ranging from modestly negative to modestly positive. Adult immigrants are normally educated at their home country's expense, making them a prima facie good deal for receiving countries. The foreign born typically use more welfare. At least in the United States, however, the foreign-born *poor* use less welfare than the native poor. This is partly due to restrictions on welfare

---

49. Wilkinson (2009) critiques a passage making the argument that immigration increases poverty and inequality by writing: "This is a sadly typical example of the distortions of analytical nationalism. If we were to assume a natural and mundane moral perspective, from which all people involved are taken into account and assumed to have equal worth—that is, if we assume the perspective of moral egalitarianism—what we would see is a profound reduction in both poverty and economic inequality. If the question is 'What happened to the people in this scenario?' then the answer is 'The poorest people became considerably wealthier, narrowing the economic gap between them and the rest.' But what actually happened seems either invisible or irrelevant to the authors, which certainly suggests that their analytical framework leaves something to be desired. Here's how the passage I highlighted might be more accurately stated: Immigration decreased inequality both directly, by sharply increasing the wages of low-skilled, foreign-born workers, and indirectly, through remittance payments to low-income relatives at the immigrants' places of origin. Due to the widespread opposition of American voters to liberalizing immigration, very large additional reductions in poverty and inequality have been forgone."

50. See Kerr and Kerr (2011), pp. 15–21.

eligibility for migrants, suggesting that further tightening would make migration a clear fiscal plus.[51] Can we generalize from the present to the world of open borders? The main concern: net fiscal effects vary widely by skill. For the United States, Storesletten (2000) calculates a $96,000 net fiscal benefit for highly educated immigrants and a $36,000 net fiscal cost for uneducated immigrants, versus a net cost of $80,000 for the typical native. However, these estimates seem pessimistic across the board; Wolf et al. (2011) find that the average newborn American native has a net fiscal *benefit* of $83,000. On balance, there is no solid reason to expect the average immigrant under open borders to be a fiscal drain. However, since immigration will sharply increase, the *total* fiscal effect could end up being highly positive or highly negative.

3.5   Effect on Crime

Empirical work on migration and crime focuses on receiving countries. The big result: open borders may well *decrease* crime rates in many receiving countries, and is at any rate unlikely to cause crime rates to rise sharply. In the United States, the foreign born have *one-fifth* the native incarceration rate.[52] This is not just a reflection of American criminality. Japan has one of the lowest crime rates in the world, but its immigrants are even more law-abiding than the rest of the population.[53] While many blame South Africa's crime woes on the end of apartheid's internal migration restrictions, the evidence suggests otherwise. Its homicide rate, though high, has dropped steadily post-1994.[54]

What about crime in *sending* countries? Open borders are a powerful lifeline for the potential victims of genocide, ethnic cleansing, and other war crimes. Imagine how many victims of the Holocaust would have survived if the United States had open borders during the 1930s. Safety, like

---

51. See Ku and Bruen (2013).

52. Butcher and Piehl (2007). See also Rubén Rumbaut, Roberto Gonzales, Golnaz Komaie, and Charlie Morgan, "Debunking the Myth of Immigrant Criminality: Imprisonment among First- and Second-Generation Young Men," 1 June 2006, http://www.migrationinformation.org/usfocus/display.cfm?ID=403, which shows lower foreign-born incarceration rates in total, within each ethnicity, and for every combination of ethnicity and high school graduation status.

53. Maciamo, "Foreign Criminality in Japan," Wa-pedia, 15 June 2004, http://www.wa-pedia.com/gaijin/foreign_crime_in_japan.shtml.

54. See United Nations Office on Drugs and Crime (2011), "Global Study on Homicide," p. 45. http://www.unodc.org/documents/data-and-analysis/statistics/Homicide/Globa_study_on_homicide_2011_web.pdf.

development, is ultimately about people, not places. Rising per-capita income also gives potential criminals more to lose. Research is scarce, but there are good reasons to expect migration to reduce non-migrants' victimization risk.

3.6 Effect on Politics

Under democracy, the quality of policy depends on the quality of the electorate. Wise voting leads to good policies, foolish voting to bad policies.[55] In absolute terms, most voters look quite foolish. They're not just poorly informed; they're predictably irrational.[56] It is possible, however, that native voters are bad, but immigrant voters are even worse. Critics who raise this concern usually equate free-market policies with wisdom, and worry about foreigners' anti-market perspective. The US-based General Social Survey (GSS), inaugurated in 1972 and still running, is probably the single best source of information on these matters. What does it tell us?

By most measures, foreigners are indeed more anti-market than native-born Americans.[57] Yet the *size* of the foreign-native gap is moderate. The foreign born are 0.11 standard deviations more liberal than natives.[58] The GSS asks, "If the government had a choice between reducing taxes or spending more on social programs like health care, social security, and unemployment benefits, which do you think it should do?" The foreign-born are 8 percentage points more likely to say "spend more on social programs."[59] The GSS also features nine questions asking, "On the whole, do you think it should or should not be the government's responsibility to . . ." regulate and redistribute in various ways.[60] Overall, the foreign born are 0.35 standard deviations more favorable toward big government. Yet there is one major issue where the foreign born are 0.76 standard deviations *more* opposed to government regulation: immigration itself.[61]

55. In economic jargon, voting has "political externalities." For an extended discussion, see "Political Externalities," Open Borders: The Case, http://openborders.info/political-externalities.
56. See Caplan (2007) and Somin (2013).
57. Pashler (2013).
58. GSS variable identifiers POLVIEWS and BORN.
59. GSS variable identifier TAXSPEND.
60. GSS variable identifiers JOBSALL, PRICECON, HLTHCARE, AIDOL. AIDINDUS, AIDUNEMP, EQUALIZE, AIDCOL, and AIDHOUSE. We summed responses to all eight variables to get an index of economic liberalism.
61. GSS variable identifier LETIN1.

Foreigners tend to combine their economic liberalism with social conservatism. The GSS features five questions about free speech for unpopular minorities.[62] Overall, the foreign born are 0.19 standard deviations less supportive of free speech. Less-educated foreigners—like less-educated natives—are especially authoritarian. Foreign-born high school dropouts are 0.81 standard deviations more in favor of regulation and redistribution, and 0.59 standard deviations less supportive of free speech.

On reflection, though, raw public opinion data make immigration look a lot more politically dangerous than it really is. Open borders give everyone the right to live and work where he likes, sharply reducing the incentive to become a citizen. Legal US residents have to wait five years before they can even *apply* for citizenship.[63] When immigrants finally gain the right to vote, they often fail to show up: migrants and their descendants have lower voter turnout than natives.[64] The worryingly authoritarian less-educated foreigners are especially abstentious. In the 2008 presidential election, for example, only 25 percent of eligible foreign-born high school dropouts chose to vote.[65] Emerging evidence in political science suggests, moreover, that low-income citizens have little political influence anyway. When high- and low-income Americans disagree, politicians cater to high-income preferences.[66]

Finally, a large literature finds that the very presence of immigrants sours *natives* on the welfare state.[67] Voters are happy to support generous government benefits for their own kind, but not outsiders. Indeed,

62. GSS variable identifiers SPKATH, SPKRAC, SPKCOM, SPKMIL, and SPKHOMO. We summed responses to all five variables to get an index of social liberalism. The GSS also features a sixth free speech question, SPKSOC, but the years in which it was asked (1972–1974) do not overlap with the other free speech questions.

63. US Citizenship and Immigration Services, "Citizenship Through Naturalization," accessed 1 May 2014, http://www.uscis.gov/us-citizenship/citizenship-through-naturalization. Spouses of US citizens must wait three years to apply.

64. Caplan (2012: 13) writes: "[I]mmigrants and their descendants have lower voter turnout than natives (Xu 2005; Cassel 2002). Looking at 2000 data, Citrin and Highton (2002: 16) found that Hispanics were 26 percent of California's adult population, 18 percent of its citizen population, and only 14 percent of its voting population. For the United States as a whole, Hispanics were 5 percent of the adult population, 3 percent of its citizen population, and just 2 percent of its voting population. Roughly the same pattern holds for Asians. Citrin and Highton (2002: 67–74) project that in 2040, whites will be just over a third of California's population but remain 53 percent of its voters. Nonlibertarians often treat immigrants' low turnout as yet another strike against them. But if you fear political externalities, immigrants' political apathy is a blessing in disguise."

65. GSS variable identifier VOTE08.

66. See especially Gilens (2012).

67. See the literature review in Gochenour and Nowrasteh (2014).

the ethnic diversity of the United States is a standard explanation for its relatively small welfare state.[68] The *net* political effect of immigration is therefore unclear. When social scientists directly measure the effect of immigration on the size of government, most detect little effect.[69] A particularly thorough recent study finds that immigration fails to noticeably change US states' spending on TANF/AFDC, education, or health.[70]

4   OPEN BORDERS: A CASE OF MORAL CONSILIENCE

Predictions about the effects of open borders are far from certain. No major country has experienced anything close to open borders for almost a century, making extrapolation difficult. One effect, however, is clear: open borders will drastically increase global production. This transformation of the world economy makes other large changes highly likely: sharp reductions in global poverty and inequality, combined with greater visibility of the poverty and inequality that remain. The effects on other dimensions—budgets, crime, and politics—are less clear, but standard estimates of the global effects range from mildly negative to mildly positive. Even if you take strong issue with some of our empirics, the overall conclusion that open borders would be a boon to the world is hard to dispute.

Does this mean that countries are *morally obliged* to open their borders? In this section, we argue that every prominent moral view yields the same answer: yes. Utilitarianism, efficiency, egalitarianism, human capabilities, libertarianism, meritocracy, and Christianity all recommend open borders.[71] For moral theories like libertarianism that prioritize individual rights, the recommendation is clear-cut. For more pragmatic theories, the enormous—and pro-poor—economic gains are almost equally decisive. Doubling GDP can outweigh a lot of sins. Indeed, even moral theories like citizenism that place little or no weight on foreigners' well-being endorse open borders when packaged with pro-native taxes and transfers.

---

68. See especially Alesina, Glaeser, and Sacerdote (2001) and Gilens (1999).
69. See the literature review in Gochenour and Nowrasteh (2014).
70. See Gochenour and Nowrasteh (2014).
71. See also Carens (2013) and "Economic and Moral Factors in Favor of Open Immigration" by Alex Tabarrok, The Independent Institute, 2000, http://www.independent.org/issues/article.asp?id=486.

4.1 The Utilitarian Case for Open Borders

The utilitarian case for open borders is straightforward: open borders swiftly and reliably enrich mankind, especially the global poor. Instead of relying on often corrupt government-to-government transfers, open borders allow everyone on earth to enrich themselves by heading wherever their talents are most valuable. As long as the rise in global GDP exceeds 50 percent, it is hard to see any offsetting harms in the same ballpark. Even in an unlikely scenario where open borders *destroy* First World welfare states, the benefits for hundreds of millions of absolutely poor foreigners clearly outweigh the costs for tens of millions of relatively poor natives.

4.2 The Efficiency Case for Open Borders

Economic efficiency measures costs and benefits purely by willingness to pay.[72] When is relocation efficiency-enhancing? Whenever it raises a worker's productivity by more than the material and psychological cost of moving. The whole point of immigration restrictions, though, is to ban immigration that *passes* this efficiency test. Unlike utilitarianism, economic efficiency counts the preferences of the rich and poor equally; an extra dollar in Haitian hands counts no more than an extra dollar in American hands. The apostle of economic efficiency will therefore disregard the pro-poor distributional effects of free migration, and treat the extra visibility of poverty as a serious cost. Still, given the huge effect on global output, the efficiency case for open borders is solid.

4.3 The Egalitarian Case for Open Borders

Migration restrictions drastically and deliberately reduce equality of both opportunity and result. The effect on equality of opportunity is almost definitional. Laws exclude the global poor from the best labor markets because they proverbially "chose the wrong parents." The effect on equality of result is more empirical, but almost as clear. To repeat: in the modern world, country of origin accounts for about two-thirds of all income inequality.[73] Without immigration laws, unskilled labor in the Third World

72. Landsburg (2012), pp. 73–87.
73. See Milanovic (2012a).

could not durably earn a fifth or a tenth as much as unskilled labor in the First World. Even if open borders miraculously toppled First World welfare systems, the genuine egalitarian should focus on the shrinking gap between absolutely rich natives and absolutely poor foreigners, not the growing gap between the world's absolutely rich natives and relatively poor natives. The Rawlsian ethical framework, which accepts inequality if and only if it benefits the "worst-off group," also implies support for open borders.[74] While egalitarians who take "brain drain" seriously could condemn First World countries for poaching the Third World's best and brightest, open borders largely dissolve such complaints by making illiterates as free to migrate as Nobel laureates. It's not surprising that many egalitarian-minded philosophers who have given consideration to the questions surrounding open borders have come to support open borders.[75]

4.4 The Human Capabilities Case for Open Borders

The human capabilities approach pioneered by Martha Nussbaum and Amartya Sen stresses that all individuals should have realistic opportunities to fulfill their potential.[76] Closed borders willfully deletes the global poor's best options for escaping poverty and living fulfilling lives. Even the well-to-do may be unable to reach their full potential because border restrictions prevent them from moving to a dream job or uniting their extended family. Supporters of the human capabilities approach unsurprisingly argue for fewer migration restrictions.[77]

4.5 The Libertarian Case for Open Borders

The absolutist libertarian case for open borders is clear-cut: Immigration restrictions impermissibly restrict capitalist acts between consenting

74. See Nathan Smith, "Rawls' Highly Unpersuasive Attempt to Evade the Open Borders Ramifications of his Own Theory," Open Borders: The Case, 28 January 2013, http://openborders.info/blog/rawls-highly-unpersuasive-attempt-to-evade-the-open-borders-ramifications-of-his-own-theory/ on why Rawlsianism requires open borders.

75. See Veit Bader, "The Ethics of Immigration," *Constellations* 12, no. 3 (2005), http://dare.uva.nl/document/50299?origin=publication_detail.

76. Amartya Sen, "Human Rights and Capabilities," *Journal of Human Development* 6(2005): 151–166; Martha Nussbaum, *Women and Human Development: The Capabilities Approach* (Cambridge: Cambridge University Press, 2001).

77. See Risse (2009).

adults. Neither government nor "society" has any right to prevent employers, landlords, or merchants from trading with foreigners. All analysis of immigration's social effects is beside the point. Proponents of a wide range of libertarian and freedom-oriented ideologies, including Ayn Rand and Murray Rothbard, have made principled arguments for open borders along these lines.[78]

What about the more moderate view that we should adhere to libertarian principles unless doing so is awful for human well-being? This, too, leads to staunch support for open borders. Empirically, open borders look like a great deal for the world, so there is no rights-utility trade-off to resolve.[79] Unlike the utilitarian, though, the moderate libertarian has to support free migration even if its vast benefits turn out to be entirely illusory. As long as the aggregate effects of open borders are better than awful, the libertarian cannot in good conscience compromise the fundamental human right to accept a job offer from a willing employer. Even if immigration predictably led to a large expansion of the welfare state, the moderate libertarian would have to weigh freedom from taxation against freedom of movement and trade. For the moderate libertarian, excluding foreigners who *might* vote for statist policies is less justified than exiling natives who *do* vote for statist policies.

4.6   The Meritocratic Case for Open Borders

Free labor markets do not guarantee that the best workers will receive the best jobs and pay. But immigration restrictions are consciously designed to protect native workers from more qualified and motivated foreigners. Meritocratic norms say, "Hire the best *person*." Immigration laws say, "No,

---

78. On Rand, see e.g. Robert Mayhew, ed., *Ayn Rand Answers: The Best of Her Q & A* (New York: Penguin Books, 2005), p. 25. In *Radicals for Capitalism*, Brian Doherty documents Rothbard's early support for free migration. During the 1950s, Rothbard broke ranks with the then nascent right in the United States led by Buckley, partly over their lack of support for free immigration (p. 258). In the 1970s, he attacked the recently formed Libertarian Party for conditioning support for free immigration on the prior dismantling of the welfare state (p. 417). Rothbard changed his mind on free migration shortly before his death. See "Nations by Consent: Decomposing the Nation-State" for the *Journal of Libertarian Studies* 11, no. 1 (Fall 1994), available online at http://www.mises.org/journals/jls/11_1/11_1_1.pdf.

79. Huemer (2010) expands on this style of argument: he starts with the libertarian presumption against coercion, notes that migration restrictions are imposed coercively, then finds that the arguments offered for migration restrictions fail to overcome the presumption. Caplan (2012) follows a similar approach, but is more focused on the empirical evidence than on the moral considerations.

you are only free to hire the best *citizen.*" The status quo does not merely allow discrimination on the basis of nationality; it mandates such discrimination. Anyone who accepts merit as a moral imperative or discrimination as a grave evil should be strongly predisposed to open borders.

Meritocratic critics of immigration occasionally argue that the impoverished inhabitants of the Third World morally deserve their fate. Their suffering is fitting punishment for creating such dysfunctional societies. But what precisely should the typical low-skilled Third World worker have done differently? One vote is astronomically unlikely to change policy even in clean democracies, much less the corrupt democracies and dictatorships that most of the Third World endures. And how can we condemn a semi-literate worker for failing to fix his polity when the world's brightest minds are at a loss for answers? You could blame the ignorant voter for failing to abstain, but lifelong, hereditary exclusion from the world's best labor markets seems a draconian punishment for voting the wrong way.[80] In any case, contrary to all meritocratic principles, immigration laws punish *indiscriminately.* Residents of the Third World face lifelong, hereditary exclusion, no matter how they vote.

4.7 The Christian Case for Open Borders

The New Testament and broader Christian tradition are a natural fit with open borders.[81] Both emphasize our common humanity and preach strong obligations to welcome and support to the needy. Consider, "I was a stranger and you took me in" (Matthew 25:35); "There is neither Jew nor Greek, slave nor free, male nor female, for you are all one in Christ Jesus" (Galatians 3:28); and "When you give a banquet, invite the poor, the crippled, the lame, the blind, and you will be blessed. Although they cannot repay you, you will be repaid at the resurrection of the righteous" (Luke 14:12–14). Even the Old Testament repeatedly urges just treatment of foreigners: "Do not mistreat or oppress a foreigner, for you were foreigners in Egypt" (Exodus 22:21); and "You must have the same regulations for both the foreigner and the native-born" (Numbers 9:14). An open borders policy is not charity. But even if it were, Christians seem obliged to support it.

---

80. Brennan (2011) plausibly argues that poorly informed voters are morally obliged *not* to vote.

81. For an extended discussion, see "Christian View of Immigration," Open Borders: The Case, http://openborders.info/christian-views-of-immigration/.

4.8   The Citizenist Case for Open Borders

Many proponents of immigration restrictions argue that immigration policy should put little weight on the welfare of foreigners. Instead, they accept what Steve Sailer calls "citizenism": governments should focus on promoting the interests of current citizens and their descendants.[82] This moral position has been embraced by a wide range of critics of open borders, including Center for Immigration Studies director Mark Krikorian, *National Review*'s Reihan Salam, and Demos director David Goodhart.

Citizenists often grant the utilitarian case for open borders, then insist that almost all of the economic benefits go to foreigners. Facts aside, their reaction is deeply uncreative. A thoughtful citizenist should not say, "Open borders would make foreigners trillions of dollars richer. So what?" Instead, he should say, "Trillions of dollars of wealth are on the table. How can my countrymen get a hefty piece of the action?" Modern governments routinely use taxes and transfers to redistribute from young to old and rich to poor. Why not use the same policy tools to redistribute from foreign to native? Charge immigrants extra taxes. Further restrict their access to government benefits. Then use the proceeds to cut taxes and increase benefits for natives. What could be simpler? From a citizenist point of view, such policies are perfectly "fair"; government is *supposed* to discriminate on natives' behalf. Less parochial moral philosophies could protest the unfairness, but they should concede that open borders, tempered by pro-native redistribution, are far *less unfair* to foreigners than the status quo.

5   RESPONSES TO OBJECTIONS

Open borders speak to every major moral outlook. Given the evidence, you would expect the approach to enjoy widespread support. Yet in practice, support for open borders is rare. The World Values Survey asked the people of 48 nations their views on migration. In most countries surveyed, under 10 percent said, "Let anyone come."[83] Why is the concept of open borders so unpopular?

82. Steve Sailer, "Americans First," *The American Conservative*, 13 February 2006, http://www.theamericanconservative.com/article/2006/feb/13/00012/ is his most definitive article on citizenism. For further discussion, see "Citizenism," Open Borders: The Case, http://openborders.info/citizenism.

83. For details on the World Values Survey migration results, see Nathan Smith, "Who Favors Open Borders?" Open Borders: The Case, 3 December 2012, http://openborders.info/blog/who-favors-open-borders.

Most of the opposition, in our view, reflects unthinking xenophobia. Nevertheless, the majority of people the authors consider reasonable have yet to embrace open borders. Every major moral viewpoint implies open borders *given our empirical claims*, so we suspect that reasonable skeptics find our empirics unsatisfactory. In this section, we try to identify and answer their overarching complaints.

5.1   Open Borders Are Far Out of Sample

All of our claims about the effects of open borders rely on (a) experience with open borders in the distant past, or (b) experience with *relatively* high immigration in the recent past. Both forms of evidence are problematic. Transportation and communication have drastically improved over the past century, so open borders today could be very different from open borders a century ago. Social changes often have nonlinear effects, so open borders could be bad even though moderate immigration is good.

This critique has a kernel of truth: each of our forecasts should have wide confidence intervals. For any given outcome, the true effect of open borders is likely to be far above or below its expected value. To estimate those expected values, however, we *must* rely on past experience. We can acknowledge wide confidence intervals, yet still safely predict that open borders will be better than the status quo, as long as *some* key expected values are enormously favorable, and the rest are ambiguous.

This is precisely what the evidence shows. The expected impacts on global production, poverty, and inequality are enormously favorable. The expected impacts on the budget, crime, and politics are ambiguous. Should *all* of these estimates prove too sanguine, though, open borders likely remain a good deal. Suppose standard estimates of the effect of open borders on global output, poverty, and inequality are overstated by a factor of five. In absolute terms, that is still a present discounted value of tens of trillions of dollars. To offset a gain of this scale, the combined budgetary, crime, and political effects of open borders would have to be horrific.

5.2   I'm Still Really Worried about X

While research on open borders is growing, many important facets remain unexplored. Research on political ramifications is especially underdeveloped. As a result, a fair-minded reader might harbor serious concerns about some of the effects of open borders.

Part of our answer, again, is that the estimated benefits of open borders on production, poverty, and inequality are so enormous that they provide a large margin of error. But we can do better than this. Let us concede for the sake of argument that—holding all other policies fixed—open borders would impoverish low-skilled natives, sharply raise crime rates, break the budget, destroy the welfare state, or unleash populist policies. Migration restrictions would remain a needlessly cruel and costly way to handle the critics' concern. Why? Because each of these problems has a "keyhole solution"—a remedy tailored to handle the alleged problem while leaving the world's borders open to peaceful migration. As Tim Harford explains:

> Keyhole surgery techniques allow surgeons to operate without making large incisions, minimizing the risk of complications and side effects. Economists often advocate a similar strategy when trying to fix a policy problem: target the problem as closely as possible rather than attempting something a little more drastic.[84]

Instead of rejecting open borders, then, critics should embrace a package of open borders combined with other policy reforms.[85] Suppose you think that open borders would be awful for low-skilled natives. Once you grant immigration's overall economic benefits, the logical solution is not exclusion, but redistribution. Government could impose immigrant entry fees and surtaxes, then use the proceeds to compensate native workers with a monthly check, a lower marginal tax rate, a payroll tax exemption, or a bigger Earned Income Tax Credit. Analogous policies could be used to deter crime; immigrants could post a "crime bond" when they enter the country, knowing that they forfeit the bond if convicted of an offense.

If you fear immigrants' fiscal effect, the natural solution is, in the words of Alex Nowrasteh and Sophie Cole (2013), to "build a wall around the welfare state, instead of the country." In short, selective austerity. Government could give immigrants reduced benefits, make them ineligible for specific programs, or exclude them entirely. This selective austerity could last for a decade; it could stand until the immigrant pays $100,000 in taxes; it could be lifelong. The fiscal burden of immigration is not a law of nature. It the result of deliberate—and malleable—policy. By keeping fiscal burdens under control, and giving natives preferential access, selective austerity also helps preserve the welfare state as we know it. Current

---

84. Harford (2007), p. 123.
85. For further discussion, see Caplan (2012), and "Keyhole Solutions," Open Borders: The Case, http://openborders.info/keyhole-solutions.

beneficiaries don't have to worry about being crowded out, and voters won't be alienated by the thought that out-groups are feeding off their generosity.

Controlling the political effects of immigration is especially straight-forward. If you really worry that immigrants vote the wrong way, don't let them vote. In the current regime, permanent residents already wait many years for citizenship. The delay could easily be extended—or made permanent. Alternately, immigrants might gain voting rights after paying $100,000 in taxes. While there is no solid reason to expect immi-grants to vote for disastrous policies, it is far better to let them in and deny them the vote than to exclude them as an act of pre-emptive politi-cal self-defense.

5.3 Keyhole Solutions Are Unrealistic

Keyhole solutions rarely win over critics of immigration. While they would work in theory, they are politically impossible—mere daydreams unwor-thy of serious consideration. Strangely, though, the same critics willingly debate a far more fantastic proposal: open borders itself. If you can imag-ine the political landscape changing enough to make global open borders a reality, what is so implausible about pro-native redistribution, selective austerity, or voting limits?

The deeper problem with critics' incredulity, though, is that countless "keyhole solutions" already exist in the United States and around the world. Legal immigrants to the United States face deportation for even minor nonviolent infractions such as marijuana possession.[86] China's *hukou* system for intranational residency restricts internal migrants' rights to collect government benefits and vote.[87] In Singapore and the United Arab Emirates, guest workers have very limited legal rights.[88] Even

86. See Linda Greenhouse, "Across the Border, Over the Line," *New York Times* Opinionator blog, 8 April 2010, http://opinionator.blogs.nytimes.com/2010/04/08/across-the-border-over-the-line/.

87. See "Ending Apartheid," *The Economist*, 19 April 2014, http://www.economist.com/news/special-report/21600798-chinas-reforms-work-its-citizens-have-be-made-more-equal-ending-apartheid.

88. See Kirsten Han, "Singapore's Exploited Immigrant Workers," *The Daily Beast*, 8 November 2013 http://www.thedailybeast.com/articles/2013/11/08/singapore-s-exploited-immigrant-workers.html, and Froilan Malit and Ali Youha, "Labor Migration in the United Arab Emirates: Challenges and Responses," Migra-tion Policy Institute, 18 September 2013, http://www.migrationpolicy.org/article/labor-migration-united-arab-emirates-challenges-and-responses.

Sweden, a country with strong pro-migrant sentiment, makes migrants wait five years for citizenship.[89] Open borders are perhaps an impossible dream, but keyhole solutions are already a concrete reality.

5.4 We Should Apply the Precautionary Principle

The policy of open borders is a radical proposal. Its consequences remain speculative. No matter how promising the proposal looks, shouldn't we move toward open borders gradually, learning more and more about the far-reaching consequences as we go? For all their flaws, modern First World societies remain the pinnacles of human civilization. Hundreds of millions of people enjoy lives that kings of old could scarcely imagine. This seems like a perfect time to apply the "precautionary principle"—to wait for definitive proof that open borders would succeed instead of betting all of our achievements on a mere idea.[90]

The precautionary principle also implies, however, that a long list of historical injustices should have been phased out much more gradually. In 1860, the effects of abolishing US slavery were unforeseeable. Who could accurately predict the results of releasing millions of illiterate slaves on the economy, crime, politics, or social stability itself? While the British had previously ended slavery in their colonies, they were not putting their home country at risk. In 1960, the effects of suddenly ending US segregation were similarly hazy. The nation's 19 million blacks had never been treated equally before. Or take the breakneck dismantling of South African apartheid in the early 1990s. Nearby Angola, Mozambique, and Zimbabwe had virtually collapsed after the end of white rule, but most observers still saw cautious phase-out of South African apartheid as moral cowardice.

The lesson: the precautionary principle may be a good rule when weighing a token gain against a fuzzy risk of social collapse, but not when the status quo impoverishes billions by prohibiting peaceful movement and trade. Yes, the current residents of the First World have wonderful lives. But the rest of the world should not have to endure preventive detention for the peace of mind of the fortunate few.

89. The wait time for stateless migrants is four years. See http://www.migrations-verket.se/English/Private-individuals/Becoming-a-Swedish-citizen/Citizenship-for-adults/Time-in-Sweden.html.
90. O'Riordan and Cameron (1994).

5.5 Why Has Nobody Tried Open Borders?

While borders were nearly open until the early twentieth century, no major First World country has had open borders since then, and none looks poised to try anytime soon. If the concept of open borders is such a great idea, why has *nobody* tried it? Even if political leaders in individual countries are irrational or face specific impediments to opening borders, the fact that *no* country has completely opened its borders seems troubling.

This is a strong objection for readers who doubt the wisdom of *all* policies that no country accepts in its entirety. In our view, though, *many* untried policies are clearly superior to the status quo. No country has complete free trade, raises most of its revenue from taxes on negative externalities, or permits a free market in human organs. If one accepts these or similar examples, ubiquitous immigration restrictions are hardly surprising. The best general explanation, in our view, is that human beings around the world have pronounced anti-market and anti-foreign biases. While the intensity of these biases vary from culture to culture, they are strong everywhere.[91] Keyhole solutions, similarly, are unpopular because human beings care far more about *visible* harm than actual harm.[92]

That said, there are a few countries whose policies and constitutional principles come quite close to open borders. Argentina's constitution recognizes the right to migrate as a fundamental human right. Anybody with a job offer can immigrate, tourists can look for jobs, illegal immigrants can be legalized, and there are no deportations.[93] In 2008, Ecuador declared a commitment to freedom of migration in its Constitution, though this has not been fully implemented.[94] Svalbard, an output of Norway in the Arctic, allows anybody with a job offer to migrate. It has an ethnically diverse population with zero crime.[95]

---

91. See Caplan (2007), as well as Rubin's (2003) effort to ground Caplan in evolutionary psychology.

92. See especially Daniel Kahneman, *Thinking, Fast and Slow* (New York: Farrar, Straus and Giroux, 2011).

93. See Hines (2010).

94. See William Wheeler, "How Not to Design a World Without Borders," *The Atlantic*, 21 July 2014, available online at http://www.theatlantic.com/international/archive/2014/07/how-not-to-design-a-world-without-borders/374563/.

95. See Andrew Higgins, "A Harsh Climate Calls for Banishment of the Needy," *New York Times*, 9 July 2014, available online at http://www.nytimes.com/2014/07/10/world/europe/a-harsh-climate-calls-for-banishment-of-the-needy.html?_r=0.

6 CONCLUSION

While we don't know exactly what open borders would do, that's the same as saying we don't know exactly how much damage the status quo inflicts. In expectation, the damage is massive. It is all too easy for us—particularly comfortable First Worlders—to forget the moral urgency of freedom of movement. Under the status quo, tens of millions around the globe live as unauthorized migrants, fearing the law enforcement that is supposed to protect them. And they're the lucky ones. Hundreds of millions *want* to seek a better life in another land, but find the black market back door too costly and too scary. Border controls tear families apart and crush countless dreams of people rich and poor. Are the risks of open borders really dire enough to continue calling foreigners criminals for peacefully moving to opportunity?

The concept of open borders is radical because the status quo is a radical abridgment of freedom based on an arbitrary distinction, propped up by status quo bias and moral apathy.[96] In the heyday of American Jim Crow laws and South African apartheid, most people meekly accepted out-group oppression as the natural state of the world. The same vice plagues the world today: nationalism blinds us to migration restrictions' grave injustice and exorbitant harm. In the nineteenth century, open borders allowed global freedom, prosperity, opportunity, and equality to advance hand in hand. A century later, the promise of open borders is greater than ever. The global poor don't need charity to escape poverty. They have more than enough talent to begin their journey to prosperity once the governments of the world get out of the way.

REFERENCES

Alesina, Alberto, Edward Glaeser, and Bruce Sacerdote. 2001. "Why Doesn't the U.S. Have a European-Style Welfare State?" *Brookings Papers on Economic Activity* 2: 187–254.

Barro, Robert, and Xavier Sala-i-Martin. 2003. *Economic Growth*. Cambridge, MA: MIT University Press.

96. See Kerry Howley, "Ending Global Apartheid," *Reason*, February 2008, http://reason.com/archives/2008/01/24/ending-global-apartheid. The examples of Jim Crow and apartheid are taken because readers are likely to be most familiar with them, but similar examples can be found around the world, many of them historically propped up by governments or local leaders. The institution of human slavery around the world, the caste system in India, and the class divisions in medieval Europe were considered normal for a long time and yet came to be considered obviously immoral by people later.

Borjas, George, and Lawrence Katz. 2005. "The Evolution of the Mexican-Born
    Workforce in the United States." In *Mexican Immigration to the United States*,
    ed. G. Borjas, p. 49. Chicago: University of Chicago Press. Available online as
    NBER Working Paper No. 11281 (issued April 2005) at http://www.nber.org/
    papers/w11281.
Brennan, Jason. 2011. *The Ethics of Voting*. Princeton, NJ: Princeton University
    Press (April 3, 2011).
Butcher, Kristin F., and Anne Morrison Piehl. 2007. "Why Are Immigrants' Incar-
    ceration Rates so Low? Evidence on Selective Immigration, Deterrence, and
    Deportation." NBER Working Paper No. 13229. Available online at http://
    www.nber.org/papers/w13229.
Caplan, Bryan. 2007. *The Myth of the Rational Voter*. Princeton, NJ: Princeton Uni-
    versity Press.
Caplan, Bryan. 2012. "Why Should We Restrict Immigration?" *Cato Journal* 32(1):
    5–24. Available online at http://www.cato.org/sites/cato.org/files/serials/
    files/cato-journal/2012/1/cj32n1–2.pdf.
Carens, Joseph. 2013. *The Ethics of Immigration*. Oxford: Oxford University Press.
Chandy, Laurence, and Geoffrey Gertz. 2011. "Poverty in Numbers: The Changing
    State of Global Poverty from 2005 to 2015." *Global Economy and Development
    at Brookings*. Policy Brief 2011–2001. Available online at http://www.brook-
    ings.edu/research/papers/2011/01/global-poverty-chandy.
Clemens, Michael A. 2011. "Economics and Emigration: Trillion-Dollar Bills on the
    Sidewalk?" *Journal of Economic Perspectives* 25(3): 83–106. Available online at
    http://pubs.aeaweb.org/doi/pdfplus/10.1257/jep.9.2.23.
Clemens, Michael, Claudio E. Montenegro, and Lant Pritchett. 2008. "The Premium
    Wage Differences for Identical Workers across the U.S. Border – Working
    Paper 148." Available online at http://www.cgdev.org/publication/
    place-premium-wage-differences-identical-workers-across-us-border-work-
    ing-paper-148.
Collier, Paul. 2013. *Exodus: How Migration Is Changing Our World*. Oxford: Oxford
    University Press.
Dobkin, Donald. 2009. "Challenging the Doctrine of Consular Nonreviewability."
    Georgetown Immigration Law Journal 24: 113–146. Available online at http://
    lawprofessors.typepad.com/files/articledobkin1.pdf.
Docquier, Frédéric, and Hillel Rapoport. 2012. "Globalization, Brain Drain, and De-
    velopment." *Journal of Economic Literature* 50(3): 681–730.
Gilens, Martin. 1999. *Why Americans Hate Welfare: Race, Media, and the Politics of
    Anti-Poverty Policy*. Chicago: University of Chicago Press.
Gilens, Martin. 2012. *Affluence and Influence: Economic Inequality and Political Power
    in America*. Princeton, NJ: Princeton University Press.
Gochenour, Zachary, and Alex Nowrasteh. 2014. "The Political Externalities of Im-
    migration: Evidence from the United States." Cato Institute Working Paper
    No. 14. Available online at http://www.cato.org/publications/working-paper/
    political-externalities-immigration-evidence-united-states.
Gonzalez, Libertad, and Ortega, Francesc. 2009. "Immigration and Housing Booms:
    Evidence from Spain." IZA Discussion Paper No. 4333. Bonn, Germany: Insti-
    tute for the Study of Labor. Available online at http://ftp.iza.org/dp4333.pdf.
Guest, Robert. 2011. *Borderless Economics: Chinese Sea Turtles, Indian Fridges and the
    New Fruits of Global Capitalism*. New York: Palgrave Macmillan.
Harford, Tim. 2007. *The Undercover Economist*. New York: Random House.

Hines, Barbara. 2010. "The Right to Migrate as a Human Right: The Current Argentine Immigration Law." *Cornell International Law Journal* 43: 471–512. Available online at http://www.lawschool.cornell.edu/research/ilj/upload/hines.pdf.

Huemer, Michael. 2010. "Is There a Right to Immigrate?" *Social Theory and Practice* 36(3): 249–261. Available online at http://spot.colorado.edu/~huemer/immigration.htm.

Kerr, William R., and Sari Pekkala Kerr. 2011. *Economic Impacts of Immigration: A Survey*. NBER Working Paper No. 16736. Available online at http://www.nber.org/papers/w16736.

Khan, B. Zorina, and Kenneth L. Sokoloff. 1993. "'Schemes of Practical Utility': Entrepreneurship and Innovation among Great Inventors in the United States, 1790–1865." *The Journal of Economic History* 53(2): 289–307. Available online at http://dx.doi.org/10.1017/S0022050700012924.

Ku, Leighton, and Brian Bruen. 2013. "Poor Immigrants Use Public Benefits at a Lower Rate Than Poor Native-Born Citizens." Cato Economic Development Bulletin No. 17.

Landsburg, Steven. 2012. *The Armchair Economist: Economics and Everyday Life*. New York: Free Press.

Legrain, Philippe. 2007. *Immigrants: Your Country Needs Them*. Princeton, NJ: Princeton University Press.

Mayhew, Robert, ed. 2005. *Ayn Rand Answers: The Best of Her Q & A*. New York: Penguin Books.

Milanovic, Branko. 2012a. "Global Income Inequality by the Numbers: In History and Now." World Bank Policy Research Working Paper 6259, available online at http://elibrary.worldbank.org/doi/pdf/10.1596/1813–9450–6259.

Milanovic, Branko. 2012b. "Global Inequality: From Class to Location, from Proletarians to Migrants." *Global Policy* 3: 125–134.

Nowrasteh, Alex, and Sophie Cole. 2013. "Building a Wall around the Welfare State, Instead of the Country." Cato Institute Policy Analysis #732. Available online at http://www.cato.org/publications/policy-analysis/building-wall-around-welfare-state-instead-country.

Ottaviano, Gianmarco, and Giovanni Peri. 2012. "Rethinking the Effect of Immigration on Wages." *Journal of the European Economic Association* 10(1): 152–197. Available online at http://www.nber.org/papers/w12497.

Pashler, Hal. 2013. "U.S. Immigrants' Attitudes Towards Libertarian Values." Available online at http://papers.ssrn.com/sol3/papers.cfm?abstract_id=2234200.

Risse, Matthias. 2009. "Immigration, Ethics, and the Capability Approach." *Human Development Research Paper (HDRP)* 2009/34. Available online at http://mpra.ub.uni-muenchen.de/19218.

Rubin, Paul. 2003. "Folk Economics." *Southern Economics Journal* 70: 157–171.

Saiz, Albert. 2003. "Room in the Kitchen for the Melting Pot: Immigration and Rental Prices." *The Review of Economics and Statistics* 85(3): 502–521. Available online at http://dx.doi.org/10.1162/003465303322369687.

Saiz, Albert. 2007. "Immigration and Housing Rents in American Cities." *Journal of Urban Economics* 61(2): 345–371. Available online at http://dx.doi.org/10.1016/j.jue.2006.07.004.

Sala-i-Martin, Xavier. 2006. "The World Distribution of Income: Falling Poverty and . . . Convergence, Period." *Quarterly Journal of Economics* 121(2): 351–397. Available online at http://dx.doi.org/10.1162/qjec.2006.121.2.351.

Saxenian, AnnaLee. 1999. "Silicon Valley's New Immigrant Entrepreneurs." Public Policy Institute of California. Available online at http://wee.ppic.org/content/pubs/report/R_699ASR.pdf.

Shaw, Kathryn L. 1989. "Life-Cycle Labor Supply with Human Capital Accumulation." *International Economic Review* 30(2): 431–456.

Somin, Ilya. 2013. *Democracy and Political Ignorance*. Stanford, CA: Stanford University Press.

Storesletten, Kjetil. 2000. "Sustaining Fiscal Policy Through Immigration." *Journal of Political Economy* 108: 300–323.

Wilkinson, Will. 2009. "Thinking Clearly about Economic Inequality." Cato Institute Policy Analysis No. 640. Available online at http://www.cato.org/publications/policy-analysis/thinking-clearly-about-economic-inequality.

Wolf, Douglas A., Ronald D. Lee, Timothy Miller, Gretchen Donehower, and Alexandre Genest. 2011. "Fiscal Externalities of Becoming a Parent." *Population Development Review* 37(2): 241–266. Available online at http://www.ncbi.nlm.nih.gov/pmc/articles/PMC3134288/.

CHAPTER 9

༺ঙ৹

Conclusion

Alternative Policy Perspectives

BENJAMIN POWELL

1   INTRODUCTION

There is a considerable gap between the public discourse concerning the costs and benefits of immigration compared to the social science discourse. This is not to say that all economists agree on all of the economic impacts of immigration. They don't. But their disagreements tend to be much narrower than those held by the general public.

For instance, as Chapter 2 documents, David Card and George Borjas have been debating the impact that immigration has on the wages of native-born citizens for years. But that debate has largely boiled down to whether low-skilled immigrants impact the wages of native-born citizens who don't have a high school diploma at all, or whether it depresses their wages by up to 8 percent and for how long that impact lasts. Similarly, as Chapter 3 documents, some reputable scholars find immigration is a fiscal drain, others a fiscal benefit, but the magnitude of the disagreements is small and clustered around zero.

The disagreements about purely economic impacts among social scientists is much smaller than the wide variation of beliefs held by the public and touted by politicians and the media. But that does not mean that all economists who study immigration agree on what a desirable immigration policy should be. As Chapters 6 through 8 demonstrated, they don't. I suspect that most of economists' policy disagreements stem from three factors: (1) disagreements about non-economic impacts that we do not have much evidence about, (2) disagreements about how well existing empirical evidence would apply to alternative policy regimes, and (3) differing views of what the appropriate social welfare function is for society.

As an example of the first of these, as this book is going to press George Borjas (forthcoming) challenged the conventional economic wisdom (Clemens 2011a) that worldwide elimination of immigration barriers would create massive gains for the world economy. Borjas does not challenge the standard economics of comparative advantage. Instead he asks how immigrants' non-economic impact might transform the economic systems. If poor countries are poor, at least in part, because they have bad institutions, might immigrants transform the political and economic institutions of richer countries in ways that lower the productivity of everyone who was already there?

Borjas asks the question, "What would happen to the institutions and social norms that govern economic exchanges in specific countries after the entry/exit of perhaps hundreds of millions of people" (forthcoming: 3)? He provides a number of simulations showing how varying degrees of importation of bad institutions impact the projected global gain from unrestricted immigration. He shows that these "general equilibrium effects can easily turn a receiving country's expected (static) windfall from unrestricted migration into an economic debacle" (forthcoming: 21). Of course these are merely simulations, based on assumptions about the importation of bad institutions. As he recognizes, "[u]nfortunately we know little (read: *nothing*) about how host societies would adapt to the entry of perhaps billions of new persons" (forthcoming: 12, emphasis in original).

This author and co-authors attempt to learn *something* about how immigration impacts economic institutions in a new working paper (Clark et al. forthcoming). Institutions that grant economic freedom, which includes the protection of private property rights and the rule of law, are important for economic growth and a host of alternative measures of standards of living.[1] The best empirical measure of these institutions is the *Economic Freedom of the World Annual Report* (Gwartney et al. 2014). We use this index to observe how both beginning stocks, and in-period flows, of immigrants impacted economic institutions in a broad cross section of countries over a 20-year period. Rather than importing negative institutions, as Borjas assumed, we find that greater immigration was associated with small improvements in economic institutions or had no effect at all.

---

1. See Hall and Lawson (2013) for a survey of this literature.

Our findings make me quite skeptical of Borjas's concerns, but I doubt our paper will convince him that a world of open borders would not lead to institutional deterioration in immigrant-receiving countries. Our disagreement would likely stem from the second reason that economists have conflicting policy positions mentioned above: disagreements about how well existing empirical evidence applies to alternative policy regimes. Our paper is based on data from existing immigration, which is subject to controls. How well does this evidence speak to a world with no quantitative restrictions on immigration? Perhaps the impact of immigration on institutions is nonlinear, or the social capital of current immigrants is not representative of the social capital of the population that would migrate under alternative policy regimes. Disagreements about how well our existing social science can inform our knowledge of the costs and benefits of immigration under radically different policy regimes can easily lead reasonable economists to prefer differing policies.

Finally, even if all immigration economists agreed that large-scale migration creates trillions of dollars of efficiency gains for the world economy, they can hold differing policy preferences based on a disagreements about the appropriate social welfare function. After all, advocating for economic efficiency is a normative position and only one of many possibilities. If someone embraces a normative view that does not count the welfare of foreigners, and has a strong preference against localized inequality, they may well favor an immigration policy that leaves trillions of dollars on the sidewalk.

The prior three chapters illustrated how reasonable social scientists come to hold differing immigration policy positions. In the following section, I briefly outline the policy positions of six other prominent immigration scholars who did not contribute to this volume. The first three can be generally classified as desiring to see policy decrease current levels of immigration and/or change the mix of the immigrants. The second three are generally supportive of increasing flows of legal immigrants from current levels. I offer my own views in the concluding section.

2   POLICY VIEWS TAKEN BY IMMIGRATION ECONOMISTS

The policy views of economists who study immigration are not often stated in their scholarly publications. Their scholarship surely informs their policy views, but the scholarship itself usually does not imply any particular position on immigration policy. Some immigration scholars also author policy studies or comment frequently in the popular press about desirable or undesirable policy reforms. Others, like David Card, keep their policy views so private that it is impossible for me to comment on them. When authored in the popular press, these views sometimes might indicate what the scholar thinks is the optimal policy, but other times might just indicate what he thinks is a policy move in the right or wrong direction given what at that moment happens to be politically possible. Furthermore, what a scholar believes is an optimal policy in one situation cannot necessarily be extrapolated to others. What a scholar wrote about policy in 1999 is not necessarily what he believes today. So, it is with a little bit of trepidation that I attempt to outline some policy views of immigration scholars.

2.1   Scholars Generally Critical of Greater Immigration

2.1.1   George Borjas

George Borjas's 2014 book, *Immigration Economics*, does not document any of his current views on immigration policy. In fact, as he put it in a 2013 email to me, "I've pretty much spent the entire last 5 years writing a very technical book on the economics of immigration where the word 'policy' shows up perhaps 4 or 5 times in the entire book and which resolutely refuses to draw any policy implications whatsoever from whatever it is that economics has to say." As for the policy debate going on at the time, "I've pretty much stayed out of the entire policy debate this time around. I've been there, done that, wrote a book on it, and decided a few years ago to move on." He certainly has "been there" and "done that" in his 1999 book, *Heaven's Door*, which contains an entire chapter outlining his views on an optimal immigration policy.

Borjas argues that it "is worthwhile to assume that immigration policy should strive to maximize the well-being of the native population" (1999: 189). He does not define well-being as merely income levels. Instead, "economic well-being depends both on per capita income and on the distribution of income in the native population. In other words, the optimal immigration policy should make natives wealthier, but should not increase the income disparity among workers already in the country" (1999: 190). Notice that this formulation of the social welfare function completely excludes any benefits that accrue to the immigrants themselves, the very group that experiences the greatest benefit from migration. Notice also that by excluding immigrants from a welfare function that includes inequality, it excludes the great reduction in global inequality that immigration causes.

This specification leads Borjas to conclude that "[a] strong case can be made that the social welfare of the United States—*as I have defined it*—would increase if the country adopted an immigration policy that favored the entry of skilled workers" (1999: 190, emphasis in original). In terms of concrete policies to achieve the goal of favoring skilled workers, Borjas desires a point system, similar to Canada's, that awards points to each potential immigrant awarded for "desirable" characteristics such as educational attainment, English proficiency, age, occupation, and experience. Then a threshold can be set, which can be adjusted up or down based on our macroeconomic circumstances, for the score necessary to obtain a visa.

Borjas favors skilled workers because they will help increase our incomes by making the businesses that employ them more productive and profitable, while they will simultaneously compete with other high-skilled native-born workers for jobs, which could lower the income inequality between high- and low-skilled native-born workers. He also characterizes high-skilled immigrants as having a greater positive fiscal externality because they generate more tax revenue and consume fewer social services, which again does more to enhance the wealth of the native born. Borjas recognizes that such a point system is "doomed to failure unless the problem of illegal immigration is also resolved" (1999: 205), so he also favors employer-based penalties for hiring illegal immigrants, asset forfeiture for illegal immigrants detained, and suggests a national ID as a method to identify who is and is not here legally. He also suggests fluctuating the number of legal visas available downward by the number of illegal entries in order to create rival political factions to agitate against businesses that benefit from illegal immigration.

While Borjas is very clear that he favors skilled immigrants, he's much less concrete about the optimal number of visas that should be issued. He believed that academic literature was "not at the point where one can estimate the relevant costs and benefits with any reasonable degree of confidence, and then use these estimates to grind out a magic number" (1999: 200). Thus he was very candid when picking a number,

> There is no objective yardstick that I can use to determine what the right number of immigrants should be. My recommendation is based less on the available evidence, and more on how I balance the value of the efficiency gains from immigration with what is "fair" to the population of native skilled workers. Other participants in the immigration debate could reasonably disagree with my pick of the magic number. (1999: 202)

His magic number: roughly 500,000 legal immigrants per year (1999: 202). That's roughly a 33 percent cut from the number of legal immigrants annually in the 1980s and 1990s and a cut of roughly 50 percent compared to the last 15 years.

Though *Heaven's Door* was published 15 years ago, Borjas's public writing in response to George Bush's 2004 guest worker proposal and the US Senate's immigration reform proposal in 2007 were both consistent with his policy preferences outlined in *Heaven's Door*. In both cases he was critical of low-skilled guest worker programs (Borjas 2004, 2007). In response to the Senate bill, he again expressed his support for a points system and dismay that he didn't expect the Bush administration to seriously enforce border security. Despite his lack of interest in participating in the latest policy debate, his recent public lectures on immigration also show a consistent preference for skilled workers and limiting entry.[2]

These policy preferences, like everyone's, are dictated by his chosen social welfare function and the social science that informs our understanding of the consequences of immigration. In *Heaven's Door*, he lays out what he believes are the stylized facts of social science that informs his policy position (1999: 189–190). I think some of those stylized "facts" have turned out to be false in the subsequent 15 years of scientific research. However, it would seem to me that there remains social science findings that could lead someone endorsing his favored social welfare function to continue to favor a skills-based limited immigration policy. The social science that seems most relevant for informing these views are that the net economic gains to the native born in immigrant-receiving countries is positive but small (Borjas 1995), that the least skilled workers might see their wages decline by 8 percent from unskilled immigration (Borjas and Katz 2007). Finally, and more recently, one would endorse limiting mass immigration of low-skilled workers if one believes that they may harm the productivity of the native-born population by importing immigrant's bad institutions with them (Borjas forthcoming).

2.1.2 Paul Collier

Paul Collier, an Oxford University economist and author of *Exodus: How Migration Is Changing Our World* (2013), has articulated policy views similar to George Borjas, though usually commenting on European immigration

2. For example, see this February 2013 lecture: https://www.youtube.com/watch?v=vCvdXFUtCMs.

policies. He favors restricting the total quantity of immigration and replacing illegal immigration with legal immigration that is chosen through a point system (2014a, 2014b).

Exodus provides a useful road map for how Collier comes to his conclusions. He recognizes the social science literature that finds that natives generally benefit economically from welcoming immigrants. But then he goes on to worry that large future migrations might have much more negative impacts. Of course, these negative impacts are speculative but could be attributed to not believing that the existing empirical evidence would apply under radically different policy regimes.[3] But as Collier put it in his popular writing, "The important effects of immigration are social and long term, not economic and short term. The key long-term social effects are probably on the size of the population and its diversity" (2014b). As outlined in *Exodus*, he worries that the diversity of the immigrants can make them culturally distant from the native population, which could undermine the mutual regard and trust that helps make our societies function well. More fundamentally,

> Migrants are essentially escaping from countries with dysfunctional social models. It may be well to reread that last sentence and ponder its implications. For example, it might make you a little more wary of the well-intentioned mantra of the need to have "respect for other cultures." The cultures—or norms and narratives—of poor societies, along with their institutions and organizations, stand suspected of being the primary cause of their poverty. (2013: 34)

This is similar to, but broader than, Borjas's (forthcoming) concern about importing the very institutions that make them poor. Collier suggests that perhaps it is the culture of the people themselves that cause their countries to be poor and that their migration might undermine both the relatively "good" culture and institutions in richer countries that are responsible for our well-being. Collier's main reservation about immigration, from the perspective of receiving countries, is not narrowly economic and is not based on current social science, but is more social and cultural, and is based on worries for which little social science data exist.[4] This leads

---

3. Though, as Clemens and Sandefur (2014) point out, existing empirical evidence that urban whites benefited from the massive movement of people from rural areas to cities in South Africa after apartheid should give one some confidence that natives could benefit similarly from large international migrations.

4. Though Clemens and Sandefur (2014) do point out that some of the limited data that do exist should make one skeptical of these worries.

Collier to favor a policy position temporarily slowing immigration to the United Kingdom. As he put it,

> There is no way of establishing whether further increases in diversity in England would be a net gain or a net cost. However, the rate at which migrants are assimilating appears to be slower than had been expected. Immigrants have tended to cluster, and this reduces social interaction outside the group. Hence, after the surge in immigration since 1997, it may be sensible to have a temporary phase of slower immigration while we take stock of its social consequences. (2014b)

If immigration is to be limited, the possibility of illegal immigration must be dealt with. Collier sees two ways to tackle illegal immigration: legalize it or reduce the incentive to migrate illegally. The first is ruled out by his beliefs outlined above because if open immigration were legalized it would induce an "unmanageably large influx" (2014a). Thus the incentive to illegally migrate must be reduced. Collier favors an automatic return for illegal immigrants without exception, an added penalty that the right to legally migrate in the future would be forfeited when someone is caught illegally migrating, tightened enforcement of access to welfare, enforcement of employment laws, and the issuance of national identification (2014a). These measures certainly could deter future illegal immigration, but what about immigrants already residing illegally? "Countries which already have a large stock of illegal immigrants will need to legalize them. . . . The point of hiring is the vital event to police: businesses that hire illegal workers have to be actively prosecuted and face severe penalties. This is only feasible if they are rare. For example, in the USA where many of the 11 million illegal immigrants are illegally in work, enforcement is impossible" (2014a). Collier, like Borjas, also favors tying increases in legal immigration to decreases in illegal immigration and using a point system and a lottery to allocate scarce slots (2014a).

2.1.3   *Victor Davis Hanson*

Victor Davis Hanson is a Senior Fellow at Stanford's Hoover Institute and, though a classicist and historian rather than an economist like the others profiled in this chapter, he has been a prominent scholarly critic of US immigration policy. He is largely silent on debates surrounding core economic issues of immigration. His main reservations, similar to Borjas and Collier, center on non-economic issues.

Hanson's 2003 book, *Mexifornia*, worried that massive illegal immigration "coupled with a loss of confidence in the old melting pot model of transforming newcomers into Americans, is changing the very nature of state" in undesirable ways (2003). Hanson sees lack of political will to stop illegal immigration as the outcome of agricultural and business interests that desire cheap labor but do not care about any long-term social costs to society and the political desires of leftist politicians, academics, journalists, and organizations such as La Raza, who see Spanish-speaking illegal immigrants as a new class of "victimhood" to promote their leftist political agendas. He views the current numbers and mix of immigrants to be a threat to our collective infrastructure, social services, law enforcement, and state budgets (2014). He instead desires that immigrants come "legally, in manageable numbers, in ethnically diverse fashion, eager to learn English and assimilate quickly" (2014).

I think some of Hanson's concerns are unfounded, based on the evidence that Jacob Vigdor documents in Chapter 4 of this volume. However, his more general implicit concern, that they might harm our culture and institutions, seems to have a general congruency with Borjas and Collier's fears.

2.2   Scholars Generally Supportive of Greater Immigration

2.2.1.   Gordon Hanson

Gordon Hanson, a professor of economics at the University of California San Diego, is widely known for his research on the international migration of skilled labor and on border enforcement and illegal immigration. He favors policy changes that would increase quantity of highly skilled immigrants that the United States admits and, unlike the above scholars, also favors legalizing more low-skilled immigration.

His position on high-skilled immigration is not particularly controversial.[5] "A binding constraint in generating innovations is the supply of highly talented scientists, engineers, and other technical personal. Immigration helps relax this constraint" (2012: 26). He documents the large percentage of foreign students earning doctorates at US universities in these disciplines and notes, "the difficulty is not attracting top foreign

---

5. Chicago Booth School's IMG forum asks extremely accomplished expert economists from a variety of subfields public policy questions. On the question of "The average US citizen would be better off if a larger number of highly educated foreign workers were legally allowed to immigrate to the US each year," 89 percent of those surveyed either "strongly agreed" or "agreed" with the statement. http://www.igmchicago.org/igm-economic-experts-panel/poll-results?SurveyID=SV_0JtSLKwzqNSfrAF.

students to America but in keeping them here after they graduate" because student visas are relatively easy to obtain but working visas after graduation are much scarcer (2012: 27). His policy solution is straightforward: "By making it easy for talented foreign students to stay on in the country once their studies are finished, their contributions could be even more" (2012: 27).

Hanson's views on low-skilled illegal immigration are more controversial.[6] He believes that low-skilled illegal immigrants help our labor market function more efficiently and that the solution to the illegality problem is a greatly expanded legal migration path for these low-skilled workers (Hanson 2009, 2010, 2012).

He argues that low-skilled illegal immigration helps our economy by making our capital and land more productive, improving the productivity of our native born high-skilled labor, particularly high-skilled women, and because the illegal immigrants are highly mobile across jobs and geography, unlike native-born low-skilled workers (Hanson 2012).

However, Hanson believes that low-skilled illegal immigrants have a small negative fiscal impact and, in particular, can be a drain on some state and local jurisdictions that provide schooling to immigrants' children while their tax contributions accrue disproportionately to the federal government (2009, 2012). However, Hanson notes that if "reducing immigration requires substantially higher levels of enforcement the drain on government budgets could actually increase. A more sensible approach than a pure-enforcement strategy would be to allow low-skilled immigration to occur but to shield taxpayer from negative effects" (2012: 30).[7]

To reform policy Hanson recommends that

> A constructive immigration policy would allow low-skilled immigration to occur in a manner that generated maximum productivity gains to the US economy, while limiting the fiscal cost of immigration and keeping enforcement spending contained. Effectively, this means converting existing inflows of unauthorized immigrants into inflows of legal immigrants. (2009: 13)

6. Though not directly on the question of illegal immigrants, in the more general case of low-skilled workers, the IMG poll of accomplished expert economists found that 50 percent agreed and another 2 percent "strongly agreed" with the statement that "[t]he average US citizen would be better off if a larger number of low-skilled foreign workers were legally allowed to enter the US each year." http://www.igmchicago. org/igm-economic-experts-panel/poll-results?SurveyID=SV_5vuNnqkBeAMAfHv.

7. He further notes that he doesn't even know if current levels of enforcement spending are justified because the government (and presumably no one else) does not provide information on enforcement costs relative to fiscal savings obtained from current levels of border apprehension.

Specifically, he recommends letting the total number of visas fluctuate from year to year because "[t]he productivity benefit from immigration is higher when businesses can choose which workers they want to hire and when they want to hire them" (2009: 13). In order to deal with any fiscal costs associated with these low-skilled immigrants, he recommends subjecting "employers [of these immigrants] to an immigrant labor payroll tax that would fund the benefits that their immigrant employees, and their family members, receive" (2012: 32). He believes that these policy reforms would be beneficial because "[t]he problem is not immigration per se but rules governing taxes and spending that fail to make U.S. employers internalize the fiscal consequences of hiring low-skilled foreign labor" (2012: 32).

2.2.2   Lant Pritchett

Lant Pritchett, currently a professor of practice at Harvard's Kennedy School, has been a major contributor to immigration scholarship. In particular, he is known for his joint work with Michael Clemens and Claudio Montenegro on the "place premium" (2008). In 2006, he published *Let Their People Come: Breaking the Gridlock on International Labor Mobility*, which outlined his immigration policy reform proposals.

Pritchett endorses a very different social welfare function than George Borjas. As he outlines at the beginning of his book,

> Normatively, I am primarily concerned with raising the well-being of the world's least well off—not just the "poorest of the poor" but all people whose standard of living is below that of those below the poverty thresholds of the world's rich countries, which is the large bulk of the world's population. Most analysis and recommendations about the policies of the rich countries presume that policies should be informed exclusively by the interests of the current citizens of those countries (for example, Borjas 1999). (2006: 2)

However, in his book he never outlines his policy stance based on that normative standard.[8] Instead, he explores what are the policies toward "labor mobility that would be most beneficial to the world's currently poor and yet are still politically acceptable in rich countries" (2006: 3). Thus his policy advocacy appears to be a balancing act in which he advocates for

---

8. Given the massive economic gains to the world's poor that he estimates in his work on the place premium, it is hard for me to imagine him endorsing anything other than a massive increase in the flow of workers from poorer countries to richer countries if this is the normative standard employed.

whatever policies that he believes can generate the greatest increases in immigration but still might be politically possible in the current environment.

His book is framed around eight immovable ideas that constrain the politically possible migration reforms and five irresistible forces that push for greater migrant flows. The five forces pushing for greater migration are increasing unskilled wage gaps between countries; differing demographic futures that indicate shrinking populations for many rich countries and rapidly growing populations in poorer countries; the globalization of everything else but labor, which dictates that globalizing labor is where the greatest remaining economic gains are; the growth of hard-core non-tradable service employment; and lagging growth in "ghost" countries that have falling labor demand and encourages workers to move. Left unchecked, these forces would dramatically increase international labor mobility.

However, political barriers allow only a small fraction of the movement that these forces could generate. As Pritchett describes,

> The real barrier to the movement of people across national boundaries is coercion—people with guns stop them. . . . This exercise of nation-state coercion to prevent labor flows is under the complete and total control of the democratic processes in rich countries. Hence the real barriers to increased labor mobility are the ideas of these rich countries citizens. (2006: 8)

He sees eight immovable ideas that constrain politically possible migration policies: that nationality is a morally legitimate basis for discrimination; that moral obligation is limited by one's proximity to someone else; that development is conceived in terms of nation-states' growth rather than individuals' well-being; that labor movements are not necessary to raise living standards; that migration of unskilled labor will harm wages or steal jobs from native workers and worsen the income distribution in receiving countries; that migrants are a fiscal drag by consuming more in social services than they generate in tax revenue; that migration increases risks of crime and terrorism; and that "they" are not like "us" so there will be cultural clash. Pritchett does not evaluate the merits of any of these beliefs. He merely treats them as given constraints in designing a politically possible migration reform proposal.

Pritchett outlines six features that are development friendly and, he believes, represent a politically possible scheme to increase labor mobility (2006: 105–137). He believes that agreements should be bilateral rather than multilateral so that security and cultural clash accommodations can be made in particular cases. He also recommends that temporary status should be granted to increase mobility in order to combat the current bias against allowing permanent low-skilled migrants. Rationing should be employed by job and/or region to address fears of stealing jobs from natives. Enhancements are made to ensure that the development experienced by the migrants also benefits their country of origin. Sending countries should be involved with enforcing temporary migration because destination countries are often incapable of doing so unilaterally. Finally, he states that reforms must ensure the protection of the fundamental human rights of migrants.

Throughout Pritchett's policy advocacy, it is abundantly clear that he desires increased migration flows. He never addresses what he believes the desirable limit is. He even says, "Clearly, any proposal for 'open borders' or 'free immigration' is simply pointless. But it is worth asking if there are not modest steps that can be taken toward realizing the potential benefits" (2006: 139). Throughout his book those modest steps are constrained by having to "accommodate the immovable ideas in the interests of increased flows" (2006: 138).

2.2.3   Michael Clemens

Michael Clemens, a senior fellow with the Center for Global Development, has become one of the leading economists studying the economic impacts of migration. In addition to his joint work on the place premium, he is best known for his provocative article, "Economics and Emigration: Trillion-Dollar Bills on the Sidewalk?" which argues that the global gains to increasing migration flows from poorer countries to richer countries are massive (Clemens 2011a). He argued, as I did in Chapter 1 of this volume, that when surveying the literature, estimates of the increase in world GDP resulting from the complete elimination of migration restrictions are in the range of 50 to 150 percent of world GDP. Such a large gain only occurs with at least half of the population of poorer countries moving to richer countries, but even a migration of less than 5 percent of the world's poor creates gains greater than the complete elimination of all remaining policy barriers to merchandise trade and capital flows.

If Clemens believes the size of these estimates (and I have no reason to believe that he doesn't), then it is hard to imagine him advocating a policy position that does not dramatically increase rates of migration or even fully embrace open borders. After all, as Chapter 8 of this volume argued, if the gains are this large, it is hard to imagine that we could not redistribute some of the gains to deal with any other negative consequences affecting other factors in virtually any social welfare function. Yet, I'm not aware of any written advocacy for a policy of "open borders" or "free migration" by Clemens.

Clemens has favored a creation of a "Golden Door Visa" to "create a legal mechanism to allow limited numbers of immigrants from the very poorest countries, like Haiti, to either temporarily or permanently live and work in the U.S." and he has suggested that these could go to some countries some years and to other countries in other years, perhaps in response to economic crises or natural disasters (Clemens 2010). But elsewhere he has embraced a variety of policies to try to capture some of the global gains that can be had through increased migration:

> There are numerous clear and sound proposals for more economically sensible migration policy. These include Lant Pritchett's proposals for bilateral guest-worker agreements, the ideas of Pia Orrenius and Madeline Zavodny for raising permanent economic visa allocations, and the proposal by Jesus Fernandez-Huertas and Hillel Rapoport for tradable immigration quotas. I suggest using migration policy as one tool to assist people in poor countries struck by natural disaster. Each approach has advantage and disadvantages, but they have in common a drive to generate triple-wins for migrants, destination countries, and origin countries. (Clemens 2011b)

One gets the feeling that Clemens is willing to embrace a variety of policies as long as they increase the total migration from poorer countries to richer countries.

In a 2013 interview with economist Russ Roberts, I think Clemens comes the closest to revealing what his own unconstrained preferred immigration policy would be. He questions what it means when people ask him if he favors open borders:

> If open borders means absolutely free movement of people without any sort of tracking of who they are or any sort of concern for free riding in public services or any concern for trespassing on private property, then, no. Open borders doesn't exist in any space that I've ever seen. I don't really want it to exist. Before we talk about open borders, I need to know what that means. Usually people mean something like a great relaxation to the policy barriers that people face right now. (2013)

He goes on to describe immigration restrictions in the past, like the Chinese Exclusion Act, and current caps on different worker visa categories, and he argues that there is no evidence that any of these limitations have made anyone better off. "So if more open borders means getting rid of provisions of legislation that don't help anyone and hurt everyone, then movements toward open borders fall into that class of things that economists love to search for—which are Pareto-optimal things" (Clemens 2013). When Clemens was asked to clarify if he would distinguish between high- and low-skilled workers in his ideal immigration policy his response was,

> I have never seen good evidence that planners in Washington are better than employers at doing that. . . . There could be very high demands for some kinds of low-skill labor relative to some kinds of high-skill labor. There could be high demands for some kinds of high-skill labor to some kinds of low-skill labor. That needs to be determined by some process. Then you have to ask: What is the best process to make that distinction? And as far as I know the people who are best able to determine how many cucumber, lettuce, and melon-pickers are needed are farmers. The people who are best able to determine how many Information Technology (IT) engineers are needed in Silicon Valley are the people who are at those firms day to day, knowing exactly what skills and type of person is required. (2013)

In a recent article in *The Atlantic*, Clemens is quoted as saying that he is "in favor of a vastly more sensible way of regulating movement," if not "a utopia of completely free movement" (Raviv 2013). So, I do not think it is unfair to infer from Clemens's policy statements that he either favors no quantitative restrictions on migration visas, or at least favors greatly increasing the quantitative caps and allowing market forces to dictate who migrates, while at the same time limiting freedom of movement under either of these scenarios with private property rights, security checks, and some form of limitation on access to tax funded services.

3   CONCLUSION

As this chapter and the prior three have illustrated, reasonable social scientists can, and do, disagree about optimal immigration policy. However, our reasons for disagreement are largely based on factors other than purely economic impacts. They revolve around non-economic impacts, differing judgments of how well existing empirical social science findings could inform consequences of much more liberal immigration regimes, and differing normative judgments about who and what count in a social welfare function.

I believe the first two reasons for disagreement are the most important. If embracing a policy that allows half of the world's population to migrate would really double the world's annual income, it is hard to believe that some redistributive policy between gainers and any losers could not be devised that would satisfy virtually any social welfare function. Thus the first two reasons for disagreement, which are interrelated, become fertile ground for future social science research.

If large-scale migration undermines a society's formal or informal institutions (culture) that are responsible for its high standard of living, this could easily erase the trillions of dollars of annual gains that economists estimate from large-scale migration. The best objection to greatly increasing immigration flows made by social scientists is that large-scale migration *might* involve immigrants importing their lousy institutions or culture to destination countries. But this objection is entirely hypothetical. George Borjas himself claims we know *nothing* about whether and how much it would occur.

Much more research by social scientists is needed on this important question. But I do think we know some things about it already. First, migrants are leaving because they are upset about the opportunities provided in their homeland. If they have any understanding that their lack of opportunities had something to do with the poor governance of their society, then it is highly unlikely that they would want to import that governance to their adopted country. Second, there is likely a selection bias in which the migrants who leave are those least satisfied with their institutions and governance and least likely to desire to perpetuate them. This is common-sense reasoning but obviously could use more social science research to back it up.

Of course migrants may undermine institutions in recipient countries unintentionally. Paul Collier worries that because immigrants are "culturally distant," that distance may erode societal trust. Some might tie this fear to the literature on the impact of ethnic and linguistic fragmentation. Easterly and Levine (1997) find a negative relationship across countries between ethnic diversity and the amounts and qualities of government-provided goods such as schooling, electricity, roads, and telephones. Similarly Alesina, Baqir, and Easterly (1999) find a negative correlation in US cities, metropolitan areas, and counties between ethnic fragmentation and shares of spending on government-provided goods such as trash pickup, roads, sewers, and education. But much of the literature draws its empirical results from places where populations were forcibly integrated, rather than the result of patterns of voluntary association that emerged through migration.[9]

It is not at all clear that the fragmentation findings apply to cases of international migration. As Clemens and Sandefur point out in their review of *Exodus*, "crime is significantly lower in the English and Welsh neighborhoods in the United Kingdom with the largest immigrant inflows and . . . immigration raises local property values in Spain and the United States" (2014). If immigration destroyed social trust, we should see the opposite. Similarly, as Chapter 4 of this volume documents, Clemens and Sandefur point out that "culturally distant" immigrants tend to assimilate. Referencing the Manhattan Institute's assimilation index, they note that "[a]fter Canadians, it turns out that the highest-scoring groups come from the Philippines, Cuba, and Vietnam—hardly countries with social institutions mirroring those of the United States" (2014). Assimilation rates that have remained high and increased in the United States should alleviate worries about migration undermining our culture and institutions in a way that would dramatically reduce the projected global gains from increasing migration.

My own new study with co-authors is the first to empirically investigate how immigration impacts economic institutions that support economic freedom. Our results indicate that immigration may marginally improve a country's institutions in a manner consistent with economic freedom. Using our estimate that a one standard deviation higher immigration stock increases economic freedom by 0.34 points and an estimate for the impact of economic freedom on growth (Gwartney, Holcombe, and Lawson 2006), our results suggest that a higher immigrant share of this magnitude will generate a 0.45 percentage point higher long-run annual growth rate (Clark et al. forthcoming). Rather than assuming that the existing literature overstates the global gains because it ignores the impact of immigration on institutions, if our results from current levels of immigration's impact on institutions can be extrapolated to a world with open borders, the opposite is true. The static gains in traditional estimates underestimate the global gains by ignoring the positive general equilibrium impact on institutions. Of course, there are reasons that our results might not be applicable to a world of open borders. But at a minimum, when starting from a baseline of knowing "nothing," our study,

---

9. In Africa's case, it was through national borders that were imposed by outside powers. In the case of the United States the integration is between descendants of people who were brought to the United States against their will as slaves and whose subsequent treatment after the abolishment of slavery has left much to be desired.

which shows current levels of immigration either improve or fail to impact institutions, should make one skeptical of Borjas's or Collier's unsubstantiated assumption that large-scale migration will negatively impact recipient country institutions.

Ultimately, we live in a world that is far from one with open borders. We must make the most reasonable policy judgments we can based on available evidence. Unfortunately, without a significant liberalization of immigration policies in richer countries, we are never going to get better empirical evidence on the impact that large-scale legal migration around the globe would create.

Judging from the social science documented in this book, it seems that most fears of the consequences of existing levels or slightly increased levels of migration are misplaced. Expanded immigration would increase world income; would dramatically improve the living standards of those who migrate; would do little to hurt and may possibly help the people who remain in poorer countries; would slightly enrich natives in destination countries; would have small to nonexistent negative impacts on the least-skilled native workers in destination countries; would not significantly impact the fiscal situation of destination countries; and would assimilate (at least in the United States), much like prior waves of immigrants.

With those stylized facts in mind, most social welfare functions, including my own preferred one, dictate, at a minimum, substantially increasing legal migration flows (both temporary and permanent).[10] How big the desired "substantially" is depends on one's degree of confidence of how far we can extend the trend line from our existing knowledge.

As long as some cap on migration, either temporary or permanent, exists, there will likely be more people who desire to migrate than are allowed. Some rationing method must be used. Although many people, including Borjas and Collier, favor a point system, like Canada's, to ration scarce permits, I think this is a mistake. A point system requires government planners to plan an international labor market where they know little about the subjective evaluations of the value of individual people in foreign lands to employers, family members, and humanitarians in destinations countries, nor do they know the subjective longing of those

10. My own normative criteria (social welfare function) includes the economic well-being of all humans, regardless of national origin, as well as respecting their natural human rights. These natural rights are negative rights, which include the freedom of association. In this context that means the ability to sell or rent a residence to, or employ, anyone without regard to national origin, whenever mutually agreeable terms can be found. This does not amount to a "right" to move freely. I believe that private property rights can and should limit movements.

wishing to migrate. Yet it is this subjective, tacit, and localized knowledge that is necessary to efficiently plan the international labor market just as it is necessary in other markets (Hayek 1945). The price system is the best system we know of for balancing all of these subjective desires against each other. As long as there are going to be quotas, some version of something along the lines proposed by Richard Vedder in Chapter 6 is the most efficient way to allocate them. Ultimately, though, without freedom of entry to determine quantity as well as price, any regulated labor market will underperform relative to its potential.

Until evidence emerges that substantially increased immigration is causing harmful impacts that cannot be dealt with by "keyhole solutions," I think we should be moving, perhaps rapidly, toward a world without quantitative restrictions on international migration.

REFERENCES

Alesina, Alberto F., Reza Baqir, and William Easterly. 1999. "Public Goods and Ethnic Divisions." *Quarterly Journal of Economics* 114: 1243–1284.

Borjas, George. 1995. "The Economic Benefits of Immigration." *Journal of Economic Perspectives* 9(2): 3–22.

Borjas, George J. 1999. *Heaven's Door: Immigration Policy and the American Economy.* Princeton, NJ: Princeton University Press.

Borjas, George J. 2004. "Making it Worse: President Bush has Tackled the Immigration Problem Wrongly." *National Review* 56(2). February 2.

Borjas, George J. 2007. "Let's Be Clear about Whom We Want to Let In." *Washington Post.* December 23.

Borjas, George J. Forthcoming. "Immigration and Globalization: A Review Essay." *Journal of Economic Literature.*

Borjas, George J., and Lawrence F. Katz. 2007. "The Evolution of the Mexican-Born Workforce in the United States." In *Mexican Immigration to the United States,* ed. George J. Borjas, pp. 13–56. Chicago: University of Chicago Press.

Clark, J. R., Robert Lawson, Alex Nowrasteh, Benjamin Powell, and Ryan Murphy. Forthcoming. "Does Immigration Impact Economic Freedom?" *Public Choice.*

Clemens, Michael. 2010. "Let Haitians Come to the US." *Global Post.* February 26. www.globalpost.com/dispatch/worldview/100225/haiti-us-visas.

Clemens, Michael A. 2011a. "Economics and Emigration: Trillion-Dollar Bills on the Sidewalk?" *Journal of Economics Perspectives* 25: 83–106.

Clemens, Michael. 2011b. "A World Without Borders Makes Economic Sense." *The Guardian.* September 5.

Clemens, Michael. 2013. "Clemens on Aid, Migration and Policy." *Econtalk* interview with Russ Roberts. July 15. http://www.econtalk.org/archives/2013/07/clemens_on_aid.html.

Clemens, Michael, Claudio Montenegro, and Lant Pritchett. 2008. "The Place Premium: Wage Differences for Identical Workers across the US Border." *CGD Working Paper 148.* Washington, DC: Center for Global Development.

Clemens, Michael, and Justin Sandefur. 2014. "Let the People Go: The Problem with Strict Migration Limits." *Foreign Affairs* (January/February). http://www. foreignaffairs.com/articles/140354/michael-clemens-and-justin-sandefur/ let-the-people-go.

Collier, Paul. 2013. *Exodus: How Migration Is Changing Our World.* Oxford: Oxford University Press.

Collier, Paul. 2014a. "Illegal Migration to Europe: What Should be Done." *Social Europe*. September 9. www.social-europe.eu/ 2014/09/illegal-migration/.

Collier, Paul. 2014b. "Now Is the Time to Slow Down Immigration." *The Guardian*. November 4.

Easterly, William, and Ross Levine. 1997. "Africa's Growth Tragedy: Policies and Ethnic Divisions." *Quarterly Journal of Economics* 112: 1203–1250.

Gwartney, James, Randall Holcombe, and Robert Lawson. 2006. "Institutions and the Impact of Investment on Growth." *Kyklos* 59: 255–273.

Gwartney, James, Robert Lawson, and Joshua Hall. 2014. *Economic Freedom of the World Annual Report.* Vancouver: Fraser Institute.

Hall, Joshua, and Robert Lawson. 2013. "Economic Freedom of the World: An Accounting of the Literature." *Contemporary Economic Policy* 32: 1–19.

Hanson, Gordon. 2009. *The Economics and Policy of Illegal Immigration in the United States.* Washington, DC: Migration Policy Institute.

Hanson, Gordon. 2010. *Regulating Low-Skilled Immigration in the United States.* Washington, DC: American Enterprise Institute for Public Policy Research.

Hanson, Gordon. 2012. "Immigration and Economic Growth." *Cato Journal* 32(1): 25–34.

Hanson, Victor Davis. 2003. *Mexifornia.* San Francisco: Encounter Books.

Hanson, Victor Davis. 2014. "Voting 'No' on Obama's Immigration Policies." *Fresno Bee*. November 16.

Hayek, F. A. 1945. "The Use of Knowledge in Society." *American Economic Review* 35(4): 519–530.

Pritchett, Lant. 2006. *Let Their People Come: Breaking the Gridlock on International Labor Mobility.* Washington, DC: Center for Global Development.

Raviv, Shaun. 2013. "If People Could Immigrate Anywhere, Would Poverty Be Eliminated?" *The Atlantic*. April 26.

ABOUT THE AUTHORS

Benjamin Powell is the Director of the Free Market Institute and Professor of Economics in the Rawls College of Business at Texas Tech University. He is the North American Editor of the *Review of Austrian Economics*, Past President of the Association of Private Enterprise Education, and a Senior Fellow with the Independent Institute. He earned his Ph.D. in Economics from George Mason University. Dr. Powell has authored or edited 3 prior books, published more than 50 scholarly articles and policy reports, and frequently writes on immigration in the popular press.

Nicolás Cachanosky is an Assistant Professor of Economics at Metropolitan State University of Denver. He earned his Ph.D. in Economics from Suffolk University in 2013.

Bryan Caplan is a Professor of Economics at George Mason University and Senior Scholar at the Mercatus Center. He earned his Ph.D. in Economics from Princeton University. The *New York Times* named his book, *The Myth of the Rational Voter: Why Democracies Choose Bad Policies* (Princeton University Press, 2008), "the best political book of the year." Dr. Caplan's recent publication on the topic of immigration titled "Why Should We Restrict Immigration?" appeared in *Cato Journal* in late 2012.

Zachary Gochenour is a Visiting Assistant Professor in the Department of Economics at Western Carolina University. He earned his Ph.D. in 2014 from George Mason University. His dissertation and current research explore the political economy of immigration.

Peter T. Leeson is the BB&T Professor for the Study of Capitalism at George Mason University's Mercatus Center. He is the North American Editor of *Public Choice*. He earned his Ph.D. in Economics from George Mason University. Dr. Leeson has served as Visiting Professor of Economics at the University of Chicago's Becker Center on Chicago Price Theory, a Visiting Fellow in Political Economy and Government at Harvard University, and the F. A. Hayek Fellow at the London School of Economics.

Herbert London is President of the London Center for Policy Research and Senior Fellow with the Manhattan Institute for Policy Research. He is also President Emeritus of Hudson Institute, where he served from 1997 to 2011. He is Professor Emeritus and the former John M. Olin Professor of Humanities at New York University, where he was responsible for creating the Gallatin School of Individualized Study. He earned his Ph.D. from New York University. Dr. London has published over 25 books during his career.

Vipul Naik is a data scientist and software engineer at LiftIgniter, a company that uses mathematics and technology for personalized recommendations. He earned his Ph.D. in Mathematics from the University of Chicago in 2013. Dr. Naik created openborders.info in 2012, a website devoted to a mixture of discussion, debate, and advocacy of steps in the direction of freer migration and more open borders.

Alex Nowrasteh is the Immigration Policy Analyst at the Cato Institute's Center for Global Liberty and Prosperity. Previously, he served as the Immigration Policy Analyst at the Competitive Enterprise Institute. He earned an M.Sc. in Economic History from the London School of Economics. He has published policy studies on immigration, including *How to Make Guest Worker VISAs Work* and *The Economic Case Against Arizona's Immigration Laws*.

Alexandre Padilla is an Associate Professor of Economics and the Director of the Exploring Economic Freedom Project at Metropolitan State University of Denver. He earned his Ph.D. in Economics from the University of Law, Economics, and Science of Aix-Marseille III. He was a member of the Executive Board for the Association of Private Enterprise Education from 2008 to 2012.

Richard K. Vedder is the Edwin and Ruth Kennedy Distinguished Professor of Economics and Faculty Associate at the Contemporary History Institute at Ohio University. He is also a Senior Fellow with the Independent Institute. He earned his Ph.D. in Economics from the University of Illinois. Dr. Vedder has published several peer-reviewed articles on the history, causes, and consequences of human migration.

Jacob Vigdor is a Professor of Public Affairs in the Evans School of Public Affairs at the University of Washington. He hold affiliations as a Research Associate at the National Bureau of Economic Research, an Adjunct Fellow at the Manhattan Institute for Policy Research, and an External Fellow at the Centre for Research and Analysis of Migration at University College London. Previously, he served on the faculty of the Sanford School of Public Policy at Duke University. He earned his Ph.D. in Economics from Harvard University. His book on assimilation and immigration policy, *From Immigrants to Americans: The Rise and Fall of Fitting In* (Rowman & Littlefield, 2009), received the 2009 IPUMS research award for the best analysis of historical Census data.

INDEX

INDEPENDENT
I N S T I T U T E

INDEPENDENT INSTITUTE is a non-profit, non-partisan, public-policy research and educational organization that shapes ideas into profound and lasting impact. The mission of Independent is to boldly advance peaceful, prosperous, and free societies grounded in a commitment to human worth and dignity. Applying independent thinking to issues that matter, we create transformational ideas for today's most pressing social and economic challenges. The results of this work are published as books, our quarterly journal, *The Independent Review*, and other publications and form the basis for numerous conference and media programs. By connecting these ideas with organizations and networks, we seek to inspire action that can unleash an era of unparalleled human flourishing at home and around the globe.

FOUNDER & PRESIDENT
David J. Theroux

RESEARCH DIRECTOR
William F. Shughart II

SENIOR FELLOWS
Bruce L. Benson
Ivan Eland
John C. Goodman
John R. Graham
Robert Higgs
Lawrence J. McQuillan
Robert H. Nelson
Charles V. Peña
Benjamin Powell
William F. Shughart II
Randy T. Simmons
Alexander Tabarrok
Alvaro Vargas Llosa
Richard K. Vedder

ACADEMIC ADVISORS
Leszek Balcerowicz
WARSAW SCHOOL OF ECONOMICS

Herman Belz
UNIVERSITY OF MARYLAND

Thomas E. Borcherding
CLAREMONT GRADUATE SCHOOL

Boudewijn Bouckaert
UNIVERSITY OF GHENT, BELGIUM

Allan C. Carlson
HOWARD CENTER

Robert D. Cooter
UNIVERSITY OF CALIFORNIA, BERKELEY

Robert W. Crandall
BROOKINGS INSTITUTION

Richard A. Epstein
NEW YORK UNIVERSITY

B. Delworth Gardner
BRIGHAM YOUNG UNIVERSITY

George Gilder
DISCOVERY INSTITUTE

Nathan Glazer
HARVARD UNIVERSITY

Steve H. Hanke
JOHNS HOPKINS UNIVERSITY

James J. Heckman
UNIVERSITY OF CHICAGO

H. Robert Heller
SONIC AUTOMOTIVE

Deirdre N. McCloskey
UNIVERSITY OF ILLINOIS, CHICAGO

J. Huston McCulloch
OHIO STATE UNIVERSITY

Forrest McDonald
UNIVERSITY OF ALABAMA

Thomas Gale Moore
HOOVER INSTITUTION

Charles Murray
AMERICAN ENTERPRISE INSTITUTE

Michael J. Novak, Jr.
AMERICAN ENTERPRISE INSTITUTE

June E. O'Neill
BARUCH COLLEGE

Charles E. Phelps
UNIVERSITY OF ROCHESTER

Nathan Rosenberg
STANFORD UNIVERSITY

Paul H. Rubin
EMORY UNIVERSITY

Bruce M. Russett
YALE UNIVERSITY

Pascal Salin
UNIVERSITY OF PARIS, FRANCE

Vernon L. Smith
CHAPMAN UNIVERSITY

Pablo T. Spiller
UNIVERSITY OF CALIFORNIA, BERKELEY

Joel H. Spring
STATE UNIVERSITY OF NEW YORK, OLD WESTBURY

Richard L. Stroup
NORTH CAROLINA STATE UNIVERSITY

Robert D. Tollison
CLEMSON UNIVERSITY

Arnold S. Trebach
AMERICAN UNIVERSITY

Richard E. Wagner
GEORGE MASON UNIVERSITY

Walter E. Williams
GEORGE MASON UNIVERSITY

Charles Wolf, Jr.
RAND CORPORATION

100 Swan Way, Oakland, California 94621-1428, U.S.A.
Telephone: 510-632-1366 • Facsimile: 510-568-6040 • Email: info@independent.org • www.independent.org

CPSIA information can be obtained
at www.ICGtesting.com
Printed in the USA
BVHW072156271119
564910BV00002B/6/P

9 780190 258795